D1480991

ADVANCE PRAISE

"René has no limitations at all and Spike is his and all of our manifestos for navigating this troublesome world of ours – you must read it at least twice"
Sir Michael Lockett, World leading communications guru

"Positively impatient for a better world without the negative energy of being fixated on our limitations – this is René. This is Spike"
Liz Ellen, Partner at Mishcon de Reya
runs the Sports Practice

"Our World is getting tougher, faster and more unforgiving and we will need all the Spikes we can get – ours and others. René makes this both clear and unforgettable"
Allan Leighton, Serial Chairman
– one of the UK's leading business leaders

"René has continuously assisted me and my team in better deploying our Spikes that has made us a much better and stronger team – and it has made our very challenging targets so much more fun"
Nomkhita Nqweni, CEO Wealth Management
– Barclays Africa

Published by
LID Publishing Ltd.
The Record Hall, Studio 204,
16-16a Baldwins Gardens,
London EC1N 7RJ, United Kingdom

31 West 34th Street, 8th Floor,
Suite 8004, New York,
NY 10001, US

info@lidpublishing.com
www.lidpublishing.com

A member of:

www.businesspublishersroundtable.com

Printed in Great Britain by TJ International
ISBN: 978-1-911498-52-0 (paperback)
ISBN: 978-1-911498-58-2 (hardback)

RENÉ CARAYOL

SPIKE

STRENGTHS • POSITIVELY • IDENTIFIED • KICK-START • EXCELLENCE

WHAT ARE YOU GREAT AT?

LONDON MONTERREY
MADRID SHANGHAI
MEXICO CITY BOGOTA
NEW YORK BUENOS AIRES
BARCELONA SAN FRANCISCO

This book is dedicated to my mother and father.
Because of their courage in leaving their home and middle class lives in Gambia back in the early 1960s, to face an unknown and difficult future, I had the opportunity to truly find and fine-tune my Spikes.

I had to find them initially to survive and then, because of my Spikes, I have thrived.

Mum and Dad, without your huge sacrifice there would be NO Spike.

This book is dedicated to the both of you.

Thank you.

EVERYONE IS A WINNER.

THERE NEED NEVER BE ANY LOSERS ANYMORE.

WHAT DID YOU SEE FIRST?

We learn best through stories. Stories paint pictures and every picture tells a thousand words. This is a book full of stories; real stories about real people that I have had the privilege and pleasure to have met on the journey to discovering and energizing my Spikes.

So, let me tell you a story…

When giving a talk to an audience you've never met before, it is always helpful to focus on finding an approving or supportive warm face within the audience. It's even better if you can identify someone friendly somewhere in the middle, and then one each at either side of the auditorium.

This is a simple tip for encouraging and eliciting reciprocal positivity throughout your talk. If you smile, the audience will smile with you. Many of us are so lost in concentration that we can inadvertently start scowling or frowning – again, the audience will reflect whatever you give off, and start scowling or frowning too.

By constantly looking for the warm faces to the left, right and centre of your audience, the speaker makes everybody feel included and interconnected. A glance is never enough, but a smile of acknowledgement can be very powerful.

Believe me, it is so much easier to listen to someone who has a smile on their face.

Whilst giving a talk in Dublin for the Association of Higher Education Access and Disability (AHEAD) a few years ago, I saw many positive and supportive faces in the quite dark Helix auditorium. Sat right in the front row was a young woman with the most sparkling of smiles, lit up by the only light in the darkness. Her obvious encouragement and delight radiated around the theatre. She nodded her approval and laughed along with all of my humorous anecdotes; during quite challenging pieces she mirrored my serious demeanour. The perfect attendee!

Not long after I had begun, a slight and confident woman entered through the side door by the stage, silently led by a guide dog that guided and sat her comfortably – and rather surprisingly – on the stage just to my right. After a couple of moments, her guide dog growled softly; the growl was instantly returned from another guide dog, I had not noticed, lying at the feet of my supporter in chief; she, too, could not see.

As the audience walked out at the end of the conference, my guiding light stood up, waited until I approached her, then gently held my arm as we walked out together. Her grip was light but secure. She was incredibly alert and she nearly anticipated my moves and direction – it was quite beautiful.

We headed out to the dining area, where a buffet lunch was being served. As I handed her a tray, I did what most of us would probably do: I instantly started explaining and describing what was on offer for lunch. She smiled patiently and politely ignored my descriptions, then chose the salmon and the broccoli. Her 'other' senses were fine-tuned and had become huge Spikes.

We sat down for lunch together and shared our stories with each other. She was charming and excited about all she had just heard and experienced.

She shared her frustration at potentially missing out on jobs that she felt she was more than qualified for. She always got on the shortlist, but as soon as she turned up for the interview, she was quickly told that the reason for her rejection was only because of the perceived cost of physical changes to the office infrastructure necessary in order to accommodate her disability.

She was not at all bitter, but determined to land an opportunity to demonstrate what she could do. She was very much aware of her Spikes: not many had taken the time to notice anything she could do, but they felt strongly about what they perceived she would not be capable of doing.

She had travelled alone on the train from Cork to attend the conference and would have another three-hour journey back.

She worked for the Irish Guide Dogs Association and was an inspiration to all who took the time to engage with her.

When it was time to leave, as we reached the door, we hugged (her dog growled quietly at me). She was still giving me positive feedback when we eventually went in different directions. I instinctively turned back and waved and she instantly waved back.

As I caught a taxi to the airport, I reflected that her warmth and poise had left a lasting impression on me. The first impression of most who met her would be to see her limitations. Those who were able to see beyond her disability would soon warm to her tremendous Spikes of instant care and a positive connection, plus an amazing ability to read people and their intentions.

How much better and more inclusive would our world be, if we all first saw the Spikes that others possessed, before we dismissed them for their supposed limitations.

"WE DECEIVE OURSELVES WHEN WE FANCY THAT ONLY WEAKNESS NEEDS SUPPORT. STRENGTH NEEDS IT FAR MORE."

MADAME SWETCHIN

CONTENTS

ACKNOWLEDGEMENTS

To...

Zakir Hussain – for all the creative inspiration, huge support, and the never-dying belief in Spike.

Anna Drizen – for all your hard work, care and passion for Spike – every book needs its passionate pedant.

Ashley Theophane – for allowing us all to read and share your story and your dreams.

Shalimar Adorno – for the full-blown support and for affording us the privilege of sharing your wonderfully uplifting story.

Paul Kearney – for just being the most concise and prepared person I know, and for sharing your instructive story.

George Stone – for kick-starting the need to explain just why the world needs Spike and the inspiration to make this happen.

Simon Benham – for appearing just when you were most needed, and then delivering.

Bernard Fisher – for being there from the first written word of Spike, and for continually challenging and provoking ever so positively.

Ray Walters – for being there from the first written word of Spike and for continually supporting and pushing, whilst always being there.

Rupa Das – for the brilliant research and ongoing support.

Raisa Carayol – for listening, reading and inspiring me to continue.

Marcellus Carayol – for not interfering but offering pride and support.

Martin Heward Mills – for reading, believing and supporting.

Prosper Williams – for reading, believing and giving continuously.

Safie Sarr – for the initial challenge, energy and support.

Chris Brady – for your continued cynicism and scepticism.

Simon Lewis – for the surprise of publishing the first excerpts of Spike.

Simon Ward – for your continuous generosity and undying support for Wolverhampton Wanderers.

PREFACE

When I try to explain SPIKE to friends, colleagues, and indeed to the audiences to whom I speak regularly, I usually struggle to articulate a precise definition. I have come to realise that's because there isn't one. Like most things that we find difficult to define – love/hate, peace/war – we can easily tell you what it isn't and we can always tell you what it looks like when we see it.

What this book isn't is another unit in the ever growing 'Strengths-based leadership/development/coaching' industry, exemplified by the excellent Gallup publications (a market leader in strengths training), focusing on exponents such as Marcus Buckingham and Tom Rath, which has dominated this approach over the past 10 to 15 years.

In fact, there is much to agree with in an interview in the Harvard Business Review from 16 January 2016, entitled, *Stop Focusing on Your Strengths*, given by **Tomas Chamorro-Premuzic**, a professor at University College London and Columbia University.

He warned of the potential dangers of concentrating on your strengths alone. He argues that, "most tools and assessments that are designed to find your strengths would simply pick up the thing that you are best at." I agree and that is precisely the point. A 'Spike' is not simply something you are good at – it is something that is your brand, the essence of what you are.

There are many people who are great at certain jobs but actually hate doing those jobs.

Many sports professionals fall into that category. They have not necessarily found their 'Spike' but have fallen into their marketable skill. This book isn't about positioning yourself for the best paying job – it's about understanding what the best job is for you.

It's not about ignoring your weaknesses – it's about recognizing them and making decisions about how best to accommodate them. When thinking of team environments this means identifying, recognizing and developing individual Spikes and balancing them in the service of the team.

What separates this book from the strengths-based theorists and practitioners is that it does not try, or even want, to provide a guidebook to success or an online 'strengths finder' or dictate the way each individual should be; it is not, in any way, a self-help book.

It does not provide a methodology; rather it attempts to develop a philosophy – not for self-help, but for self-discovery. It does this through its use of real and emotionally connecting stories and through its simplicity.

Through my work and life over the last 25 years, I believe that I have earned the right to tell the stories that have informed my Spike philosophy and, more importantly, that will allow readers simple, but not simplistic access to Spike, through that greatest of learning vehicles: the story.

This book also is not about data-driven deep, impenetrable lists, charts and amateur psychometrics. That is the IQ approach of management, and there are more than enough good books covering this already. *Spike* is all about engaging your EQ, your Leadership of yourself and your future.

Management is concerned with 'doing things right', where Leadership on the other hand, is about 'doing the right things'. Management is all about tasks, plans, strategies and activities, leading to their ongoing measurement of how these factors affect the tangible and demonstrable results.

Spike, however, like all Leadership approaches, is much more about attitude and mind-set. Spike sets out to provoke a completely different mind-set about our real natural assets and how we best capitalise upon these.

When I'm on stage, I always say, "If you want to know what your Spikes are, just ask a loved one." Not a work colleague, but someone who has unconditional love for you – mother, father, sister, uncle, partner, niece, gran, husband, wife, daughter, brother or wife. They will want you to succeed, so will not play games or compete with you. They will not use management speak but will kick-start your journey of self-discovery by using terms like, "you're generous", "your patience is your Spike", "you're firm but fair", and so on.

Understanding the Spike approach also enables us to tackle the implicit biases to which we are all vulnerable. Far too often, our first impression of someone will negatively colour our ongoing judgement of them.

This implicit bias can be very damaging, especially for women and minorities, and is a constant barrier to greater social mobility. The Spike philosophy can help.

By looking for an individual's Spike from the outset, we will care less about their 'first impression'. Searching for someone's Spikes takes us beyond their gender, race, religion, disability or social status.

But what does a Spike look like when you see it? As will be the pattern for the bulk of the book, I will answer this question by telling a story.

Forgive the footballing analogy – while this is not a story about football, it provides the perfect example of an individual who, at first impressions did not quite look the part. It's the story of an individual with obvious limitations, but most of all, it's a story of Spike.

It is the story of Ferenc Puskás, a Hungarian footballer of the immediate post-war period. Ferenc Gyurcsány, the Prime Minister of Hungary, speaking after Puskas' death in 2006 said, "There is not one Hungarian who will be left untouched by the death of Ferenc Puskás. The best-known Hungarian of the 20th century has left, but the legend will always stay with us."

Puskas scored 83 goals in 84 games for Hungary between 1945 and 1956. He was nicknamed the 'Galloping Major' because he was nominally a soldier in the Hungarian army, but it was only as a player with the Hungarian army team, Budapest

Honvéd SE, that he really found his calling. He was to become an integral part of the Mighty Magyars, who bestrode the footballing world in the early-to mid-1950s.

They became the first overseas team to beat England on home soil in 1953. As they were warming up for the game, an unnamed English player looked across at Puskas and said, "Look at that little fat chap. We'll murder this lot!" Hungary beat England that day 6-3 (Puskas scored two goals) and then took them back to Budapest for a 7-1 thrashing.

After the collapse of the Hungarian uprising against the Soviet Union in 1956, Puskas escaped to the West, surfacing in Spain to sign for mighty Real Madrid. In the ensuing years, he became central to the Madrid team, winning the first five European Cups, culminating in the almost mythical 1960 final against Eintracht Frankfurt at Hampden Park, Glasgow, watched by a crowd estimated at 127,000.

Madrid won 7-3 and Puskas scored four goals.

But what has any of this to do with Spike? Well, another tribute to Puskas by Sir Tom Finney, the England and Preston North End legend, holds a tiny clue. Puskas, he said, "had a roly-poly physique, but a wonderful left foot and he was a brilliant finisher. I would put Puskas in any list of all-time greats."

He didn't look like a footballer but, unlike the other England player, Finney looked past the obvious and marveled at Puskas' 'Spike': that 'wonderful left foot'.

Most respected football coaches work on the premise that all footballers will have a favoured foot, which they will naturally try to play every ball with, and they work hard to push all players to work on their weaker and less used foot.

When Puskas was asked why he didn't practise more to make his right foot better, he explained that he practised all day, every day on his left foot to make it near perfect, and to worry too much about his other foot, would have taken time away from perfecting his left. He understood what his Spike was, and appreciated that concentrating on a weakness would have been counterproductive.

In so doing, that 'little fat chap' became *the best-known Hungarian of the 20th century*. Not bad for a guy with 'only one foot.' Puskas did not ignore the deficiencies of his weak foot and worked to make it adequate, but he decided that a 'perfect' left would be more valuable and a competent right foot would be sufficient.

"PLEASURE IN THE JOB PUTS PERFECTION IN THE WORK."

ARISTOTLE

MAKING YOUR SPIKE SPIKIER

Spike is the most straightforward and perhaps radical approach to:

- building self-esteem and confidence
- enabling success in all you do
- identifying roles, jobs and careers that are right for you
- building truly inclusive high-performing teams
- ensuring no-one is left behind

The vital and essential ingredient of the Spike philosophy is that absolutely everyone has at least one inherent Spike, one characteristic talent, that if identified and released, can enable lives to be genuinely fulfilling by energizing and mobilizing them for your own and everyone else's benefit.

I believe passionately in the principles incorporated in this book, as these messages are embedded within all aspects of everything we do and at all levels.

This book will uniquely prepare you to fulfil the ultimate dream of every student, employee, or business leader:

"FIND A JOB THAT YOU LOVE AND YOU WILL NEVER WORK A DAY IN YOUR LIFE."

"Spike" will lead you on an enjoyable and pragmatic journey, utilizing great and memorable anecdotes, case studies and research-led statistics and data towards the 'Virtuous Spike Circle' of:

THE THINGS I TEND TO DO WELL

SPIKE

THE THINGS I TEND TO ENJOY

Ernest Shackleton's memorable 1914 advertisement in The Times was oversubscribed, with over a thousand applicants. Shackleton was brutally honest about the skills required; consequently, only those with the appropriate Spikes applied.

qualified. M. L. Barker, 1408 Chapman Bldg.

MEN WANTED

for hazardous journey, small wages, bitter cold, long months of complete darkness, constant danger, safe return doubtful, honor and recognition in case of success.

Ernest Shackleton 4 Burlington st.

MEN—Neat-appearing young men of pleasing personality, between ages ... and 40 to work

Nearly all organizational Performance Management systems, as well as Employee Appraisal systems and their associated methodologies, are designed and implicitly biased towards identifying weaknesses or areas for development.

Consequently, every employee becomes fixated on working nearly exclusively on raising their (sometimes obvious) weaknesses to a decent level – with 'decent' usually prescribed by the prevailing Performance Management system. Not many achieve this, despite years of frustrated effort and focus, and continual negative feedback! Most are not confident enough to break out from the pack on their own, and actually focus on honing their strengths to a formidable standard.

My experience of working with some of the world's best leaders of this generation: from President Bill Clinton, Prime Minister David Cameron, Mikhail Gorbachev and Sir Richard Branson to world champion boxers, David Haye and Ricky Hatton, and many others (despite the Queen telling me not to name drop, I will share their stories, their Spikes and more), informs me that none of them are flawless or 'all-rounders'.

But they all tend to know their 2 or 3 Spikes, and have taken the time and focus to fine-tune them to near Olympian standards.

Spike will encourage and provide the pathway for an intelligent and strong-willed focus on your key strengths that will deliver the following:

Your very own key to your unique and sustainable Leadership Code:

- Finding Your Spikes – in PART ONE
- Balancing Spikes – in PART TWO
- Spike for Change – in PART THREE
- Spike is Persistence – in PART FOUR
- The Story of the Stories – in PART FIVE

Nothing is best done alone anymore. Keep your friends close and your complementary Spikes closer still: exploit their Spikes to yours and everyone's benefit.

PART ONE

FINDING YOUR SPIKES

CHAPTER I
~~HERITAGE IS EVERYTHING.~~
FAST HISTORY

When the world around us is changing at such a relentless pace, recognizing your own Spikes provides confidence and enhances performance. What are your Spikes?

Before any organization can become adjusted to one change, it is hit by several others. We're living in a constant period of transition, and our shelf life keeps getting shorter.

'What works' becomes history in a hurry. How will we ever keep up? Our skills feel as though they are being eroded with every week that passes.

Where is all this change coming from? Well, to begin with, people create change. So let's look at what's happening to the head count on Mother Earth.

Human beings have been around for some six or seven million years. It has taken that long for the population of the earth to reach 7.3 billion people. But the predictions say it will take only about 50 years for the next 7.3 billion people to be here. If people create change – and obviously they do – then we should expect a rapid increase in the rate of change as the population doubles over the next few decades.

This growing crowd of people is armed with another source of change: technology. And technology feeds upon itself. So let's review what's happening in the area of science, inventions and technology in general. Word has it that more than 80% of our technological inventions have occurred just since 1900. Within the first 15 years of the 21st century, we have seen as much technological change as had been observed in the previous 100 years. Don't think of technological change as something that keeps merely adding up – think of it as multiplying on a daily basis.

Still another source of change is knowledge. Information. In 2010, Eric Schmidt, the CEO of Google, stated that "every two days now, we create as much information as we did from the dawn of civilisation up until 2003… The real issue is user-generated content, pictures, instant messages and social media that all add to this".

More people, more tools, more knowledge. And here's the bottom line: maybe you think you've seen a lot of change lately, but you haven't seen anything yet. The future promises us more change than we've ever experienced before, and it will come at us faster and faster. The question is, will we give our culture permission to change in such a way that the organizations can survive in a world of fast history?

Change has no conscience. It doesn't play favourites. It takes no prisoners. And change ruthlessly destroys organizations with cultures that don't adapt. Just look around – it's happening to companies everywhere.

In years past, we could get by with a slower response time. Change didn't happen as fast; competition wasn't as stiff. Also, the world gave us more room for recovery. There was enough space between major change events for people to catch their breath and collect their senses. Many of the normal human reactions to the stress of change worked well. Our old culture could cope. But those days belong in the history books now.

A world of high velocity change calls for radical shifts in behaviour. Specifically, we must think differently: reorder our priorities, develop faster reflexes, give the culture an entirely new set of responses. We can't afford to ignore change and just do what comes naturally. We must face reality and do what works.

But we are no longer alone – armed with the Spike philosophy, change becomes our friend and our weapon for progress.

In 2010, the BBC afforded me the privilege of presenting an eight-part series called *Business 2025*. We took eight corporate leaders from eight completely different businesses in a variety of sectors and asked each of them the same, straightforward question: "What will your business look like in 2025?"

The series examined and challenged their responses and predictions.

Some two years later, in 2012, we revisited the initial responses and predictions from our business leaders, and every one of them had predicted wrongly. Everything (and more) they thought would take fifteen years to accomplish was actually completed within two years of the filming.

The power and unpredictability of disruptive innovation had transformed their businesses beyond recognition.

The best strategy for our disruptive times is not trying to predict 10 or even 5 years into the future, but to identify our Spikes and then add "a little more, a little faster and a little more quality every day".

"THERE'S NO OFF-SEASON ANYMORE"

NOLAN RYAN,
TEXAS RANGERS' PITCHER AND WORLD RECORD HOLDER FOR NO- HITTERS

SPIKE SPARKS

Listen and listen again – Make time for frequent chats with a teenager. It might just give you an insight into how well you listen and offer an opportunity to learn from someone with no authority, but loads of contemporary know-how.

Under 25s know more – When was the last time you asked an under 25-year-old for advice? Are you making the most of your smartphone? Ask a teenager to give you a demonstration of what it could really do for you.

Create aspirational 'high-flyers' clubs at work and worry less about misplaced egalitarian principles – it will drive ambition and pride and deliver your next generation of leadership.

Businesses don't change; people do – Businesses rarely change, the people within them do – much more so when they have been given positive opportunities to capitalize upon their Spikes.

Make tough decisions quickly – by the time you have decided to act, you are already late.

ON THE SAME PAGE

The Digital Disruption means that "Uber, the world's largest taxi company, owns no vehicles. Facebook, the world's most popular media owner, creates no content. Alibaba, the most valuable retailer, has no inventory. And Airbnb, the world's largest accommodation provider, owns no real estate. Something interesting is happening." Tom Goodwin[1], TechTarget.

With increasing disruption in business models, diminished trust in leaders, and escalating employee expectations, it is essential that we rethink what it takes to lead well. Today's leaders are required to have even more of the 3 A's than ever before as described in *Leadership Thoughts at the Conclusion* by Wright L. Lassiter, Jr[2]: Agility (to lead in the face of uncertainty rooted in a sense of purpose), Agency (sense of control and ownership of choices) and Authenticity (taking responsibility for actions taken in line with one's own convictions, as well as the organization's vision and mission).

"Leadership of the future is less about the theory of an idealized leadership model and more about the practical ability to navigate a journey of authenticity and inspiration; energizing and equipping oneself and others to make the right choices for the situation at hand." – Giles Hutchins[3]

---

1 Goodwin, T. (2015) "The Battle Is For The Customer Interface." [online] Available at: http://techcrunch.com/2015/03/03/in-the-age-of-disintermediation-the-battle-is-all-for-the- customer-interface/ [Accessed 22 Mar. 2016].

2 Lassiter, W. Jr. (2014) *Leadership Thoughts at the Conclusion.* [ebook] Trafford Publishing.

3 Hutchins, G. (2012) "Leadership for the future: diversity, creativity and co-creation." [online] *Guardian Professional.* Available at: http://www.theguardian.com/sustainable-business/leadership- future-diversity-creativity-cocreation [Accessed 22 Mar. 2016]

CHAPTER II
~~SOME ARE JUST USELESS.~~ ALL BRAINS ARE BRILLIANT

It pays to focus on a positive solution rather than a negative problem. How? By making all your observations, when things don't go to plan, much more positive. Then take note of just how much more positive the responses you gain are.

This isn't a self-help book. It's a help yourself book. Go figure.

You are the most amazing thing in the world. Nothing else in nature, or made by man is more amazing than you. What you're doing right now, as you read this, is absolutely phenomenal. There are words printed on this page, which you are translating into thoughts and language and ideas. You're doing this as you read. As you flick your eye along the lines of print, you're pulling out meaning from marks on a piece of paper.

You're figuring out things moment by moment, second by second. Sights, sounds, smells and sensations, made entirely of symbols are rushing in, and you're analyzing it all in real time.

You are live and online, right here, right now doing the most amazing thing ever: being.

Rocks are 'being' too, of course, but in a way that is markedly different from you.

You're conscious.

You're aware that you are reading this. You understand that there's another consciousness out there somewhere, that is writing this, and that you are reading it.

So, unless I'm a figment of your imagination, and I have no way to prove otherwise, there are at least two of us.

Let's agree, right now, that I could be a part of your imagination and may well have no independent existence at all. We should explore your imagination further.

First of all, let's try and figure out what makes you different – because of course you are different. You look different, you sound different, you like different things, you have different tastes: maybe you can juggle, maybe you can whistle, maybe you can grow orchids or help a cow give birth.

Whatever. You're different. You know you're different and you've always felt that way, because your head is wired up differently.

What if these differences became inherent strengths – Spikes?

Imagine a round white ball, the size of a basketball. Take a felt tip pen and write words for every human quality that you can think of on the surface of the ball. It doesn't matter which way up or where you write the words. Draw rings around each one if it makes things look tidier.

On my list there are skills like cooking, dancing, juggling, adding up, recognizing words, comforting the dying, doing crosswords, being logical or an excellent driver, or a big picture person; having empathy, sympathy or a sense of humour, liking Chelsea F.C; being good at communicating, listening or jumping; having an ear for melody, being good with children, growing orchids and birthing cattle.

So, now we have a white ball with lots of words written on the outside. Now, imagine the centre of the ball, and then move out towards a word you recognize as a part of you. Let's say you have a sense of humour. Move from the centre of the ball towards 'sense of humour'. Now look around for another word you recognize as part of you. Perhaps, you like tunes, so move towards 'ear for melody'. Do this for long enough, ticking off all the words that apply to you, and you'll arrive at the point that is uniquely you. It is somewhere within the surface and away from others.

Some people are a long way from 'handy with a hammer' but quite close to 'chess grandmaster'. Others are quite close to 'juggling' but a longish way from 'recognizing words'.

Everyone is different, but we are all made up, to a greater or lesser extent, of the same abundance. And yet, who is recognized by others as being exceptional?

Some of us can't read. Something happens when word signals hit the brain that the brain can't quite figure out what was not with came round the back with a spade happening on the wordage four eggs or nine, Jimbo.

It's a wiring problem. You can try and find a workaround, and sometimes that helps, but most dyslexics are stuck in a world where words don't work. And they feel ashamed and afraid because they've been made to feel that way by people who've told them they ought to try harder, who, incidentally, are themselves a long way from the word 'empathy'.

The point is that we're all different: no-one is better than anyone else. Our heads are simply wired up differently.

Sometimes our wiring fits our culture and sometimes it doesn't. Imagine having the wiring of a top computer coder, but being born a nomad near Timbuktu. What good is that Spike going to do you out in the desert where the Spike for spotting signs of water and finding trails through the rock will serve you far better?

Imagine being potentially the best shepherd in the world, but being born in Brooklyn.

Our wiring decides what we can do. Our environment presents us with choices and possibilities. Sometimes, we have Spikes that are completely useless for our culture, that are unremarked and unrewarded and may even be seen as a handicap. Sometimes our culture throws up Spikes that we could never have imagined, like video games or hover boarding.

What did people do before they discovered they could yo-yo? Is there a point on our white ball that says 'yo-yoing'? Sure, why not? It's our ball and we can write what we like on it.

What's interesting is that there are places on the surface of our ball that don't have anything written on them because we don't know what the Spike is, yet. Equally, there are places where the Spike, or ability, or quality, has been with us forever.

There's a point of view that says that some of these things are reinforced by heredity. If your mother was a good singer, then maybe you are too. If your father was an accountant, then maybe you have a feel for numbers.

One thing is certainly true. If you don't practise, you don't get better at the things you're good at. Practicing may help improve the skills you find challenging. But in those areas where you are completely and utterly inadequate don't even get off the bus.

Some teachers have a lot to answer for. Love of a subject at school can be the result of a single teachers' enthusiasm. Equally, a less than sparkling presence in the classroom, hunched over their notes and a little too focused on control, can kill stone-dead any spark of interest that might have been.

A dismissive sentence can drop a barricade or build a wall, or, worse, convince the listener that he or she is stupid.

It's not stupid, stupid! It's wiring.

Some teachers don't have the necessary teachers' wiring at all. We've been there, in that room: understanding nothing, at the back, and baffled. So now in our lives there's a great big 'Unknown' around that subject. We didn't get it when we were eleven – by twelve it was slipping, and by fourteen it had GONE.

Yet kids with (almost) the same wiring as us HAVE got it. Are we stupid or what?

What if all teachers could work through our wiring until they found a way to connect what they want us to know with our ability to know it?

Go and watch a good basketball coach. He IS the sport. How many teachers are their subject?

A lot are – yes a lot. They connect their subject with our ability to know it. And it feels amazing. Sometimes in the classroom EVERYONE is paying attention. The buzz of a bee outside sounds loud. We're all focused, we're all there and we GET it.

Maybe you weren't so lucky. But with the right attention to detail and a little encouragement, you can go back to an old subject and discover that actually, yes, you can learn it. Mostly.

Just don't ever ask me to look after chickens. They outthink me at every turn. They're better than a German goalkeeper. I go left; they go right. I close the top of the gate; they're out of the bottom. A chicken in an apple tree is more agile than a squirrel. Their tails go up just before they let it all out, but I don't notice till I've been well and truly decorated.

I'm no good at chickens; neither do I want to learn. I also don't get maths particularly well. I'm inadequate at both. I don't know what numbers ARE. Something happens when I'm faced with a list of numbers, which makes my head spin. But I have hope.

I have hope because Bill has the same problem with numbers but can do one very cool thing, which I just don't get. Bill can give you a three dart finish on any number lower than one hundred and sixty-three, in the time it takes you to say the number. "Bill, One Hundred and Seventeen." "Treble Nineteen, Twenty, Tops."

Any number lower than 163 and Bill will be there with his three dart finish. Yet Bill has big(ish) problems figuring things out otherwise. His wiring is not as easy to diagram as yours or mine. The blueprint is certainly unique. He's brilliant. But then, all brains are.

WIRING

There are lots of ways that you can try and figure out what something is made of, or consists of, or if you insist, what something IS.

Figuring out what brains are is a tough one. We can shoot at them, we can fall in love with them, we can operate on them; we can try and copy them; we can try and train them, we can try and make them think or stop them thinking; we can show them slogans, tell them what to believe and what to fear; we can even hypnotise them. After all this, we still may not know everything that a brain is.

What we do have though is a model. A model is a way of thinking about something easily. It's an idea that we can criticise, modify and argue with until it works, or until something better comes along.

Our model is Spike and it forms the basis of that white ball. On the ball, we've written all the human qualities and we've said that each of us occupies a unique spot within the ball.

So let's step inside our white ball now and look out, look around. We can read the words from the inside of the ball too – they're hanging in space all around us, defining the edge, the perimeter of us.

Some words attract us – we have no control over this yet – others send us drifting away. We are seeking equilibrium, that place which is us, uniquely us, with everything that is not 'us' being different, separate and 'out there'.

Our equilibrium determines how we see the world, the filters that we employ and our points of 'blindness'. From here the world looks the way it IS. There isn't anything else. How could there be?

This balance can change. We can learn things, pick up experiences, go through traumas, live through hell and come out the other side.

We can emerge bitter and hurt. We can emerge nursing bruises and scars. The pain can sometimes drive us to numbness and Nothing. We can find ourselves walking in the dead of night to the place where Nothing waits and for a while can be held by Nothing and know Nothing and perhaps decide we want to stay where there is Nothing.

Turn around. When you stare into the Abyss, the Abyss stares back at you. Every suicide is a VIP. Be lucky. Just remember this. Walk Towards.

Nice to see you back. Nice night. How loud did you shout? Not bad. We should have hooked up and done the shout thing together. It might have helped. I'd certainly have known there was someone else out there who felt the way I did.

We're not meant to feel things. We're allowed to be angry and hurt but there's no reward for giving a reward. We have become emotional traders and it's only very seldom that we get beyond these transactions.

Walk towards your Spikes.

You either walk towards your Spikes or away from them, not both. That's it. There's nothing more to understand. Walk towards your Spikes. Walk towards healing, not away from pain.

Pain has you looking over your shoulder. Healing is the Better You. Walk towards wisdom, not away from stupidity.

Stupidity has you worrying about everything. Wisdom is wanting to know more.

Walk towards your Spikes.

SPIKE SPARKS

Embrace difference – For centuries people who are 'different' have been given a hard time. The Spike approach thrives on difference – diversity must be valued and embraced, not mistrusted and marginalized.

Be honest with yourself – Be brutally honest and open about your Spikes.

Understand what you're great at – Know what you are great at (your Spikes) and do that thing often, so that your Spikes become spikier.

Optimism works – Live each day positively through your Spikes.

Humility works – No leader is flawless and every Spike demands support, but if we always cut off their heads when they fail, who will want to be a leader?

ON THE SAME PAGE

Changing career trajectory tends to lead to greater innovation, success and finding meaning in one's work. It is a way to stay engaged and innovative – pushing leaders to keep agile by learning through new challenges. This helps one to maintain a fresh perspective and, ultimately, to find meaningful work so as to leave behind a lasting legacy.[4]

"Employees are attracted to organizations that will value them and that make a difference in the world. When they are capable of doing that, they will attract the best people. Business is better when relationships are better. Culture is great when the people have a say." Lolly Daskal[5], founder of Lead from Within – a global consultancy firm.

An organization can only prosper if its culture is designed from the ground up, to enable ongoing development for all its employees. The critical ingredient for achieving its ever-greater business aspirations is through its employees' continuous development: maximising organizational performance along with individual fulfilment.

---

4 Gardner, J. (1996) Self-Renewal: *The Individual and the Innovative Society*. Re-print, New York: Norton & Company.

5 Daskal, L. (2014) "Building Relationships and High Performing Teams." [online] Intuit. Available at: http://quickbase.intuit.com/blog/lolly-daskal-building-relationships-and-high-performing- teams [Accessed 18 Mar. 2016].

CHAPTER III
~~NO GOLDEN DOOR.~~
ALL IMMIGRANTS ARE WELCOME

How aware are you of your unconscious or implicit biases? Overriding them is key to success in any team selection. You need to look beyond them for a deeper impression when you first meet someone. Try to guess their Spikes.

The real danger of doing a job that you love is that it is seriously difficult to take time off – you're voluntarily and delightfully 'always on', constantly utilising your Spikes.

It is a sad fact that I've rarely ever taken my full allocation of annual leave and yet never feel bad about it. Every now and then, it is worthwhile switching off, even from the job that you so love.

Sitting at the beach bar just next to the beautiful fishing village of Tanji, on the stunning Atlantic coast of my beautiful birth place, The Gambia, life could not have been more tranquil.

However, my peaceful slumber was woken up by voices speaking in the local language, Wolof; but these weren't Gambians. They were obviously Senegalese. We are the same people, sharing the same heritage, culture and language. But after Vasco da Gama 'discovered' Senegal and Gambia in 1497, just as Columbus was discovering America, the British, the French and the Portuguese squabbled and fought over the strategic naval ports of Dakar and Banjul. As history would have us believe, a British gunboat sailed down the River Gambia and fired a cannon both north and south of the river. The borders offered to the French were within the reach of the British gunboats that patrolled the River Gambia – gunboat diplomacy at its earliest.

The French settled for Senegal, the British took the little fertile bit around the River Gambia and the strategic port of Banjul, leaving the Portuguese to the relatively barren lands of Guinea Bissau. Whilst the cultures have remained very close, the language has moved on. The French vocabulary has hijacked Senegalese Wolof, while many English colloquialisms have crept into Gambian Wolof.

The voice was shouting and demanding all the money be paid up front. I stood up to watch what was going on; it was a sickening and gut wrenching sight. Over 100 men were clambering on to a small wooden and hardly seaworthy vessel, which was going to try and sail for the Spanish Canary Islands.

They had no room for any belongings. The cargo was just a bunch of scared men with their lives literally in the hands of these profiteering gangsters and traffickers, who might even pay with their own lives should the boat go down. Most of these men never make it. Far too many Senegalese and Gambian young men, especially those with new-found access to the internet, feel as though they have no hope in their rural villages which probably haven't changed much over the past 500 years.

Armed only with outrageous hope and, usually, the collective life savings of most of the people in their village, the men pay these peddlers in human tragedy the price of a one-way trip, usually to oblivion, but on rare occasions, to a refugee camp on the island of Las Palmas in the Canaries… if they are very lucky.

This heart-rending sight is frequently played out on many coasts around Africa, where the 'have nots' will risk their lives in order to rub shoulders with the 'have lots'.

The sight made me realise just how strange life can be. I was born in Gambia and, under different circumstances, it might well have been me clambering aboard one of these wooden pirogues and risking all in order to give my family a chance.

Some 50-odd years ago, my parents had a similar, but tellingly different dilemma. Unlike many of these rural villagers my parents grew up in the colonial capital of Bathurst, which, after independence in 1964 was renamed Banjul. My parents were married in 1956; my father had a good white-collar job working in the meteorological office of The Gambia. They had three young children, and came to the stark realisation that the local educational system in The Gambia was beginning to creak as the British were starting to pack up and leave. They could see few positives in terms of their children's formal education. There was decent primary education but hardly any secondary schools, and no tertiary education whatsoever.

What also worried them was the unintended consequences of British rule. All the British African colonies were forced to comply with the onerous but effective 'British' way of doing things; civil service, judiciary, policing, education – even etiquette and manners were strictly controlled. There were many advantages (mainly for the British Governors of the day), but the miserable legacy of this colonization is still playing out today.

In my parents' estimation, by far the biggest issue was that Gambia had become a nation of acquiescent 'followers' – by force.

In order to obtain a decent civil service job (most of the available white-collar work was within the civil service), you needed the bare minimum of a decent secondary school education. Former British Africa is still to this day overly obsessed with formal qualifications – in contrast to the new world, where people are qualified based on their own merits.

In the new world, if you're capable – you are qualified!

This desire to work in the rarefied atmosphere of the relatively well-paid civil service left no other choice but to conform. Anyone who dared to be different was out. Any spark of challenge or maverick behaviour was also quickly ejected.

Progressive organizations have a culture of "challenging up and supporting down". The British built a culture of the direct and dangerous opposite "support up and challenge down".

My father recognized that he would not thrive or even survive in this environment. His Spikes would never flourish in a command and control regime.

This culture soon became pervasive across British Africa and this has bred the 'Big Man' legacy. As soon as the British left, the Big Men were quick to replace the authority figures. And due to the acquiescent and benign populations, they could easily grab power – and never have to relinquish it.

My parents were lucky: they were both born into devoutly middle class Roman Catholic families and there were a few Catholic schools founded by the missionaries and run by priests and nuns. The Gambia was nearly 90% Muslim and there were just not enough schools to cater for the fast growing young population.

My father had already travelled widely and spoke 4-5 languages fluently. An opportunity arose for my father to take a diplomatic posting in London. Given his Spikes of being a natural people person, gregarious and an Anglophile, my parents decided he would boldly go to London. He would make the same journey to Las Palmas for which many of these later generation Gambians would risk all. But my father would not travel in a wooden boat in the dead of night.

There were no scheduled airlines from The Gambia to the UK, but there were a few cargo ships making the trip up along the west coast of Africa up to the Canary Islands, going on to Casablanca and then to Spain, Portugal and France, before entering into the British port of Southampton. There were usually some meagre cabins available, for the very few who could afford them.

Times have changed but maybe not that much at all!

My parents made an unbelievably tough decision at that time: my father was going to take one of these cargo ships and see if he could make a life in London.

At this stage, there were hardly any black people in the UK and the very few that were there had mainly come under completely different circumstances from the West Indies. Many of them had been 'invited' to come and do the low level and rather menial jobs that the Brits didn't want to do in the new post-war era.

For the travelling Africans, it was very different. There were few invitations and most who came (like my father) felt that they were loyal subjects of the Queen, and looked to the Mother Country for direction and support. As far as my father was concerned, in the early '60s, this was a logical but bold move, which made complete sense, as in his view, there were strong and unbreakable ties between Britain and its colonies.

After an arduous and expensive six-week journey, he arrived fresh-faced and hugely naïve, but he confidently stepped out towards the exciting and wealthy metropolis that was London.

In Gambian terms, my father had never been anywhere near deprived, but he was now instantly poor. He had always lived in large houses, there were always maids and hired hands and he usually got whatever he wanted. He'd come with his life savings, thinking that he could buy a property and then send for his wife and his children.

In many respects he was beautifully naïve and that's just where the beauty ended. Along with some Gambian friends that arrived just before him, he managed to rent rooms in the old and dilapidated parts of the east end of London. At this stage, the Gambian men were lonely, without their partners left back home. They all had great plans to send for their loved ones, but they were lonely and isolated and consequently, suffered terribly.

Britain was not yet ready for its colonial friends, and these young men on their own found themselves the targets of ignorance and hatred. They were forced to live and band together. Whenever possible, they travelled together, as at least there was some safety in numbers.

Many years later, my father and his friends would describe what London was really like when they first came over. Many were attacked and beaten up by marauding gangs of young 'Teddy boys' out for a good laugh. It was brutal; many returned early and broken to Gambia. My father would never give in – it was his dream; it was his Britain.

He never shared the horror stories with my mother, and eventually, he sent for her and for the three of us.

We made a similar trip on a French cargo ship, where my mother had a tiny cabin, shared with my two sisters and me. My mother spoke seven languages including fluent French, which helped, as the French sailors would sneak food down to Mum and her three young kids. I remember Mum had no sea legs whatsoever, and was ill every day. For six long weeks, all four of us cried constantly.

If only Mum had known what she was letting herself in for: all my parents could eventually afford was a tiny two-bedroom ground floor flat in Church Road, Harlesden, a disadvantaged and run-down district in the north west of London.

Mr and Mrs Wilshire were in their late sixties; a wonderful Welsh couple whose children had grown up, married and moved away. This meant they had two bedrooms to rent, with a small kitchen and a lounge on the ground floor. My father ignored the 'No Blacks' sign on the window. My parents were greeted by a polite, proud and well-educated man, with whom they instantly hit it off. The Wiltshires were friendly and always kind to my parents.

Mr Wilshire seemed to have a story for everyone and every occasion. He had fought proudly for Britain in both World Wars, and on Sundays would take out his bugle and blow it as hard as his old frame would allow.

This recognizable screeching blast always coincided with the Boys Brigade band marching in the street outside our house. All the neighbours would line the streets, clapping the boys, who were joyfully playing their instruments. As they went past our house, Mr Wilshire would blow his bugle and we would all know it was time to go back into our homes. Along with my father, Mr Wiltshire was my hero – yet his only discernible Spikes were his ability to (just about) blow the bugle and his wonderfully uplifting stories. However, that one weak blast was all it took, and it fueled his enthusiasm for another month, until the Boys Brigade returned. We loved his Spikes, nearly as much as he clearly did.

I had no idea we were poor. From where I sat things were more than okay. There were five of us by now – my two brothers were born in London. We five children shared two single beds in a tiny bedroom. It never felt cramped; it never felt odd. In fact, we were much better off than most of our relatives.

By now my father had at last got his dream job at the Gambian High Commission in London; he was massively proud, but probably never realised just how Anglicised he had become. Mum was all and always African; she never really settled in London. She despaired at the fact that she was a 'nobody' with few resources, no network and zero influence in this monstrous and unforgiving city. Dad playing to his Spikes, was gregarious and massively inclusive; he made friends of every colour, race and religion – he was made for London.

Every summer, Mr and Mrs Wilshire would rent out the spare room upstairs and they would place a badly-written sign in the window, which would say 'Room to Let – No Jews, No Blacks, No Irish, No dogs!'

It would make my father's blood boil, but he grew up in a colonial Africa that was totally deferential, if not subservient. He could never totally break free of being institutionalized into believing that it was not his place to argue; he had been taught to avoid conflict and confrontation and, like far too many Africans of that era, was far too accepting of the status quo.

One summer, when the stupid sign was up again, I was coming home from school and I saw Mum pleading with my father not to say or do anything. I had never seen him so angry: he was shaking with rage (and Dad was one of those men who rarely lost his temper). I was sent inside whilst Mum coaxed Dad back into the lounge. He sat down with a tear in his eye; the glass in his hand shattered as he gripped it angrily.

Something inside of me changed that day forever: I knew this was never going to happen to me. I decided that I wasn't going to be deferential or subservient, and I never have been.

Going to school involved buying many things; fortunately, Mum was a genius with the very tight housekeeping budget – the most crucial and vital of Spikes to have in those most punishing of times. She could make exciting dishes from the most frugal of ingredients. Because we couldn't afford expensive uniforms, my Mum made mine. She had to buy the cap and the blazer, but she'd knitted my jumper and sewed my shirt and shorts. I knew no better, but as far as I was concerned I looked the part. With a satchel that my sister had outgrown, I could not have been more excited about going to school.

Where we lived, in run-down Harlesden, over 50% of the population was non-white; the housing was decrepit, the schools were not the best. There was very little investment in any sort of infrastructure and the big brands on the high street were already leaving.

As I was about to leave the house with my older sister who was only 7 years old (we all used to walk to school quite safely, without a care in the world), Mum gave me the usual lecture that I know many well-meaning immigrant mothers gave their children before they left for school: "You be twice as good as that white boy sitting next to you." I wasn't sure quite what Mum meant, but I was far too excited about school anyway.

My sister and I skipped off to school and I remember her just leaving me at the gate and running off with her friends, I was very quiet until shown in to the compact classroom. There were over 40 of us in the class. I sat silently, loving every moment.

When suddenly I remembered what Mum said, something about being "twice as good as the white boy sitting next to me," I froze for a moment and then looked around: there were NO white boys in the classroom.

Perhaps this was just as well, as my well-intentioned mother was in danger of giving me an inferiority complex, and perhaps planting the first seeds of victimhood in my unprepared mind.

This was tremendous learning for me, as from now on, no one was ever going to force me into being someone I didn't want to be. From this moment, I realised I had choices: no matter what the disadvantage, I became determined to make it an advantage. I was to encounter many opportunities and many disappointments, but now that I was beginning to understand the total sacrifice my parents had made for us, I was never going to be denied.

I went in search of anything that would give me a competitive advantage: without my knowing it, the search for my Spikes had started.

SPIKE SPARKS

Find yourself. Many descend on London from all around the UK and from abroad, bringing their very own ambitions and appetites to the city where 'you can be who you want to be,' in the relative anonymity of the metropolis.

Difference is good. Victorian London had the bad habit of continuously correcting new arrivals and demanding they conform. This is being replaced with a new desire of wanting to positively connect with and embrace diversity and difference.

Get out and about. No one territory has a monopoly on culture or talent – travel makes that so obvious and unforgettable.

Life is not a rehearsal. Don't waste it trying to live your dream constrained by the only place you know – dreams have no boundaries, but might come to life better elsewhere.

Love one another. Ultimately, the key motivator for great friendships and relationships is love. So don't be embarrassed to show your love, and show it as often as you can.

ON THE SAME PAGE

Research shows that there is no one perfect recipe for Leadership. Great leaders come in all shapes and sizes, with a variety of personal styles. Some have strengths in certain areas, while others complement them with their strengths in other capacities. The key for exceptional leadership within a successful organization is the ability to assemble the perfect blend of people with ample diversity and talent, to maximize the collective influence of the team.[6]

"Top-performing teams need diversity in personalities and talent. They need members who don't just settle for pleasant conversation but who respectfully challenge and ask, and members who build relationships and bring people together." Lolly Daskal[7], founder of Lead from Within – a global consultancy firm.

One of the critical reasons for pursuing diversity programmes is for innovation. For this, diversity of thought is essential. When diversity of thought is the goal, then one has to bring in people who have diverse experiences – in other words Diverse SPIKES. This is not simply an 'old school' understanding of diversity, in terms of race, gender and socioeconomic background, but focusing more on diversity in learning styles and professional experience.[8]

"Diversity: the art of thinking independently together." – Malcolm Forbes

---

6 Zenger, J. and Folkman, J. [2014] "Key Insights from the Extraordinary Leader." [White Paper] Available at: http://zengerfolkman.com/wp-content/uploads/2013/03/Extraordinary-Leader- Insights-Excerpts-from-The-Extraordinary-Leader.pdf [Accessed 05 Mar 2016]

7 Daskal, L. (2013) "The Honest Truth About Teams. [online] Lead from Within." Available at: http://www.lollydaskal.com/leadership/the-honest-truth-about-teams/ [Accessed 19 Mar. 2016].

8 Brescoll, V. [2011] "What do leaders need to understand about diversity?" [online] Yale Insights, Yale School of Management. Available at: http://insights.som.yale.edu/insights/what-do-leaders- need-understand-about-diversity [Accessed 26 March 2016]

CHAPTER IV
~~GET READY~~.
GET GOING

It all begins with understanding your Spikes, and is followed by understanding your limitations even better. Focus on these things when you're winning. What are you not so good at?

Rapid change calls for a rapid response, but many people often get bogged down in planning how they will react. They confuse getting ready with actual progress. They diddle away precious time in preparing to do something.

You can analyse the situation to death. Weigh the facts… Consider your options… Get organized… Calculate the best plan of attack… Then take forever to debug that plan.

Meanwhile, the beat goes on. Change – and the problems it creates – won't wait on you to come up with a fool-proof approach. A moving target allows little opportunity to take aim. By the time you come up with a perfect plan, the problem may have developed – and possibly even grown bigger. Getting ready gets dangerous when it creates a culture of delay.

You can take time to roll up your sleeves, but that's about it. Today's rapid rate of change calls for a culture of mobility. Put your faith in those whose Spikes prefer action rather than analysis, in pursuit of finishing instead of painstaking preparation.

But don't ignore the need for 'critical friends': those who are not afraid to challenge openly and ask the necessary tough questions. The action-oriented person still requires some constructive questioning, and by combining these two differing approaches, you could make the winning combination. Having only one of these Spikes can be fatal to the organization.

Your job together is to help the organization dramatically shrink the time it takes to achieve goals. This means you must be willing to improvise, to respond and react, and to accept each other's Spikes.

To ensure you go faster, do less; but do it better together.

You can't afford to just stop and study the situation from all angles before you make a move, yet you shouldn't simply dive in. Instead of trying to analyse every last detail, again and again, and plan your way through problems, learn your way through the situation. But you'll need each other's complementary Spikes – and all the time.

Inertia is more crippling than mistakes. Inaction is the costliest error. So get going! Mobility will be your best teacher. It's the fastest way to find out what works and what doesn't. But be courageous enough to recognize when it's not working – and quickly.

But don't just keep moving. When you foul up, pause and fix it. Learn from your mistakes and then plough on. The only mistake is the one you don't learn from.

This is how you energize the organization and build momentum. Create a culture of intelligent action, which can keep up in a world of constant change.

But remember: even the fastest and best racing drivers have a team behind them, constantly checking for problems and issues. They are empowered to stop the car when they believe it may be in danger of crashing and endangering everyone.

'Finished' beats 'perfect', but every dissenting voice in the team must be heard.

"NO PLAN SURVIVES CONTACT WITH THE ENEMY."

FIELD MARSHAL HELMUTH CARL BERNARD VON MOLTKE

CAMILA – 'NO CHILD IS BORN A CRIMINAL'

I was lying awake on a hot summer night in London, barely listening to the radio and worrying about the usual things: kids, the business, Mum, Chelsea FC, but most of all, the diary from hell (and how it was all going to be 'shoe horned' in again this week). It was yet another day, in yet another flashing week and another disappearing year.

No matter: the BBC World Service radio has always been consistently brilliant at getting me to sleep. An assertive and friendly voice was speaking with passion and authority, despite the annoying interruptions from the BBC interviewer, desperately trying to trip her up.

Her calm but forceful voice could not be denied. It demanded my attention and, more importantly, it pushed the flotsam in my mind completely out of the way.

Her name was Camila, and she was an expert, a visionary and, most of all, different. After ten minutes, it was no longer possible to remain lying down: this was not well-practiced rhetoric, and it was real. Very real.

Camila delivered a graphic and moving picture of her charity, Kids Company, and the tough and unforgiving London that she knew only too well. She had become the expert witness for the Metropolitan Police during the tragic and high profile Damilola Taylor trial.

Damilola was a 10-year-old boy from Nigeria, who was brutally murdered in Peckham, London in November 2000. The tragic and senseless nature of the killing shocked the nation. There was a large public outcry for justice. Camila was vocal and well-informed about the circumstances that are prevalent in the inner city and that can lead to these tragedies.

The Metropolitan Police had learned to trust her knowledge and experience and had come to rely on her judgment calls, especially when it came to dealing with the kids from the streets of inner London.

I, too, in an instant of meeting her, would become inspired by her knowledge, focus and colossal generosity.

A feeling raced through my body: this was not just information, it was not just wanting to care and help. This was much more than that. This was inspiration.

Camila had surrendered so much of her time and care to these kids, in a way that no one else had in their short lives. In a world of dysfunctional families, class 'A' drugs, violence and abuse, she had become their guiding light.

In a matter of moments, she had lit my fire, broadened my thinking and compelled me to want to know so much more. And most of all, she encouraged action.

I'd arranged to meet Camila at the offices of Kids Company, in a small terraced house in Peckham, a disadvantaged part of south London. It was clean, tidy and orderly and at the same time, lived in and homely. The phones rang constantly, with children seeking out Camila's soothing voice and authenticity. She was providing incredible advice and warmth in two-minute doses and appeared to know them all intimately.

She had a drop of magic for all the faceless kids on the phone; most of all, she had time for them all. Even without seeing them it was possible to feel their growing comfort, and to see the warmth that radiated from Camila's care. Inspirational.

She offered me tea and, whilst pouring it out, she shared the invigorating story behind her founding of Kids Company. She had a strong sense of self-belief, which was balanced by her self-effacing manner – but she could not hide her humour or generosity. This is a special story and one that needed telling, and she told it marvellously. She was an arch communicator.

However, nothing could have prepared me for the moving and hurtful experience we were to share when we arrived at Kids Company.

Kids Company was founded in 1996, under some dilapidated railway arches in Peckham. Railtrack (who at the time were responsible for running the UK's rail infrastructure), made the space available at a reasonable rent to Camila.

This soon became a 'rent-free' deal after they had visited Kids Company, and saw the inspirational leader and her team in action first-hand.

There were various classrooms and workshops carved out underneath the arches for the kids. It was a little dark, a little dank, but genuine human warmth radiated from every worker. Kids Company offered the children a safe haven where they could be cared for and taught.

Many of them had been expelled from school, and had no capable or caring adult fighting their corner. The authorities were far removed from these street kids.

They were left to their own devices and regularly fell prey to drug dealers, abusers and a whole host of desperadoes who cared nothing for their interests and betterment – until Camila. Until Kids Company.

My tour of Kids Company was a total revelation, and it served to make me feel both honoured to be amongst them, and also totally and abjectly shamed by a lack of understanding and prior knowledge of their tragic predicament.

TWIN PEAKS

A quiet and seemingly shy boy of 13 was standing next to a near-life-size papier mâché statue of himself. There was an aura of pain surrounding him. After watching for a few minutes, it became clear that he was really hurting.

Camila caught me feeling his anguish and shared his story with me.

He was one of identical twin brothers, and they were often to be seen tearing around on their BMX bikes, delivering crack cocaine for one of the many local dealers. They used to regularly stop off at Kids Company and stare through the gates at the kids inside. They were street smart, but had missed out on any formal education and the necessary love and camaraderie that all children need to develop.

Like many of their street peers and others in the neighbourhood, their paths were set, and their story would surely end in tragedy. Camila appeared to be their one chance to break free from the pack.

She engaged with them on a regular basis, and they began coming by more and more. They were keen to come inside and join in the fun and warmth that were tangible, even from the other side of the gates.

They eventually plucked up the courage to quietly enquire about joining Kids Company. They were warmly welcomed, but on the condition that they gave up their 'delivery' business. They had a huge decision to make, and their circumstances and their dealers would not make this easy, or without risk.

A few weeks later, one of the boys joined up. He said confidently that his brother had "a few more deliveries to make over the coming days," but then he would also be joining up. Hope was on the horizon, but fate would deal them the cruelest of blows.

On one of the last of his errands, the youngster handed over the substance, but the client was less than impressed, complaining that it was not genuine stuff; he angrily chased the boy away. Not knowing good stuff from bad, the boy took the addict's word and threw the rest of the stuff away.

On returning to the dealer, all hell broke loose: he demanded his money and then just wanted the stuff back. Neither was available, and he resorted to the only method of feedback known to him: violence. The boy, now petrified, jumped on his bike and rode for his life. The dealer wanted revenge – payback is the unwritten law of the inner city streets. He enlisted the help of one of the local 'crack heads', who was to be rewarded for finding and 'sorting' the boy.

After much searching and asking around, he came across the boy's twin brother, who had, by now, settled in at Kids Company. Mistaking the boy for his twin brother, the crack head savagely attacked him. He was found dead later that day.

I was still watching his brother standing next to the papier mâché statue of his departed twin that he had created. He joined Kids Company soon after the tragedy, and was cared for; they helped to come to terms with the fact that his twin had paid his debt with his own life. Now the boy was alone, and his world was just about as bleak as it could get – without Camila and Kids Company there might have been two tragedies.

It soon became clear that there were far too many of these stories of destruction on the streets. All the kids shared the harrowing experience of a lack of care and understanding, with no support from their parents or any of the governmental authorities.

It's in desperation that many leaders are found.

Camila was an inspired, visionary leader, who aimed to deliver extraordinary results. She had the amazing Spike of being able to remain utterly steadfast and adamant about everything she believed in, no matter what barriers lay in front of her. This took courage and a tremendous resolve, as there were many who challenged and doubted her approach and direction. She soon (dangerously, but perhaps impressively) grew beyond listening, and took on all comers with an increasing tenacity and assertiveness.

Whilst many admired her 'iron' will and her resolve under fire, some started worrying about 'checks and balances'. She couldn't always be right, could she?

Even Batman needed a Robin, both for support and challenge.

CHECKS AND BALANCES

Camila had been born into a wealthy Iranian family that had to flee the country with nothing, after the overthrow of the Shah of Iran. Her family eventually came to the UK, and being experienced and gifted business people, they soon had built successful businesses again.

But this path was not for her; she had a different calling. She had an inspirational and compelling vision, which became Kids Company. By saving her monthly mortgage payments, she was able to breathe the necessary financial life into what had become her charity.

In her own words: "What children need, more than anything, is a stable home life, love and attention. Kids Company was founded in 1996, in response to the growing number of kids who do not have these advantages."

Camila was adamant that "every child should have a chance. It makes sense for society, as well as for each one of these vulnerable children. Kids Company has already made a huge difference to the lives of thousands of kids, thanks to the support of all our friends and benefactors over recent years. But there is more work to be done and more kids who need their childhood back."

We were all, in the main, so enamoured and inspired by Camila and Kids Company that we just had to assist her cause in any way that we could.

Camila had amazing Spikes, and they were on clear display all the time. However, Spikes as prominent and as strong as hers scream out for the necessary – but perhaps opposite – balancing Spikes.

It was December 2006, and our next Inspired Leaders Network evening was to be in honour of 'Woman of the Year'. Camila was a (very) late entrant into the voting by our network.

We invited 200 VIP executives from our network to the gala dinner, with Kids Company as the chosen beneficiary of the evening. Camila, alongside the other two powerful women in our top three, would be interviewed by me. After a short break, I would then facilitate a fast-moving and challenging Q&A session with the live audience.

At the end of a stimulating and provocative session, we asked our audience to support Kids Company in any way they felt was appropriate.

We had a very full house at the Imperial War Museum in London on the 12th December 2006. Camila was a difficult interviewee: she would take any question as a cue to launch into a long, brilliant monologue on another aspect of the conditions and potential solutions for London's street kids. Whilst, at times, it was spellbinding, some in the audience were starting to ask whether she could be right about everything – well, could she?

As we broke for refreshments and something to eat, Camila was mobbed by well-wishers and those who had become mesmerised by her rhetoric. She was turbo-charged, and hardly drew breath as she had time and poise for everyone.

As we regathered for the questions from the audience, Camila was in her element.

She was sharp, very focused and without any sense of doubt at all. Real people – real leaders – like Camila, inspire us to do the things that others say cannot be done.

However, there were a few occasions where some of Camila's 'facts' were not quite right or were misquoted. But all who noticed would have felt churlish in picking her up on these relatively small points.

Again, as we were forcefully confronted by her all-consuming dogma, it was noticeable that even her phenomenal and very well intentioned Spikes, would require a strong and complementary team around her. Kids Company didn't need any more visionaries, but they would need managers who were far more focused on the exploding costs, the operational delivery and the execution of the services that were being offered.

As the electrifying evening drew to a close, we asked for anyone who wanted to 'give' to Kids Company, if they could leave their business card with an outline of their offer written on the reverse of the card.

Camila was a fundraiser extraordinaire. Nearly everyone left a business card. The offers were breath-taking: from a year's free consulting from Accenture, volunteers from The Post Office, ASDA, Santander, with many individuals donating sums of money. It was collectively worth a huge amount to Kids Company.

Everyone left feeling better. Camila's unique and evangelical delivery – never with notes, but always from the heart – had proved compelling and irresistible, once again.

After the event, we spent a few days calling around and firming up the generous offers of support, then producing a well-defined document, with everything itemised, including names, companies and all contact details.

I delivered three copies of the document in person to Camila at Kids Company. She was both gracious and grateful.

We all felt moved and uplifted by our small involvement in helping Kids Company to continue making such an important difference to the lives of London's inner city children.

A couple of months later, a few of those who had offered services or resources other than money, began chasing us to find out what was happening as they had not heard back from Kids Company, despite enquiring directly.

I began making enquiries, and was also left a feeling concerned and dissatisfied.

I decided to visit Kids Company again. Camila was away and I sat with some of the team members and chatted about the company. It became very clear that Camila's span of control was beyond the means of any individual to master.

Whilst all the individuals I met were impressive in their own way, there was no one with the presence or profile to really challenge or 'manage' Camila – no one to balance her Spikes.

The documents were largely untouched from where I had left them.

Camila's belief system was impervious to cynics and doubters alike, but what started out as a tremendous strength, unchecked, had started becoming a limitation. Force of will, and even a force for good – which she obviously was – still required checks and balances.

This lack of a strong willed, but more cautious and process-driven executive at her side, or within her top team, would cost the once brilliant charity dearly. Sometimes a huge Spike requires as strong a compensating Spike. This was an opportunity missed, which would eventually result in the unravelling of Kids Company in late 2015.

THE BITTER END

Throughout the ordeal of the worrying and troubling demise of Kids Company, Camila appeared to be in the media all the time and maintained a defiant stance, refusing to accept accusations of mismanagement of the charity.

The Conservative government – along with its Labour predecessor – had fallen under her spell and appeared mesmerized by Camila's charisma and captivating rhetoric.

She admitted to "bending the law slightly" over using redundancy money as revenue cash: "I never break the law but just stretch it. The correct law is to take care of these children. If the law is not correct, we have to bend it slightly. I'm playing chess with psychopaths."

However, she also blamed "the collective madness of the media and politicians" for the demise of her charity, adding: "And I was supposed to be killed off too."

The government had given over £40 million to Kids Company and had embarrassingly authorized another £3 million, on the condition that Camila resigned as CEO, the day before Kids Company became insolvent. She refused to resign.

Asked for her thoughts, when she learned that donors were pulling out, she replied: "The media have been generating so much poor publicity that our philanthropists have freaked... A poor reputation has made me seem as if I am a person who mismanaged. And now we are being accused of child protection failure."

Camila said her only regret was that she did not raise a greater amount. "I'm not sorry that I gave the kids holidays and money," she stated.

This brilliant initiative should not have ended in such disrepute, but a more inclusive approach, which valued diverse Spikes in the top team at Kids Company, would have served to challenge some of the well-intentioned excesses that led to the company's demise.

Here was an organization that hurtled towards good work, in various forms, without pausing to consider the consequences of some of the decisions. It required some differing Spikes to challenge the leadership to not simply continue 'doing the right things', but to also 'do things right'.

Simply knowing Camila and experiencing her inspirational magic has been life-enhancing. She encouraged – and sometimes provoked – everyone she met to honour the children. After all, as she constantly reminded us, "no child is born a criminal".

Camila's devotion and motivation have never been in question, but queries regarding mismanagement, misjudgment and the alleged misuse of donations and government money deserved better answers.

Many people felt a growing frustration, disappointment and sadness, as Camila refused to back down and simply admit that there had been gross mismanagement. After all, it was there for all to see. She simply found it impossible to accept that she had done wrong in any capacity.

It is impossible not to admire and support the brilliance and genuine care that motivated the beginnings of Kids Company – to bring the love of a family to the troubled lives of inner city children, who did not have this vital foundation of support.

Camila has always been motivated by the best of intentions towards the kids, but she eventually became carried away by the unchecked power she was able to wield.

The biggest issue was that Camila herself required 'managing', whilst she continued to provide her rare magic.

Every Spike deserves a complementary Spike, and some need this far more than others.

"NEVER HIRE OR PROMOTE IN YOUR OWN IMAGE. IT IS FOOLISH TO REPLICATE YOUR STRENGTH AND IDIOTIC TO REPLICATE YOUR WEAKNESS.

IT IS ESSENTIAL TO EMPLOY, TRUST, AND REWARD THOSE WHOSE PERSPECTIVE, ABILITY, AND JUDGMENT ARE RADICALLY DIFFERENT FROM YOURS.

IT IS ALSO RARE, FOR IT REQUIRES UNCOMMON HUMILITY, TOLERANCE, AND WISDOM.

DEE W. HOCK,
FOUNDER AND FORMER CEO OF THE VISA CREDIT CARD ASSOCIATION

SPIKE SPARKS

If all you bring to a problem is hope, you have already played a vital part in its eventual resolution.

Being right all the time (and dangerously wanting to prove that you are right) can be destructive.

Ambition is apparent in all great leaders – but what separates the Inspired Leader is their ability to put the ambitions of the organization above their own personal goals.

Our minds are like parachutes – they function best when fully opened and are ineffective when fully closed. The most dangerous leader is the one who is 'parachuted' in with a completely closed mind regarding what needs to be done.

Identify the Spikes you need in your team and never stop developing them. Can you imagine a top sprinter, ballerina, or pilot who stopped training and developing?

ON THE SAME PAGE

Founder's Syndrome has been aptly described by Elizabeth Schmidt as "The first is a sense of grandiosity – that the organization is the founder's, and it exists to serve his or her ego (or pocketbook). The second is an inability to delegate – poor management on the part of the founder. The third is an inability to make a smooth transition from the founder to new leadership. And the fourth is an unwavering dedication to the original vision for the organization."[9]

Complementary-leadership structures are common and, in some cases, even institutionalized.[10] An executive dream team is essential for repeated success, as can be seen by Pep Guardiola bringing along his trusted four-man backroom team (Personal assistant, Assistant coach, Fitness coach, Scout and video analyst) to Manchester City to face his biggest challenge of transferring his high-intensity, possession-based paradigm to a new arena.[11]

In the *Guardian*, Kristina Keneally states, "Hillary Clinton's policies look good. But she lacks authenticity and the kind of charisma required to unite a nation."[12] Maybe the balance that her political team requires is someone like Bill Clinton with a charismatic ability to explain policy, as demonstrated while speaking at an event in Hell's Kitchen NY, "Clinton proved that he remains a great asset for his wife's campaign – blending obvious star quality and the ability to communicate almost willfully detailed policy arguments in a way that still keeps an audience hanging on his every word."[13]

---

[9] Schmidt, E. (2013) Rediagnosing "Founder's Syndrome": Moving Beyond Stereotypes to Improve Nonprofit Performance. (online) Non Profit Quarterly. Available at: https://nonprofitquarterly. org/2013/07/01/rediagnosing-founder-s-syndrome-moving-beyond-stereotypes-to-improve- nonprofit-performance [Accessed 21 Apr 2016]

[10] Miles, S. and Watkins, M. (2007) "The leadership team: Complementary strengths or conflicting agendas?" (online) *Harvard Business Review*. Available at: https://miles-group.com/sites/default/files/article_file_attachments/hbr_article_leadership_team.pdf [Accessed 22 Apr 2016]

[11] Pollard, R. (2016) "Meet Pep Guardiola's backroom team: The four men behind the incoming Man City manager." (online) *Mirror*. Available at: http://www.mirror.co.uk/sport/football/news/meet-pep- guardiolas-backroom-team-7308504 [Accessed 20 Apr 2016]

[12] Keneally, K. (2016) "I can't get excited about Hillary Clinton's campaign – it lacks a raison d'être." (online) *The Guardian*. Available at: http://www.theguardian.com/commentisfree/2016/feb/03/ i-cant-get-excited-about-hillary-clintons-campaign-it-lacks-a-raison-detre [Accessed 20 Apr 2016]

[13] Siddiqui, S. and Taylor, D. (2016) "Bill Clinton still boosts Hillary's campaign despite clash with protesters." (online) *The Guardian*. Available at: http://www.theguardian.com/us-news/2016/ apr/11/bill-clinton-hillary-campaign-us-election-2016 [Accessed 20 Apr 2016]

CHAPTER V
~~BELIEVE IN THE PROBLEMS~~. HAVE FAITH IN THE OPPORTUNITIES

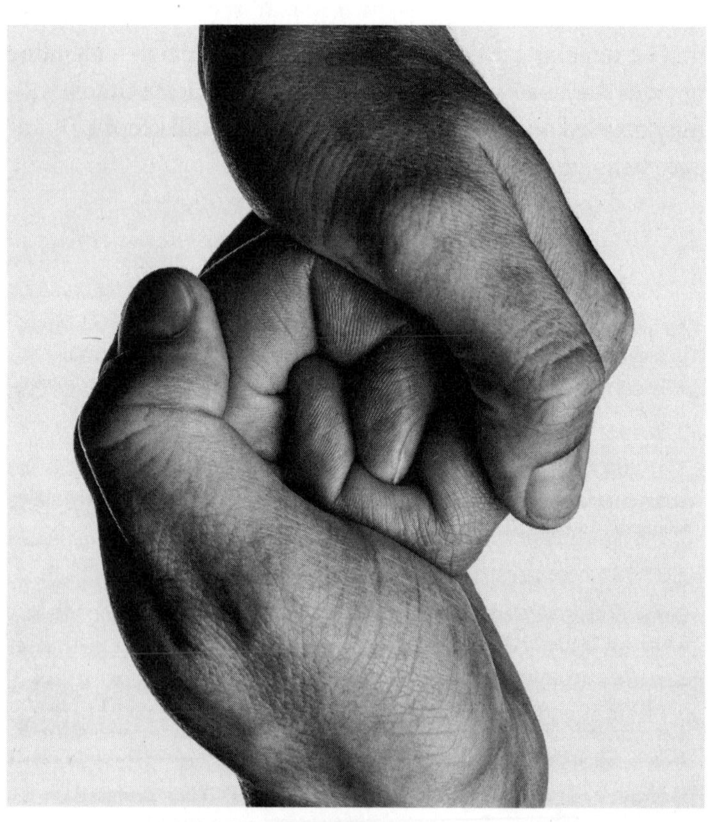

Despair is readily available to all of us. Hope is so much tougher to access every day – but it's so worth the effort.

What's your personal vision or mantra that keeps you full of hope and moving forward every day?

Change can be hard on hope. Problems, which are the natural offspring of change, fill our field of view. It's easy to focus on what's going wrong instead of searching out the possibilities and opportunities.

Trouble naturally draws attention. As soon as change starts throwing off sparks, people become preoccupied with the various headaches, aggravations and fears.

As they say in the newspaper business, "Bad news drives good news away."

Believing in the problems destroys our faith in the opportunities. We get discouraged. We lose our spirit. Our energy drains out through the cracks in our self-confidence.

We are left disempowered and cynical in a culture of despair. It's a dangerous way to face the future.

But we need to remember that opportunity often comes disguised as trouble. Rather than dwelling on the negatives, we need to attack problems with a 'can-do' attitude. We do the best job of managing change when our mind-set is relentlessly positive. Hope for tomorrow enables us to transcend the problems of today.

This adversity will reveal those with the Spikes of strong determination, resilience and a steely resolve – but most will be fixated on avoiding the pain of change. Despair can erode and blind hope – and very quickly. Notice those still standing tall and empower them to inspire others, no matter how challenged you may personally be feeling.

It's no longer feasible for the leader to be 'fully rounded' in these turbulent times, but a team that has been selected and integrated for its complementary Spikes is, by design, fully rounded.

The way you think – the way you frame the situation – heavily influences your ability to deal with tough problems. Look beyond the bleakness of the moment and envision a brighter tomorrow. Think in terms of possibilities rather than limits. Search for openings that can lead to a better future. Believe in the opportunities, and you will help them to appear. Keep the faith and you will contribute to a culture of optimism, hope and expectancy.

Having those around with the necessary path-finding Spikes of resilience and resolve will help the whole team to navigate the tough times.

Think team and think Spike.

"THE PERCEPTION OF A PROBLEM IS ALWAYS RELATIVE. YOUR HEADACHE FEELS TERRIFIC TO THE DRUGGIST."

RAMONA E. F. ARNETT, PRESIDENT, RAMONA ENTERPRISES, INC.

THE WORLD BANK

Far too rarely, I've had the opportunity of working with an organization where its mission and purpose is crystal clear to all who work there. The World Bank is the finest example of such clarity: with its fixation upon ending global poverty, it is probably the most uplifting professional environment I've ever had the privilege of working in.

My job was to help coach the Senior Management Team (SMT), and that meant working closely with the President of the World Bank Group. The world of development was going through an enormous period of transformation. This would threaten the very survival of some organizations.

The President of the World Bank was incredibly focused and somehow coped with the huge demands on his time, both externally and internally.

The World Bank had become far too bureaucratic and was perceived as being too slow to meet the increasing demands of this ever-changing and unforgiving world. There were no 'off weeks'. It was highly intense and hugely pressurized – all the time.

Change would not be easy in an environment with such a prolonged average length of service (nearly 20 years) and such low attrition rates (3%).

The President was a supremely efficient leader: always on time and readily available all around the world. His constantly demanding schedule was only matched by his endless energy and desire to keep the Bank relevant and agile in these testing times.

Shalimar was the amazingly appropriate point of contact for the President's Office. She was always charm personified. She possessed an instant, golden smile and the most incredible and consistent professionalism. No matter what time I called or arrived, she was always available and alert.

We were to forge a unique relationship, where our Spikes worked in unison and in a complementary fashion – especially when the pressure became intense.

JOB TITLES AREN'T NECESSARY

Shalimar and I routinely worked very closely together, as with so many events running concurrently, it was vital that I had access to the President – sometimes at very short notice. It was rare that I had to explain in detail; she somehow always 'read' what was on my mind and better still, the situation.

She was discreet and thorough with everything, no matter how trivial it might have initially appeared.

She had an obvious Spike of charm, a good nature and was very service-oriented. She was also intelligent and perceptive.

Her skills of observation meant that she saw everything and was always a move ahead of all those who might have less than straightforward intentions.

Her other Spikes were rather well hidden. She is one of the most resilient and determined people I have ever had the pleasure of working with. She was also the most natural of team players.

I have never known her job title.

There was so much more to Shalimar and I knew that her story would reveal a great deal about her dynamism, her resolve, and most of all, her golden Spikes.

This story needed telling in her very own words.

SHALIMAR'S STORY – AN EXTRAORDINARY OPPORTUNITY

At one point, I chaired an interview panel where one of the candidates told me that I should feel proud to be in my position, working so close to the President and being a part of decisions that mattered.

It wasn't the first time I had heard this, but, for some reason, it had never resonated as strongly as it did this time. I smiled and nodded my head in agreement and told her that it was a privilege – something I had said many times before as well. She told me she was a huge fan of his and would give it all she had, if provided with the opportunity.

I could tell that she was excited to be there and wanted to convey her sincerity and enthusiasm. She had high energy and for a split second I saw a reflection of myself in her attitude.

But for some reason, I wasn't totally convinced. I had a hard time believing in her and her intentions. I concluded the interview by telling her that we would be in touch and waved good-bye as she got in the elevator.

I went about my day and, long after the meeting had concluded, I couldn't stop thinking about her comment. "How lucky was I"? It dawned on me that perhaps I was indeed lucky, but why was it so hard for me to digest this? Was it that I felt undeserving? Or was I indifferent to my role or my title? Either way, it was food for thought.

Perhaps the truth was that I was in a position of power and yet hadn't quite put it all together in my head. I was processing it as completely new information.

From the outside, my role appears to be powerful. I sit at the pinnacle of an organization as the aide to the President – one of the most powerful and influential people in the world. Many people like him and work in his best interest. Others are drawn to him for their own advancement: they confuse their role of subordinate or colleague for that of a 'friend' or confidant looking for an opportunity to further their own careers.

Still others are determined to destroy him for daring to change the banking culture and for challenging its inefficiencies.

My job, as I see it, is to be his eyes and ears and to always let him know the temperature and mood of the room. I'm the first person he sees when he reaches the office and I'm the last one to see him out.

He trusts me and knows that I would never betray him. He also knows that I treat everyone with dignity and respect. He realizes that I'm humble enough to ask questions, but have no issues having difficult conversations as and when necessary.

My role requires a delicate balance of building relationships that are based on trust and at the same time, being his gatekeeper. I have to be the funnel between him and the team. Always thinking ahead, anticipating the positive and negative outcomes of any given situation and having appropriate solutions ready for when he asks.

He also knows that I 'get' him and come from the same adversity that he and our clients come from, something that not all in the organization can relate to.

I am his ambassador. But this isn't the job I applied for. A role like mine isn't advertised; it's created, based on trust and respect. This doesn't mean I'm in anyway indispensable, but rather that I work tirelessly to ensure that he's surrounded by the right people with the best of intentions.

I cross all my 'T's' and dot all my 'I's' and ensure that the team runs like a 'well-oiled' machine. This is also the first time I've worked in the public sector after spending six years in Investment Banking. To say the two are worlds apart is a huge understatement.

I come from an incredibly humble background and have worked very hard for every single opportunity that I have been afforded. I know that no matter how difficult things were for me, they were far more difficult for many others, so I didn't use my circumstances as an excuse to slack, but rather as encouragement to forge ahead.

I clearly understood that what had been my life for so long, didn't necessarily need to be the rest of my life. I knew that there was so much more to be had.

Every morning when I wake up, I'm grateful to have a roof over my head, have food on the table and clothing to wear. This ritual takes place every morning without fail. Once I've digested these thoughts, I start going through a mental checklist of things that I need to tackle as soon as I walk through the door and those that I need to address before the end of the day.

I have a sense of responsibility to get things done well and find solutions to those that can be done differently. With that said, there's seldom time to really think about how much power – if any – lies within my role or title.

Unlike most, I see the President as a human being, who cares deeply and is compassionate; he is this person well before being the "45th most powerful person in the world."

It's seeing things through that lens that allows me to stay grounded and focused and not get caught up with being in the same room or photograph as the various heads of state, Queens, Kings and many other dignitaries that he meets with regularly.

Are they powerful and perhaps have some of the most brilliant minds? Yes, but I see past that. As far as I'm concerned, they are human beings, like you and I. They have good days and bad days and perhaps deal with pressures I could never relate to. It's as simple as understanding that this is their life and not mine. I don't ever confuse my world with theirs. I'm meant to do great work in ways where many don't even know that I exist.

I continuously strive to lead and be a voice to those that perhaps don't believe they have one.

Humble Origins

I came from poverty, with little emotional support to inoculate me from the constant violence and addiction that plagued my every interaction with the world.

I was raised by my mother, grandmother, step-grandfather and three crazy uncles, two of which took turns going to jail for stealing or selling drugs.

On the only occasion I spent time with my biological father, he took me to Central Park in my stroller and started selling "loosies" to anyone who wanted a quick fix of marijuana. I can only imagine what the people who walked by my stroller thought about what my future – if any – would look like.

I doubt they imagined me gaining an education at a highly competitive university, working in investment banking, being the body-woman to a Latin American Billionairess and then the right-hand person of the President of the World Bank Group.

The reality is that I was given the right ingredients to make all the wrong decisions in life. However, a life filled with tumult and adversity had cultivated an indelible sense of resolve in me. I learned how to quickly check the temperature in the room even when many had no idea what was truly happening – some might describe it as being 'street smart' and others would call it emotional intelligence; I'm not sure what it really is but I've learned to trust my perceptions and live by them.

I learned that some people are so rich that all they really have is money. I also learned that what I enjoyed doing the most

– connecting and understanding what made people tick – was seldom practiced in most circles. Few people appeared to ever care about scratching past the surface.

Most importantly, I learned (and felt) that although I was raised with only the bare essentials, I was wealthier than many.

I have a sense of purpose and an incredible drive, which money can't buy. It takes very little to make me happy. In fact, I felt like I had arrived when I could go to the movies and afford to buy anything on display. This may not mean much to someone who's had it all, but to me, it was everything.

Now, I am privileged to wake up every morning and aim to break the vicious cycle of poverty by injecting hope into the hearts of our world's most grief-stricken people, and to be an inspiration to those that don't believe they have a voice.

It's a wonderful and very fulfilling feeling.

Bronx, New York – 1978

My mother left my biological father six months into her pregnancy with me because she didn't want me to grow up in an abusive household. She was just 16 years old when she summoned the strength to break free, and she vowed that she would never allow anyone to treat her like that again.

She went to live with my grandmother, where she remained until I was six years old. I was very close to my grandmother and her older sister, Carmen, who lived across the street. Carmen would go on to be one of the most inspiring people in my life. She didn't have any children and so she spent a significant amount of time and energy contributing to my upbringing by ensuring that I understood the importance of having a relationship with God.

We lived in the South Bronx and I went to school two blocks away from our apartment. At the time, the neighborhood was made up of mostly Puerto Ricans, Mexicans and a handful of Dominicans, and was plagued with drug dealers on every corner. Speaking in Spanish was the norm and, as a true bilingual, I don't remember a time when I didn't speak both languages. I was very close to my grandmother: everywhere she went, I went.

One day we were walking down the stairs of her apartment when we both realized that the landlord was coming to collect the rent. My grandmother immediately pulled me to the side and whispered in my ear (in Spanish): "Tell her that I don't have the money for the rent – she'll have to wait till next month." I did as I was told and proceeded to spend the next five minutes translating back and forth between the two of them.

I was five years old and, although I don't think it's appropriate to give this kind of responsibility to a child, it was a completely normal way of life for me then.

I've always enjoyed being able to provide for my family and became the person they turn to when they're going through tough times. I feel a sense of duty to help solve all their problems, which at times can be draining.

My brothers routinely refer to me as their 'second mom', because I not only helped my mother raise them, and worked from the age of 12 to help buy their school clothes and put food on the table, but because I'm their #1 fan. I'm always willing and available to give them advice or talk them 'off the ledge' when they're unable to see the light at the end of the tunnel.

I have always felt a sense of responsibility for everything and anything I do, and I thrive in environments where I'm in charge and I am able to help others. It's what I love to do most in life: help those in need.

Grandma's Guide & Translator

While I was living with my grandmother, my uncle, Cookie, went to a minimum security prison for the umpteenth time. But this time no one wanted to go see him but her and me. So it was decided that I would accompany her.

It was 6:00am and it was time to get ready and head to Grand Central station.

My grandmother held on to my hand fiercely: this was the first time she would be entrusting me to guide her from our tiny apartment in the South Bronx to 42nd and Grand Central station, where we would take the Amtrak train four hours north to upstate New York.

My grandmother came here when she was 14 years old, and immediately started working in the factories. She had no interest in learning English; therefore, in times like these, she had no choice but to depend on others; in this case, that meant me. I was seven years old and knew how to read well, having just memorized 23 pages of the book, Rapunzel, for a reading competition in school.

It was totally up to me to get us there and back, and for some reason, it didn't feel like such a big deal. We arrived at Grand Central station and I showed a conductor our tickets; he pointed us in the right direction. Once on the train, I ushered us to a corner seat, where I could face in the direction the train was going. I am incredibly susceptible to motion sickness – even to this day, so I didn't want to take chances. I was elated to be going on this journey, even if it meant going to a jail.

I knew it then – and now even more so: I was completely in charge, and my grandmother was completely comfortable with that. Four hours later, we arrived at the train station, where we were picked up by prison officials, who gave us a ride to the prison.

No one said a word in the car, but I sensed that my grandmother was nervous. She was a chain smoker and had gone through half a pack of cigarettes on our train ride up (you could smoke on the train back then) and inhaled another two during the 10-minute car ride.

Once inside, my uncle greeted us. I could feel a huge weight lift from my grandmother's shoulders. He was asked to sign a notepad when he walked in and I noticed that all he drew was an 'X'.

My uncle was illiterate, so I thought it appropriate to take the opportunity to teach him the ABCs, so he could at least spell his name going forward. I also decided to recite Rapunzel for the 10th time that day, just to ensure he wouldn't forget how smart I really was.

On our way out, he handed me a piece of wood about a foot long with my name hand carved on it. I was so surprised! Unlike most kids' names, mine was uncommon, so the chances of finding anything with my name on it, in stores, was slim to none. It was the coolest thing I'd ever seen, but I couldn't understand how he made it if he didn't know how to spell.

I would later learn that, in jail, they have a barter system.

My uncle had agreed to buy his cellmate snacks for a month if, in return, he would carve my name onto that piece of wood.

Isabela, Puerto Rico – December 1988 "New Encounters"

My parents decided to move to Puerto Rico half way through my fifth grade. There wasn't much advance notice: one day we were living in the Bronx, the next day we were moving. I was ecstatic about this! I knew how to read and write in both Spanish and English so I knew my studies wouldn't be negatively affected – even then, academic achievements were very important to me. We lived in Isabela for a year and a half and it was by far the most fulfilling time of my entire childhood. We moved in December and I started school in January. Making friends immediately. I also met my brother, Mikey, for the very first time in school. He was my biological father's son and was a year older than me. I was his only sibling. His mom had abandoned him when he was born, and so my father put all his energy into him, ensuring he was not only academically inclined, but a star athlete. He was living with our paternal grandmother at the time, due to some "illness" my father had. We were instantly inseparable and, for the first time in his life, he felt like he belonged to a family. I had yet to meet my father.

I went on to finish fifth and sixth grade on the honor roll. I was a star athlete, playing basketball, volleyball and even became the faster runner on the track & field team. As far as I was concerned, the world was my oyster. We didn't have much food or even clothing, but I barely noticed. Finally we had a normal childhood, where I could play outside, ride my bike and even learn how to ride a unicycle to and from school.

In May 1990 my mom called me to the living room to tell me that I needed to go visit my father. I was floored. I saw her go through a pack of cigarettes that morning but had no idea what had stressed her so. My father had never been a part of my life and my mom despised him. It turned out that my father had AIDS and had asked a mutual friend to speak to my mom so she would allow me to see him, as he didn't think he had too long to live. My father was in the military in the late 1970s; he had developed an addiction to heroin and would often share a syringe with his best friend who, unbeknownst to him, was infected with HIV.

I still remember being really nervous as my father's mother drove me to his house. I walked into his home, where I was welcomed by his companion. She was incredibly kind, but I immediately sensed that my grandmother didn't like her. She was black and, as far as my grandmother was concerned, she wasn't good enough for my father. This was despite the fact that my father had been an alcoholic, and his companion was the person who had taken him in and helped him back on his feet when she found him in town sleeping on the floor of the plaza. My grandmother couldn't be bothered.

As I made my way to his room, I stared at the pictures of me he had hung on the wall. Who had given these to him? He had a picture for every year, up until my 10th birthday. My mom would fume if she knew he had them – was all I could think to myself.

I walked into his room and couldn't believe my eyes; this stranger was my father. He was a big man who demanded respect – that was clear. He had an attitude but it quickly dissipated the second he saw me. He immediately asked me to come closer – he could no longer walk. All he could do was stare and tell me how sorry he was that this was how we had to meet. He gave me a piece of advice: "Don't ever take shit from anyone, and never let a guy touch you inappropriately."

It would be the first and last time we would meet. My father passed away on May 23rd 1990, three days before my 12th birthday.

My brother was devastated. His hero had died and the world as he knew it would cease to exist. This would soon translate into his life spiraling completely out of control.

Atlanta, GA – August 1990 "Rock Bottom/True Hunger"

It was summer of 1990 and my parents had decided that they would move from Puerto Rico to Atlanta, in the hope of a better future.

My dad – my mother's partner – left in June, and found a job in a factory. He has been the "dad" in my life since I was aged two.

He saved every cent he earned, so he could secure an apartment and bring my mother, three brothers and myself over before school started at the end of August.

Soon it was time to leave for Atlanta; I was devastated. I loved living in Puerto Rico where everyone knew each other and you could actually ride your bike outside, without fear of getting shot. My mom was desperate to leave; she had spent too many nights worrying about how she was going to feed us and didn't think things would ever get better. Moving was the only option. I could already feel myself missing Mikey and felt terrible that he couldn't move with us, as we had grown incredibly close and I was the only next of kin he had.

It was August and as soon as we arrived in Atlanta, my dad greeted us with the biggest smile and his eyes filled with tears; we were finally together as a family. When we got to the apartment, we could see that it was brand new – but strikingly bare. There were no beds, no furniture and most importantly, not much food. But we were grateful to have a roof over our heads and finally be together.

We were dead tired from the trip, so we each picked a corner and fell asleep.

The next day, we took our clothes and lined them up against the wall. My dad's niece lived in the same neighborhood, so she drove my mother and me to Lilburn Middle School so my mom could enroll me in school and ensure that they would provide transportation. I'd always either walked or ridden my unicycle to school, so getting picked up by a bus in the morning was a luxury.

A few days went by and I noticed my father becoming increasingly quiet. He seemed distant and wouldn't really interact with us. He would wake up, go to work, come back and go straight into his room.

I knew something was bothering him but I wasn't quite sure what it was, and my mother didn't seem curious about finding out. Something wasn't right. I would later learn that my dad would go into his room, as it was his only means of dealing with the stress and embarrassment of not being able to feed his family.

It was our fifth day in Atlanta and there was no food left in the apartment.

My mom and I had spent the night before looking through the brochures that came with each appliance. Apparently the microwave could make really amazing pancakes drizzled with syrup, powdered sugar and raspberries, while the oven made the most amazing lasagna and turkey.

We were so hungry and, because there was nothing to eat, we decided to fantasize about all the food we wished we could be eating at that very moment.

I was 12 years old, but I now know that I was far beyond my years in terms of maturity and knew that, as the older child, I had to partake in decision-making and problem-solving for the family.

To say that I felt a strong sense of responsibility is an understatement.

I knew this was very difficult time for my parents. My dad went to his room and closed the door so we would think that he was sleeping. I stayed up with my mother, who, true to form, had no desire to hide her feelings.

The following morning, we were too weak and famished to get up from the floor. With the exception of my youngest brother who'd had formula, we hadn't eaten in two days and had no energy to move.

A few hours passed and we heard a knock on the door; none of us moved. The knocking continued and grew louder, so my mother finally stood up and walked to the door. I followed and stood behind her as she opened the door.

We stared at each other for what seemed like five minutes trying to understand who these strangers staring back at us were. They started by saying that they were here to deliver some items that were sent for us – could they walk inside to drop them off?

It was all very surreal and I could see that my mother was just as confused as I was. My mother was much more vulnerable than I was; she was emotionally drained.

It turned out that my father had gone to work and his boss had found him crying by his machine.

He'd asked him what was wrong and in his broken English, my dad explained that he didn't have money to feed his family or buy them clothes. His boss immediately took my dad off the floor and phoned his wife who had given birth just a few days before, and asked her to make some calls. She got on the phone with their church and told them about this Puerto Rican family who had just moved into the neighborhood from the island and had no food or clothing.

These people standing in front of us were from her church, and they had come to deliver boxes of food and clothing to us. We literally couldn't believe our eyes!

There was no way to convince me that these weren't true angels sent from heaven. In that moment, I knew my life had changed forever and that this experience would never leave me. In fact, it would go on to shape the way I thought of poverty and the way in which I envisioned my future.

I had been raised in the Catholic religion and had been diligent about completing most of my sacraments, with the exception of my confirmation, which I could only complete when I turned 14 years old. For as long as I could remember, I had never gone to bed without praying (I still do) and felt a duty to God. The bond was sacred and I didn't share these thoughts with anyone.

It was my faith back then – which still holds strong today – that leads me to believe that, even when you can't see a way out of a situation, things always have a way of falling into place.

However, that morning, I couldn't see a way out, I had lost hope and no longer wondered if there was more to life than these circumstances.

Later that afternoon, my dad's bosses' wife came by the house and took us (mom, me and the three boys) shopping. She spent $100 dollars on each of us: that was a fortune and I could tell that, although my mother was grateful, she was also embarrassed that this is what her life had come to.

Bronx, New York – Summer 1992

After living in Atlanta for a year, my parents decided it was time to move back to New York to be near family.

Although my father had a steady job in Atlanta, it wasn't enough to cover the bills and support a family. So moving back to the Bronx, meant that, although it was not the most ideal of circumstances, we would be next to my grandmother and Carmen again.

I was going into the eighth grade and mom was worried about enrolling me in the local public junior high school. So she decided that I would go to St. Jerome, across the street from where my aunt and grandmother lived.

I was thrilled at the idea of going to a private Catholic school, but didn't know where my parents would raise the money. My mum said, "We're going to enroll you and we'll figure out where to get the money from later."

My mother was on public assistance her entire life. That meant that she would receive food stamps to buy food and a minimal amount of cash for household items, like detergent and dishwasher soap, that you couldn't buy with food stamps.

She made an executive decision that she would trade her food stamps for cash so she could raise the school tuition fees every month. That meant that we had to figure out how we would eat.

To my mother it was important that I receive a good education, no matter the sacrifice. She had become pregnant at sixteen and didn't want me to follow in her footsteps. She wasn't the type of parent to hover over me and ask if I had done my homework. She knew that she could trust me and I never let her down.

I also knew that I couldn't afford not to be great in life.

She had invested in me and I, in turn, was responsible for my future – and ultimately hers.

By the summer of 1993, my parents found an apartment in Brooklyn, so we moved again. This time, my mom enrolled me in public school JHS 126.

The school was one block away from our apartment, so it took me no more than five minutes to get home. With that in mind, I would stay after school and befriend the various teachers and counselors.

There's something that has always intrigued me about how people think. This was a perfect time to find out more about who my teachers were and why they were there. Did they really like being teachers? Because, from where I stood, it didn't seem like fun.

One day, a counselor stopped me in the hallway and said: "Shalimar, I think I have something you will be interested in." I walked into his office and he said: "Have you heard of a scholarship called Student Sponsor Partners?"

I hadn't heard of the scholarship, but naturally, I was ready to know more about it now it had been brought to my attention. The scholarship was designed to provide a better education for those that were at risk of failing or dropping out of high school.

I was neither failing or at risk of dropping out of high school, as I seldom got anything but A grades, but I knew that this would be the only way to get a good high school education at a private school, which would ultimately give me an opportunity to apply to decent university.

Even then, I was always thinking ahead. The counselor encouraged me to apply and told me that if I got accepted, I would be awarded a scholarship to go to a private Catholic high school.

I immediately jumped at the idea and within weeks I received notice that I had been accepted. I was elated beyond words! This scholarship meant that I could not only receive a solid education and increase my chances of going to college, but I would also have a sponsor to guide me the whole way.

I was ecstatic!

On the first day at St. Michael Academy, an all-girls school, they held a reception so every student and their families, could meet their sponsors. My mom, dad, grandmother and Carmen came.

We all met in the cafeteria and I can't tell you how excited everyone was to meet Tanya.

They were completely and utterly grateful for the opportunity that I was given and everyone wanted to express their thanks in person to Tanya. The scholarship was set up in two parts. There was a financial sponsor, who actually paid the high school tuition fees, but whom I never got to meet. Then there was a mentor, in my case that was Tanya and her role was to mentor and guide me through high school, although our relationship would continue beyond high school and she became like family.

Till this day, 22 years later, we eat Christmas dinner together every year.

I did very well at St. Michael and was the first senior to receive an acceptance letter into a university. Right before my senior year, I got news that Mikey had disappeared for a few days. Since my father had passed, he had struggled emotionally and succumbed to selling drugs and hanging with the wrong crowd to compensate for his loneliness and unhappiness.

I was worried about his disappearance, but Mikey was a

handsome guy and always had a girl hanging around his arm, so I assumed he was laying low with one of them. But on July 10, 1996 the owner of an empty lot near the beach, noticed a body in the distance. Mike had been murdered and left for dead, two days prior. He had been stabbed, hung, burned and even had battery acid pumped into his veins. 10 years had passed before he came to me in a dream pleading for me to let him rest in peace and not relive his tragic ending every moment of the day. I have since found peace in appreciating the childhood memories that we shared.

Penn State

On November 7th 1995, I was accepted into Pennsylvania State University. I didn't know it then, but this would be a complete game-changer for me.

I had hoped to go away and have the full college experience, as well as a much deserved break from my parents, who had become completely overbearing. Penn State has 23 campuses, and so I decided to go to the furthest one, in Erie Pennsylvania – nine hours away from home!

Once on campus, I was in for a rude awakening. For starters, my room was in the LIFE (living in a free environment) dorm, meaning that you weren't allowed to smoke or drink and no guys were allowed to visit, unless they were escorted at all times.

I wasn't allowed to date, nor did I smoke or drink so this didn't present itself as a problem to me, but apparently it was a problem for everyone else on the floor, so they spent a good amount of time on the weekend, trying to get around this. I had been surrounded by drugs and alcohol my entire existence and had seen firsthand how it destroyed my entire family, so I didn't smoke or drink and refused to keep acquaintances that did – it was a deal breaker!

At the time, the campus housed a total of 3,500 students of whom a handful, including me, were Hispanic.

It didn't bother me at all, however there were times when I felt like a science experiment, especially when my roommate's entire family came to visit and meet 'the girl from Brooklyn' that was living with Chrissy.

Chrissy lived in Erie, a town so tiny that her dad's signature was actually on her high school diploma – he was the principal.

She was incredibly kind, as were her family, but vulnerable in a way that I couldn't understand. She was allowed to sleep over at her boyfriend's house (something my mother just couldn't wrap her head around) but she wasn't allowed to have black friends – it seemed bizarre.

I often wondered what great lengths they must've gone to, to switch her out of our room, once they realized that, not only was I from Brooklyn, but I was Hispanic and could potentially, in their view, have a 'negative' effect on their daughter.

Classes started and it became clear to me that I was a small fish in a big pond. I had to work and study twice as hard as everyone else if I wanted to survive my freshman year. I stayed up all night to digest what seemed like hundreds of pages of reading material.

I had no idea what I wanted to study but I knew I wanted to go into law enforcement, so I majored in political science.

All the while, I was adjusting to living away from home, but it soon became apparent that my parents still needed financial support.

I had worked since the age of 12, always sharing any money I earned with them, if not giving it to them outright. But now I was away at school and couldn't help financially. So I did some research to investigate ways I could get my hands on money and discovered that I could borrow from the financial aid office – a sort of loan. It would be added to my school tuition package, so I wouldn't have to pay it back until I was out of college.

As soon as I received the money I would ask a friend to drive me to the nearest Western Union, so I could transfer the money to a branch near my parents.

Again, I felt a sense of responsibility for my parents' well-being. It meant everything to me to hear the excitement in their voices when I could help, which usually meant feeding them for a few extra days.

Since being at school, I no longer worried about not having food, because as soon as I got on campus, I signed up for the biggest meal plan which enabled me to eat six times a day: this was a great relief.

What I hadn't planned for, was dealing with the loss of my brother Mikey. I was away from my family and had plenty of time to reflect. I couldn't understand why or how people could be so cruel.

I kept replaying mental pictures of how it must have happened, and it would literally take my breath away. I realized quickly that I needed more than just a prayer every night; what I really needed was help.

I was soon to learn that the best 'help' in the world for me was to face a challenge, but I could no longer function in isolation. I needed and wanted support: not traditional 'management' but someone to believe in and an organization to belong to.

I had started to forge my own path. It wasn't always clear but I now knew it had to be uniquely mine.

Until this point, I had lived my life happily for the many others who mattered to me. I was finding it strangely hard and complex to think just about myself. I struggled with this and soon realized that without the added ability of making an actual difference to people's lives, I lost a part of myself and a great deal of my drive.

I've always felt hugely ambitious but this energy was never solely focused on myself. I was at my most driven and motivated if I could help change the situation for those I knew and cared about.

I was so much more self-aware, but perhaps not experienced or aware enough to better understand my Spikes, and therefore how much potential might lie within me.

Investment Banking

Throughout my career, I've had the opportunity to learn from each person and environment I've worked in.

When I was in investment banking, I worked for someone who was known as one of the toughest Managing Directors on Wall Street. Upon meeting him, I knew I had my work cut out for me, but I was ready to face the challenge.

He would sleep a minimum of two nights a week on an airplane bouncing from one meeting to another, never missing an opportunity to establish a new relationship and get the job done. He had no issues dismissing people on the spot if he thought they were wasting his time or were unable to meet his demands.

I found that curious. I wondered where that stemmed from and why he felt the need to be so unforgiving with people.

I decided to be my most authentic self and treat him the way he wanted to be treated. When he was snippy, I was snippy back. When he would yell, I was calm.

Eventually he realized that he didn't intimidate me, and that I was ready to work just as hard as he was, towards the same goal, bringing in new business. I needed him to understand that I was trustworthy and had his best interest at heart.

A few months into the job I realized that our business in Brazil was growing and that my boss didn't know how to speak Portuguese. As his gatekeeper, I knew that one of us had to learn and he didn't have the time or bandwidth to do so. I reached out to Human Resources department, explained the circumstances and asked if I could bring a professor in from outside. Within a week I had my first class.

My boss was impressed, even though he never told me, that I took the initiative. This step allowed me to build rapport with our Portuguese clients, and to increase our presence in South America. It was a 'no brainer' as far as I was concerned.

I knew that if I wanted to be taken seriously, I had to think ahead and not wait to be told what to do. I wanted to have a

BlackBerry and be a vital part of the team that he called on to get things done at all times, so I jumped at every opportunity that presented itself.

He was one of the hardest working people and led by example, even when everyone in the room disagreed with him. He was incredibly strategic, even if he stepped on a few toes along the way.

I knew there was more to him than this, and that if he continued behaving in this way, he could ruin his reputation, but it was my job to ensure he was seen in the best light. I was his buffer. People warmed to me very easily and would stop by my desk – only when he wasn't around. They couldn't understand how I could work with him: we were polar opposites in attitude they'd say. I found this comical.

My story was always the same: I had a great deal of respect for him and couldn't think of a better boss. When anyone spoke ill of him, I would defend him and say they just had to get to know him better. I was officially his ambassador.

A Billion Lessons

Our interview took place at one of her apartments off Madison Avenue. I had spent most of my career working in a corporate environment, therefore I didn't quite know what to expect when I was told that the interview would take place at my home. I knew she was one of the upper echelons and had homes all over the world, but how I would fit, as an extension of her, into the scheme of things wasn't so clear.

There was a light knock on the door before she let herself in. I had seen pictures of her online, but she was even more elegant in person. Regal to say the least!

She was incredibly kind and was taken aback by how polished my Spanish was, so she went right into it by asking me where I learned to speak it so well. I told her that I had been raised by my mother and grandmother, and so I would only speak to my grandmother in Spanish and to my mother and everyone else in English.

She was intrigued and decided to press further: were you raised in Puerto Rico? I explained that when I was 10 years old I had lived in Puerto Rico for a year and a half, but was born and raised in the Bronx and, later, in Brooklyn.

I could tell she was curious. I told her that I had first learned how to pray in Spanish and would normally only go to the Spanish mass with my great aunt on the weekend, because no one else in my family was religious, so I'd always oscillated between the two languages without ever really giving it a thought.

She wanted to understand what a typical day looked like for me and whether I was used to juggling multiple tasks at once.

She had a husband, children, grandchildren and a very extensive art collection. They were very important pieces of her life and she needed someone who could manage them all without letting anything fall through the cracks. She wanted someone who could handle it all in a "graceful" manner.

I could tell that what she really wanted to know was whether she could trust me to do a good job.

She'd had an assistant for 12 years that now no longer fit with the style she needed, and so against her will, she followed her coach's advice and started interviewing potential candidates. It was important that I be authentic, so I decided to share my background with her.

I told her all about being born to a single mom and how my grandmother and great aunt had played very important roles in my life. They had taught me to be respectful and courteous at all times, as well as teaching me how to remain safe. She seemed to take to this. She too was a grandmother, and understood the importance of that kind of relationship.

I also explained that, although I was raised with the bare essentials, I knew there was more to life. As such, I had always aspired for more and so I welcomed the idea of a new challenge.

She asked me why I was interested in the job. I told her I was excited about the opportunity to try something new where I could use my bilingual skills and connect with the various people across the organization.

I knew I would need to work in close proximity with personnel in the various homes, as well as colleagues in the various family offices, drivers and butlers. Therefore, this appeared to be the most appropriate fit for someone like me who loved to connect with others.

She wanted to know what my boss, at the time, was like. I told her that he was someone for whom I had a great deal of respect and admiration. He was hard working and always found a way to accomplish tasks. He forged relationships everywhere, even when he didn't necessarily agree with people, and he taught me everything I knew about finding a common ground with others. He had, in essence, taken me under his wing and shown me all the strategies and pitfalls of business, without explicitly branding himself as my mentor.

I also explained that, although he'd be disappointed to learn that I was leaving, he would be supportive, knowing that I've always wanted to do more.

She was impressed with how well I spoke of him. She struck me as someone who built her relationships on trust. There was something about how I only had good things to say about him, even though he was the toughest boss I'd ever had, that inspired her to believe that I would be a good fit. I got the job!

The employment and induction process was managed by a recruiter/coach they had hired to find the perfect match for the role of an 'extension' of her. It was a unique role in that the incumbent needed to have a balance between being quick on their feet, always understanding the cultural sensitivities of each country, and keeping all information very close to their chest, all the while building relationships with everyone.

I knew that in order to be successful, it was not only vital that I be bilingual, but it was also important that I pick up on the things that weren't said. Being perceptive was key!

I realized that those I connected with immediately were the staff in my employer's various homes. They were incredibly humble and had a deep sense of respect for the family.

I wanted them to feel open to come to me, whether it be to ask questions or to let me know when something was problematic, so I could help them sort things out. We were a team and I needed them to understand that when one of us succeeded, we all succeeded and when one of us failed, we all failed.

I was in my element. The idea that I could work so closely with everyone gave me a great sense of satisfaction. I worked long hours but it never truly felt like work, I enjoyed what I was doing.

This was the first time I had worked with a coach and I was completely fascinated with this line of work. Till then, I didn't really know this role existed. It made all the sense in the world to me, to have someone come in, really understand the role they were seeking to fill and onboard-coach the person and ensure they had all the necessary resources to succeed.

This was also when I gained my first insight into some of the personalities I would come to encounter. For starters, I learned that there were people who wanted to get close to me in order to reach my employer.

There were others who were less than enthused with me working in the most intimate of settings. Their obsession with my employer meant that they would stop at nothing to find a way to communicate directly with her. Everyone knew the rules: any and all communication had to be filtered through me, but some would find a way to get around this.

Within a few weeks I began receiving praise for all the good work I was doing and for "turning the office around". I divided my time between being my employer's bodyguard and mentoring those that had incredible potential, but felt as though they didn't have a voice.

I developed a healthy relationship of trust with her, but others didn't quite understand how. She was very particular about how she liked things done and didn't mince words – even when at times it may have offended others. Unlike her detractors, I admired this.

When people looked at her, they saw someone who 'had it all.' Many would forget the possibility of her being only human and fallible, having good days and bad days. They imagined she didn't have a care in the world.

This was the furthest from the truth. Soon, I would learn just how much 'wealthier' than her I truly was.

Conclusion

There's absolutely nothing that brings me more joy than to look someone in the eye and empower them, to believe that what has shaped their life thus far, doesn't necessarily need to mould the rest of it. I've had the privilege of traveling all over the world to donate time, money and clothing to people who are less fortunate. I feel that it's my duty to do so. I share my story with anyone who's willing to listen, in the hope that they might understand that titles don't make us any worthier than others, nor should they set us apart.

Once you've experienced poverty, not having food to eat, clothes to wear or a place to live, it never quite leaves you. In fact, it's shaped me and serves as a constant reminder of the importance of being humble and grateful for absolutely everything in life.

I couldn't have dreamed that this is where I'd be today, back when we lived in Atlanta and had food and clothing delivered to us by the church. Bringing my personal and professional goals together isn't something I'd envisioned either, I didn't know it was even an option. Now, my days and nights are devoted to assisting the President of The World Bank in being the voice of the poor when decisions are being made amongst the world's leaders.

These are the experiences that fuel me and get me out of bed in the morning.

WE ARE ALWAYS STRONGER TOGETHER

My role is to be appropriately challenging and a little pushy but in a supportive manner. Having a natural sense of urgency coupled with a 'finished beats perfect' philosophy can be quite a formidable and unwelcome force for some.

Shalimar and I were a seriously good team – we naturally had a common purpose, as we both had the future of the organization and the success of the President's vision and strategy on our minds – all the time.

This was a far bigger deal than the President per se: we were inspired by what he could achieve. This was about changing our world for the better and continuing to tackle world poverty. The President was so committed and selfless in all he did; it was an honour for both of us to be in his service.

We always defended each other – and we were both committed to serving the President.

He could be generous – to a fault. A medical doctor by profession, he just could not walk away from anyone in trouble. His approach of being consistently accessible and always available was not always shared by those around him. His work ethic and drive was phenomenal.

Shalimar matched his work ethic and was also always alert to every event that might impact on the President or his work.

Her EQ antennae and her 'nose' for falsehoods or inappropriate situations were integral to the intelligence around which we focused our joint plan of action. We never needed to write a physical plan, or to know who would do what – our mutual goals and shared understanding made the tasks natural and easy, and hugely effective.

Shalimar constantly demonstrated and displayed her Spike of sociability: she possessed a genuine curiosity about people and exploring their various motivations and what makes them tick – she engaged with anyone and everyone – all would feel special and cared for. Easily said, but done with sincerity and a rare 'common touch' at the bank – that could not be simulated.

This complemented and supplemented my 'need for speed', and ensured that our 'balanced out' approach functioned nearly kinetically.

When Spikes are so complementary and in sync, it is heady and compelling stuff. We also had some Spikes in common and this was additionally advantageous – we always backed each other, no matter the size or scale of the adversity.

Shalimar is a consummate new age leader, while being 'born to serve'. Not so long ago, these two key attributes might have been seen as opposites and perhaps incongruous, but it is far more recognized today that the best leaders serve their people, not the other way round.

"OUR DOUBTS ARE TRAITORS AND MAKE US LOSE THE GOOD WE OFT MIGHT WIN BY FEARING TO ATTEMPT"

WILLIAM SHAKESPEARE

SPIKE SPARKS

As leaders we have to recognize there is no longer Them vs Us: there is only We.

You can learn much more from setbacks than you can from successes – then you never have to fear failure.

The foundation of any team is strong relationships, based on trust.

Focus on doing your personal best – never just for yourself, but always for the team.

Always try to give YOUR best, and you will always be THE best.

ON THE SAME PAGE

"To command is to serve; nothing more and nothing less."– Andre Malraux

Trust is built over time. Once lost, it is difficult to regain. Robert Bruce Shaw states, "One key component of trust in a leader is the belief that they truly care about constituents as people, not just what they can do for the leader or the organization."[14]

"Great leaders are forged on the anvil of adversity: beaten into shape under intense heat. That's why there are so few of them. There are no short cuts – ego, talent, bravado or charisma are no substitute for prolonged, humbling experience."– Mark Ashton (CEO at Resolve)

Harvard Business Review spotlighted influence and leadership in *Connect, Then Lead*, where Amy Cuddy et al. identify the importance of influence over leadership. Leadership rises from authority, but influence is born of connection. If people feel connected, they open themselves up to the influence of others.[15]

"Aspiring leaders would do well to stop focusing on control and figure out how to expand their influence." – Michael Hyatt

Peter Northouse explains that great leaders are concerned about their followers and put them first, assisting with personal development and inspiring them to take on responsibilities and personal growth.[16]

---

[14] Shaw, R. (1997) *Trust in the Balance: Building Successful Organizations on Results, Integrity and Concern*. San Francisco, CA: Jossey-Bass, Inc.

[15] Cuddy, A., Kohut, M. and Neffinger, J. (2013) "Connect, Then Lead." *Harvard Business Review*

[16] Northouse, P. (2013) *Leadership: Theory and Practice. 6th edition*, Thousand Oaks, CA: Sage Publications

PART TWO

BALANCING SPIKES

CHAPTER VI
~~SLOW DOWN.~~
SPEED UP

No single person can achieve everything in isolation. Our world today is far too fast-moving and complex. It's no longer possible for the leaders to be truly broad, but a team ***can*** be that diverse.

When change hits, a common response is caution. Faced with the unfamiliar, surrounded by uncertainty, the organization gears down. On the surface this makes sense. You really can't do much to reduce the speed of change. But if you slow down, you somehow feel a little safer. So most people put on the brakes, hoping to buy some time.

But change won't wait on you. You simply don't have time to take your time. 'Carefulness' actually becomes dangerous when it creates a culture of caution – paralysis sets in, the organization loses momentum and problems start to multiply. Under today's conditions, slowing down is the most hazardous move you could make.

But hey, not everyone is afraid of rapid change; some thrive in ambiguous times. The so called 'change agents', who can bend to any change of direction, love the 'new' and embrace doing things differently.

Only problem is "we don't have those change agents in our organization." Well, we beg to differ. EVERY organization has them, but they are usually labelled 'mavericks' or unreliable, sometimes even 'flaky'. They are deemed as "never seeming to settle or follow through. They are not stable, they're high maintenance".

Yes, they might be all of the above and more, but they have different Spikes. This might just be their moment.

But after perhaps not recognizing that they are not just useful, but integral to your ability to thrive in these turbulent times, the big question is, "How do you find and engage them in this new unforgiving world?"

The answers are found in energizing all in the team and the wider workforce by utilizing the Spike methodology. This may sound a little grandiose, but it really is very straightforward and can be achieved just by changing our challenging viewpoint to start 'catching people doing things right'. Search for everybody's inherent Spikes; if someone is continuously outstanding at a particular activity or task, that's a huge clue as to their Spike. Now act and mobilize them by giving them roles and responsibilities that play to these Spikes.

Identify those for whom rapid change is natural – for whom merely picking up the pace a little won't work. Competition moves so fast. Markets change so quickly. Technology advances at a dead run. The world wants instant everything. The result? Good goes bad in a hurry. And the level of performance that qualifies you as a winner today can make you a has-been tomorrow.

Find those who do everything possible to accelerate – this will help to create a culture with quicker reflexes. Respect those who hustle. They will help put speed and responsiveness into every aspect of the business. Help get rid of bureaucratic practices and 'busy work' that bog down productivity. They naturally network and assist in breaking down the boundaries between work groups, so communication flows fast and freely. They understand that the organization can't afford to carry any extra weight and that downsizing and de-layering may be needed to create a leaner, fleeter, more agile outfit. They never resist change, because that's a drag on them and the organization. The culture can count on them to give it a sense of urgency.

Slowing down gives some the feeling that you're safer, more in control. But the feeling is false. Picking up the speed protects you better from today's world of high velocity change. Find those who have escaped the pull and safety of the past – forever.

Spike philosophy enables 'the faster' to identify a safe pathway for the more deliberate. Everybody has a Spike to display and bring into play, but the leader needs to have been 'Spiked' themselves and therefore practice diversity and inclusion, without ever having to mention the words.

They are then bravely prepared to identify and invest in every team members' Spikes, no matter how many glaring areas for development they may have.

"TIME USED TO BE A TYRANT. TODAY IT'S AN ASSASSIN"

FROM AN R.R DONNELLEY & SONS COMPANY ADVERTISEMENT

SWIMMING WITH THE DOLPHINS

Having recently resigned from the board of IPC Media during the successful sale of the business to Time Warner, I found myself, frustratingly, on six months gardening leave. It sounded like a great opportunity to refuel and refresh after over 20 years of non-stop working.

How wrong could I have been!

It took a couple of weeks to realize just how institutionalized I had really become. No matter how I conditioned myself, and despite the nightly pep talks I gave myself before retiring to bed each night, I still just jumped out of bed alert at 6am every morning.

On most days, I would start preparing for work: on one particular occasion, I even got into the car and started driving to the office before realizing I no longer worked there!

I would get increasingly angry as I forced myself to break free and cut loose, because there just had to be more to life than just work. Wasn't there? How sad had I become?

I had become dangerously defined only by what others paid me to do.

This was, of course, somewhat true, but I had seriously underestimated the true significance and power of what I had become attuned to doing and being – it was magically, all the things I was very good at doing – my Spikes. I had fortunately built a first class team around me that was incredibly talented, with huge Spikes that differed massively to my own, thankfully.

Yes, I had become a creature of routine – but what a routine! Every day at IPC Media (née IPC Magazines) involved portraying all my Spikes, all the time. My colleagues, Bill, Jeremy, Tony and especially, my super-organized and extremely pragmatic PA, Jill, were completely different to me, blessed with just the Spikes necessary to enable my own Spikes to be ultra-relevant and well oiled.

Despite being on gardening leave, part of my severance package that had been negotiated with the Non-Exec Chairman, David Arculus, was to continue doing (his) external talks for IPC Media, as and when was necessary. The Chairman was astutely playing to his Spikes, and even more, to mine.

I thoroughly enjoyed (and began to live for) the adrenaline rush of turning up to speak to an audience I had never met before, and having only an hour to convince them to move in a different direction or, better still, exploding some myths that were holding them back. I lived for this sense of potential danger and the jeopardy that played out in the space of an intoxicating and high-octane hour.

My final talk for the Chairman was going be at the prestigious and very high profile CBI (Confederation of British Industry) Conference in Birmingham. This was going to be an enormous event. The audience consisted of the good and the great of British businesses, including Chief Executives of most of the top multinational companies operating in the UK and many more.

The headline speakers were the Prime Minister, Tony Blair, and the Chancellor of the Exchequer, Gordon Brown, and they were to be followed by the leader of the opposition, William Hague. It didn't get much bigger or much better. I suppose I should have been very nervous, but I just had this tremendous feeling of excitement and anticipation.

These speeches would be followed by two master classes on business leadership. The first was being delivered by the learned professors, Charles Handy (London Business School) and Gary Hamel (Harvard Business School). Heady stuff and two 'thought leaders' I really admired and respected. I'd read most of their books and I had to pinch myself at the thought that I might be sharing a stage with them.

They were both hugely well-known and feted as probably the best in the world at what they did. Having a soft spoken, but hard hitting Irishman juxtaposed with a power packed and rather adversarial American, made for a spicy and memorable mix.

At the time, they both had books in the bestseller lists: Charles had *The New Alchemists* and Gary had 'Leading the Revolution'. I just couldn't wait to hear them both. I had no idea that I would actually meet them and get to know them.

The second of the master classes was to be delivered by Nicholas Negroponte (Massachusetts Institute of Technology – MIT) and myself! I would speak in front of some 300-400 captains of industry, following Charles and Gary. I just could not wait.

It was a packed house at the National Exhibition Centre in Birmingham, in central England. Tony Blair and William Hague were amazingly good, and they appeared to be so natural and so eloquent; vitally, both were self-deprecating with wit and an easygoing, natural humour. I watched everything they did. Little did I know that William and I would cross paths in the near future – and I would be giving him insights and tips on how he could build a career on the business speaking circuit! Even he hadn't realized his real Spikes!

Charles and Gary were a couple of old pros, who knew the game inside out. They were just awesome and made it look so easy. I was learning that if you're not making it look easy, then you're just not working hard enough. This was to stay with me for the rest of my speaking career.

And now it was down to Nicholas and myself. Talk about having tough acts to follow? But I could not wait, as I have always thrived on competition and being on the vulnerable edge.

If I had learned anything about public speaking in the previous months, it was to stick to your areas of expertise, know your audience and give them what they're looking for.

This was far easier for me at this particular summit, as I was living and working in the UK, than it was for Nicholas, who would have found it easier if he'd managed to find out more about the strange folk here in the UK.

I was soon to find out that he was far too busy with his seminal book, *Being Digital*. But he was also far too much of an unrepentant iconoclast to take the time to discover who was actually in the audience.

His speech was hardly anything to do with them.

We were at the peak of the dotcom boom in 2000, and Nicholas and I were talking about the winners and the losers amongst the heroes and heroines of the dotcom 'wolf pack'. He was truly a genius, but, despite having led all of IPC Media's fledgling internet 'businesses', his language and jargon was nearly all lost on me – and on many in the audience.

Nicholas had completely (and wantonly) overestimated how much this (or any) audience knew about the internet, and he was a good three years ahead of where his audience were. His blistering, full throttle keynote was delivered in relative silence. He spoke at the audience, which was mainly British, and therefore far too reserved to challenge him and desperate not to appear totally stupid, but they really did not have a clue what he was talking about.

Sitting quietly in the wings, it was painful to watch this hugely talented and unique expert completely fail to connect or engage, or even care what the audience was experiencing. He left the stage to subdued, but respectful British applause.

Nicholas had many Spikes. Public speaking did not appear to be one of them.

I had prepared some slides and some case studies regarding what we had learned at IPC Media, on our recent journey in trying to commercialize our many star brands and huge archive of quality content for the web. But it soon became abundantly clear to me that what the audience really wanted was the equivalent of the not-yet-conceived '*The Internet for Dummies*' guide to thinking about building internet businesses.

It's always been said, "Never follow a tough act", and in this respect Nicholas was quite generous towards me. It was now starkly obvious that my slides were also a little too ambitious. So, abandoning the slides, I sat on the edge of the stage and shared simple stories of fear and failure, and boldness and success. The 45 minutes flew by, and the allotted 15 minutes for questions carried on well beyond the allocated time.

It appeared to go quite well and was warmly received by a now enthusiastic audience.

We were now all gathered in the speakers' room, exchanging anecdotes and feedback about the event. I was obviously the 'new boy on the block', while Charles, Gary and Nicholas were old veterans, who knew each other very well. I was listening intently and gulping in the oxygen of this rarefied opportunity to be amongst the very best in their field.

Then Nicholas did something that I'll never forget and will always admire him for – he wandered over to me and said, "Hey René, that was not bad at all. I really enjoyed what you said, and even more, how you said it, and thank you so much – you saved the day." This was absolutely fantastic feedback, coming from the Master Blaster of all things digital, and a Master who had seriously exacting standards.

He then went on to ask, without flinching: "What did you get paid for today?" I just looked at him blankly, and, being British and finding the subject of money extremely vulgar, I would have struggled to answer this question with my best friends, let alone someone I'd met for the first time a couple of hours ago. But on this occasion the answer was relatively simple. "Paid? What do you mean Paid?" Nicholas looked at me aghast. Not comprehending at all, I innocently continued: "I drove myself up here last night, checked myself into a hotel and I'm about to go and buy myself a sandwich."

He now looked startled and angry. He bellowed: "Charles, Gary, come over here and listen to this shit!" He then demanded that I repeat what I'd just told him. I now, quite nervously, repeated the fact that I was not being paid anything at all. In actual fact it was costing me to be there!

Nicholas now reverted back to the showman he had been on the stage and asked Charles, "How much are you being paid for the event?" Charles quietly replied: "£30,000." I nearly fell over. Just about maintaining my balance. Nicholas then barked the same question at Gary, who shocked me even more, by replying, nonchalantly and without hesitation: "$50,000, two return Concorde tickets and two weeks' stay at Claridge's Hotel."

By now, my ears were popping and I was struggling for breath.

Nicholas then looked at me and explained proudly that he was also being paid $50,000, with two return Concorde tickets and two weeks at the eye-wateringly expensive Claridge's Hotel. He then grabbed me by the lapel and said: "Let this be the last time you speak for nothing. I don't care if crap people want to speak for nothing, but when good people start speaking for nothing you're ruining our industry." He then went into his pocket, pulled out a business card, scribbled something quickly on the back and handed it to me. It was the contact number for his speaking agent who did all of his European bookings; he said to give it 24 hours and then call him. "He will be expecting it."

I left Gary, Nicholas and Charles in deep and thoughtful conversation. I sat in the Speaker's Room all alone but awestruck, excited and humbled yet again. Being British, I just could not understand why anyone would want to pay for me to speak at their conference.

We Europeans, in the main, are just not wired to do what Nicholas had just done, and I would be eternally grateful for his American chutzpah.

The British are far too polite to be honest and the Americans are just far too honest to be polite.

A NEW BEGINNING

It was a drizzly and grey Thursday and I found myself standing in a grubby little office in the City of London. There were grubby PCs, grubby telephones and faxes, and, right at the front of the office, a grubby man, who was growling down one of the telephones and simultaneously snarling at his staff.

I stood politely for what seemed an eternity, but was nearer five minutes. I kept coughing politely and they kept ignoring me impolitely. Eventually the grubby man looked up and said, "Yes?" It took me some time to realise that "Yes" was actually a question.

I explained that Nicholas Negroponte had recommended me to him.

At that moment he reached into a huge pile of papers stacked on his desk; he miraculously tugged at the right sheet and started reading out aloud whilst constantly looking up at me and then back at the papers. He was desperately trying to reconcile what he was reading with the person before him.

Eventually he demanded, "What are you doing tomorrow morning?" Hardly hearing or caring that I didn't respond, he then barked some commands. "You will be on the 7.00am British Airways flight to Nice, and you'll be closing a conference for McKinsey and Co. Thank you."

I stared at him in disbelief. Crude and rude with zero warmth, no formalities and certainly no sense of customer service. I asked, respectfully, "What will they want me to talk about?" He had by now lost interest: as far as he was concerned, his work was done.

I coughed quietly and repeated my question. He was now even more irritable than when I had first walked in. "It's quite straightforward. At Nice airport, you'll catch a helicopter, which will take you to a hotel in Monaco and you will be briefed by the Chief Executive on your arrival." This was a shock and a half. But in actual fact, it wasn't really that intimidating at all. For me, it was exhilarating, but I still could not believe the rudeness of this grubby man. While I waited politely for further instructions, he barked at me again: "That's it! I'll have the tickets couriered to your house this afternoon." At that moment he picked up the phone and started speaking to someone else. I had evidently just been dismissed.

Service with a snarl.

As I was boarding the BA flight to Nice, it dawned on me that I didn't know much about the audience, or the subject matter and I had forgotten to ask about the fee! In my excitement, it had escaped my mind to even ask if I was going to be paid.

The helicopter touched down in Monaco and I was met by two men who were very formally and smartly attired – but both looked worried.

They spluttered out that the two previous speakers had "seriously underperformed" and the 400 partners in the room were now "becoming agitated."

This was clearly vital information, but it meant little to me.

We were hardly a few yards away from the loud spinning blades of the helicopter, when they broke into a trot and explained that this was "the third and final day of the Annual Partners Leadership Summit and many of them are threatening to grab their bags and head for the airport now. You must go on now and close the conference before lunch."

They dragged me along behind them and, raising his voice, one of them remarked, "It's a little volatile in there at the moment and they may not be at their most receptive, but you can close it anyway."

As I ran behind them I just had the presence of mind to shout back, "What about the briefing? I was told I'd be briefed prior to closing the conference, at about 16.00hrs?"

"We've just f***ing briefed you! Now get on with it."

I should have been wobbling all over the place, but I now ran faster, straight at some glass double doors, which I hadn't noticed. Fortuitously, they opened suddenly and automatically as I approached. I was instantly hit by a wall of loud, slow hand-clapping, jeering and the throwing of rolled up bits of paper, which were directed at the stage. I just continued running and jumped on to the platform. I started speaking breathlessly into the microphone at the lectern. And suddenly, the auditorium had become brilliantly silent.

With no slides and no script (and no real idea) 45-50 breathless minutes later, I was greeted with a standing ovation. This was a phenomenal adrenaline ride, and I just knew I wanted and needed more of it. Lots more.

Within minutes of finishing, I couldn't remember anything I had just spoken about. It was all born of passion and enthusiasm, and came straight from the heart.

On the way out, the two senior partners who had briefed me came in from hiding behind the two glass doors to shake my hand vigorously and slap me on the back. I sensed that they were more than a little pleased.

Over lunch, many of the partners in the audience came over to generously provide me with positive feedback. Little did they know just how much that meant to me, on my very first professional engagement. As lunch drew to a close and I gently came down from my huge and brilliant high, one of the senior partners asked me what my fee was, as all of this had been arranged by their Head Office.

They were incredulous when I said I had absolutely no idea. One of them pulled out his brief case; they looked at each other and out came his personal cheque book. Then he wrote me a personal cheque for $10,000. I couldn't accept that. We smiled at each other and we swapped business cards, and before I knew it, I was heading back to the helicopter.

This was unbelievable; I started to realize that I was quite good at this; even more importantly, I loved every adrenaline-soaked minute of it.

I started dreaming of the possibility that all my future days could be like this. It didn't take me long to realize that they would not be, unless I made some very tough calls.

By now, tragically, my wife, Yvonne, was suffering from what would prove to be terminal cancer. This was the most crushing of blows. Life was simply not fair and it could never be the same again. I had little else to lose now.

Alone now, I soon realised just how much I would miss Yvonne's brilliant and caring Spikes.

I couldn't take another full time job. I needed to be at home for our children.

By complete chance, through a combination of atrocious loss and happenstance, I had started out on the next phase of my career.

Little did I know that, over the next few years, I would speak on every continent, for many different industries and in front of the most diverse audiences one could imagine.

I would work with the best in the world, in the most exotic locations: from a platform behind the cascading Victoria Falls in Zambia, to on top of the Great Wall of China near Beijing.

For the first time in my career, I'd be exposing my Spikes by design, empowered by the huge confidence that focusing upon your Spikes can bring to all of us.

My limitations were no longer relevant, and in many respects were completely covered by my capable and well-chosen professional team.

When I thought back to my ten years at Marks & Spencer, three years at PepsiCo and five years at IPC Media, my appraisals and performance management experiences – whilst revealing my limitations – all consistently highlighted the three things I was really good at: I was capable of seeing the big picture; I could communicate effectively and I was usually by far the most passionate person in the team.

Amazingly, these Spikes lend themselves perfectly to my chosen career. The work I now do most often – and still get that necessary adrenaline rush from – is the one that, unsurprisingly, demands all my inherent Spikes.

"DO A JOB THAT YOU LOVE AND YOU NEVER WORK A DAY IN YOUR LIFE."

SPIKE SPARKS

The biggest benefit and greatest enemy of change is speed. Many still take time to adapt to change, but you cannot wait for the slowest or set the pace by the fastest.

Are you a creature of habit or an early adopter? Newness is an enemy to the mind – sameness is its friend. Challenge your mind constantly. Take yourself to somewhere new and continue enjoying the diversity and richness of our world's varied cultures.

If it ain't broke – break it quickly – in a low risk environment. Never get comfortable; become the 'fire starter'.

Live each day through your Spikes.

Practice failing fast. Never expect it right first time anymore, otherwise it will take far too long and with far too many committees. If you really want speed, learn to balance out your failings with the Spikes of your team.

ON THE SAME PAGE

"We need to cultivate Leadership that is ready and willing to drive innovation and lead progress towards the clean revolution."– Richard Branson

According to PricewaterhouseCoopers[17], in our increasingly global and high-speed business environment, a leader's agility is a core competence for an organization. A leader needs to be nimble and flexible in order to "have the foresight to spot change on the horizon, anticipate what comes next, and take the lead in developing future strategies to address evolving market demands to make it to the winner's circle."

"Change is a must. It's a business must, a brand must, and a consumer must. As leaders, the key is to bring the team along with you. Be transparent and speak with integrity. Be true to your word, and don't apologize for implementing change. I have learned that people want to follow an influential leader, and well-guided change is energizing and motivating."– Kathy Collins[18]

"Once you understand how powerful you are within, you exponentially increase the power and potentiality of everything outside of you."– Steve Maraboli

---

17 "PwC (2007) How leadership must change to meet the future. (online) US Human Capital Effectiveness Report." Available at: https://www.pwc.com/us/en/people-management/assets/future-leadership- change.pdf

18 Collins, K. (2015) "3 ways to embrace change at your company." (online) Available at: http://fortune. com/2015/07/01/kathy-collins-lead-transition [Accessed 03 Apr 2016]

CHAPTER VII
~~WAIT FOR INSTRUCTIONS.~~
TAKE THE INITIATIVE

When feeling deeply challenged, the act of surrounding yourself with people with Spikes that complement your own will encourage you to take the initiative. What Spikes do you need around you most to complement your own Spikes?

Change can easily create a culture of dependence. Maybe you feel uncertain or confused, so you decide to sit back until you get a new set of directions. You've got questions that need answers. You want help.

It could be that you're disgusted. Let's say you don't buy into certain suggested changes, so you figure you'll hold off until somebody comes around and tells you specifically what to do. After all, "doing nothing" is one of the popular ways people fight changes they don't like.

Of course, it might be that the culture hasn't required you to think for yourself.

Maybe you assume you're supposed to wait for guidance, to always turn to your boss for assignments, so you've just naturally come to depend on the boss for your marching orders.

Those days are over. The shift towards a culture of initiative and collaboration means you can figure out with your colleagues just what the organization needs. Then, you must take action.

Team-directed behaviour is essential in today's world of accelerating change. For one thing, organizations are learning to run lean, which means every person must become more self-sufficient. But you can't count on having someone to come around and hand-feed you instructions on a regular basis. Together the team is so much stronger, but only if the team is made up of a collection of interdependent Spikes, which cover all bases.

Besides, higher management may not be in a position to help much. Often the boss doesn't identify problems as quickly as the collective team. Or the boss doesn't understand how to fix issues as well as you all do. Plus, the boss often isn't there when the opportunity arises to improve the situation.

So put yourself and the team in charge of problem-solving. You don't have to have all the answers. Nobody does. But the team can. Just show some initiative. Come up with your own answers and there's a good chance you'll be okay. It would all be much easier and more straightforward if we had some direction and someone to turn to when difficulties arose. That's not at all unreasonable. In fact, that team support is absolutely what's needed in times of high-velocity change and the associated stress it can bring.

However, the wrong boss can crush all this goodwill with one withering put-down. Conversely, the perfect inspired leader can multiply the impact of all the positivity.

You feel let down by the organization when you go looking for help and none is forthcoming… When you depend on someone to tell you what to do, but you don't know who they are … or when you give up and wage a sneaky war against change by waiting patiently for instructions.

"IF YOU COME TO A FORK IN THE ROAD, TAKE IT."

ATTRIBUTED TO YOGI BERRA

SCHOOL DAZE

Geraldine, the recently appointed, vivacious and brilliant Head Teacher of Cardinal Hinsley School, happened to hear about my unforeseen award of an MBE for Services to Business.

She became aware of it when she discovered that I was an old boy of Cardinal Hinsley Roman Catholic Boy's school. She immediately telephoned me to find out whether I would be a guest at that year's academic achievements awards evening.

I blushed, unsure how to respond, but before I could speak, she continued to say, with sparkling charm, "This is the first instance of any previous pupil of the school receiving an award from the Queen."

How could I even contemplate not being there? By now, I was blushing even more, and flattered beyond belief.

I would soon learn and experience Geraldine's truly phenomenal Spikes of spotting the right talent and creating environments where they were empowered, exploiting their own Spikes, and subsequently, thrived.

We pulled up early and parked in the still-ramshackle teacher's car park. This was a special novelty, as it had always been 'out of bounds' and out of reach, for the seven years I attended Cardinal Hinsley School.

When I first became a pupil here, it was one of the most sought-after schools for miles around. There was always a waiting list, and many never made it; consequently, there was a huge feeling of pride for every boy that was accepted at the school.

Most of the boys at the school had come from the few local Catholic primary schools in and around Brent, which was the London Borough where Cardinal Hinsley was situated.

The school was surprisingly cosmopolitan, but perhaps not in the way that we think of cosmopolitan London today. By far the largest community represented at the school were the sons of Irish parents, who, in the main, had come to London to escape the deep recession that had blighted Ireland for many years. There were many Italians, Spaniards, Poles and lots of other Europeans with predominately Catholic home populations.

The two minorities in the school were the English and the non-whites. There were very few boys with English parents in my class and only three black boys.

That seemed like a long bygone era as we drove up to the school. The Irish had nearly all moved onwards and upwards. By now, the area had large Brazilian and Portuguese communities, with a recent large influx of Somalian refugees. It was far more run-down, with a lot less hope in the air.

The school, like the area, had now changed beyond recognition. The once smart and spotless exterior was now unrecognizable with many 'bolted on', temporary looking buildings. It was ugly and archaic.

Once inside, it was strikingly tidy, but not smart or well designed. As we proceeded through the school, following the signs to the awards evening, we passed many rushing but never running schoolboys – all smartly turned out. It felt like the majority of the school consisted of black boys.

It was now failing by every measure, and the national education standards authority, OFSTED, had the previous year placed it under the serious category of 'Special Measures'. This of course served to further stigmatize the school. Therefore, the only parents sending their sons there were those who either didn't know any better, or simply had no other options available to them. After struggling in its previous school inspection, it was now 'drinking in the last chance saloon'.

Geraldine was the inspirational Head Teacher that had recently successfully turned around the local Catholic girls' school, The Convent of Jesus and Mary. She had built a first-class team, inspiring many of the teachers she had inherited, who responded to her unwavering belief in them. She had identified their Spikes and repositioned them accordingly.

When she was offered the opportunity to become Executive Head of both schools, no one seriously thought that she would take on this now broken establishment. Why would she want the hassle? Perhaps because engineering tough transformations is another of her wonderful Spikes.

When I attended the school back in the late 1970s, there were 200 boys in each of the academic years. When I returned, the entry year, now called Year 7, had only managed to attract 76 boys! There was no bigger negative indicator of a failing school. Anyone who had an alternative took it.

In my now faraway and distant times, nearly all immigrant parents believed that education was the best and (sometimes only) positive platform they could provide for their children. Then it was up to them. My generation of the children of immigrants at this school, consequently, gave it absolutely everything we had.

There are very few things more satisfying than being an active part in the educational development of our children, and seeing them take full advantage of the real opportunities that will hopefully come their way.

We would grow up knowing that we could potentially achieve so much more than our parents had. Firstly, because of them we had a British education, which enabled us to navigate the employment landscape with that much more knowledge and confidence. But probably, just as vitally, we were able to establish home environments far more conducive to learning and developing the wide range of capabilities; environments that would enable our own children to flourish.

BACK TO FRONT

It was quite eerie, coming back to a school that had had such mixed expectations of me when I was there. Most of the teaching staff during my time deserved medals. They were natural optimists, who gave everything for their profession, and had endless patience for the boys.

They worked especially hard with those who were, perhaps, a little more focused on playing football, than concentrating in lessons. These willing teachers persevered, despite suffering from the lack of any sort of leadership, and having no semblance of a unifying team force to support them.

However, there were a few teachers who seemed to specialize and trade in despondency. With just the odd damaging word, they could remove all hope and belief from any pupil.

It always amazes me how much just a few 'inappropriate' managers can ruin the environment and corrode the culture of any organization.

I was shown into the Head's office, which, in my time you only entered to have the pleasure of a caning from the grim and stone-faced Deputy Headmaster. It was strange; I still felt a little anxious when walking into Geraldine's office.

Not only was the school physically very different; the style of leadership was totally altered. There was a warmth and a collective desire for success. Something very special was beginning to take place here: you could just taste it in the air. The teachers reveled in the belief that they were 'part of something special.' This was due to the sparkling and inspired vision of the future that Geraldine was so fond of sharing and injecting into everyone she met.

Back in the 70s, all the Heads of Department and the Head Teachers were male, tough, straight-talking and distinctly 'old school' – excuse the pun. The toughest and most disagreeable 'hard nuts' (as we used to call them) were always tense, in their dark three piece suits, crisp ties, shiny brogues, and they all wore the pin badges of the various teaching unions and associations they belonged to. Discipline was absolutely the main thing (and sometimes the only thing) on their agenda. We had to stand up in class in order to speak; uniform was a must and no one dared answer back – in fact, it never even occurred to us.

A new generation of teachers was joining and starting to transform the school back then, despite the very 'old school' Heads of Department, and a distant and aloof Headmaster. But without the leader being part of the embryonic transformative process, it would be very difficult to get the necessary traction.

I always wonder why people think about the good old days at school – they weren't that good at all. Some of the old 'hard nuts' were at their most creative when it came to corporal punishment. There were many different implements to be caned with: sticks, straps, wooden tennis bats, and plimsolls. The only good thing I can remember about this dismal experience was that you had the dubious pleasure of choosing your favoured instrument of punishment.

On the same day that I started at the school, a new Head of Physical Education joined. Perhaps unbeknownst to him, he was to assist in initiating a new culture of inclusion and confidence. Ken was completely different to all who had come before him. He was strikingly younger, handsome and, most of all, had a uniquely positive disposition.

It was the first time that we would encounter inspirational leadership.

He proudly wore the very swish purple tracksuit of his alma mater, Loughborough University. The University was building a strong and unique reputation in the UK for sports mastery.

All the school's representative sports teams appeared to derive a lift from this 'force for good' and improved beyond belief.

He was a huge and pivotal Spike practitioner. He could somehow, after minimal observation, appear to have worked out not only what sport, but what position or approach you should adopt. He was a very different sort of disciplinarian. He set boundaries for acceptable behaviour and forgave all who gave their all. He practiced sanctions, not corporal punishment, he would threaten to remove you from your Spike position or sport. It rarely ever occurred – instead, we all responded positively and with enthusiasm.

He was hugely isolated as Head of Physical Education. Slowly but surely Ken attracted other like-minded teachers to his cause. There were about 10 or so of this 'new wave' of educators. They made their lessons hugely interactive, innovative and, most of all, fun. No one was ever late when one of these passionate sharers of knowledge weaved their magic spells.

How much more could have been achieved, if we – and they – had been led by a figure like Geraldine, who embraced and inspired others' Spikes.

Still fit and still handsome, but that bit more rugged, Ken was the first face I recognized as I walked through the school. On seeing me, he instantly walked over, with that brisk and purposeful walk I knew so well and he hugged me heartily. I hadn't seen him for 25 years but his warmth dissipated any potential awkwardness. Another one of his Spikes: he made everyone feel recognized and part of something special. And he'd just done it again with me. I now was really pleased to be back here and feeling warm and engaged with the task at hand. Ken was still very special indeed.

The atmosphere and energy present everywhere was so different, everyone was charming, everyone was on first name terms, and if there was ever living proof that women lead differently to men, Geraldine was it.

She was welcoming, sophisticated, so accessible and so human. No sign of any ego or competitive zeal with her colleagues – quite the opposite, in fact. She was a red headed ball of positive energy. She appeared to be everywhere, and she appeared to leave behind her a drop of concentrated courage for everyone she touched. In just under a year, the school was finding its 'mojo'. Many young and ambitious teachers were drawn towards the opportunity to work for such an inspired leader like Geraldine, despite the less than exciting salary on offer.

I had a pleasingly short briefing on what was expected of me, but she had fired me up more than enough from her initial telephone call. Inspiration coupled with sincerity can invigorate for a very long time.

KARL – ONE DOOR CLOSES AS ANOTHER OPENS

Before long I was standing in front of a gathered 'assembly' of parents, teachers and pupils in the same school hall where we had attended a 'hard core' morning assembly, and in an instant, I felt really proud to be part of this school again.

Geraldine had accurately assessed my Spikes. I was, by this point, a decent veteran at the speaking game, but this experience was different. It was important to me, because I remembered standing in that assembly hall so many years ago, hardly understanding a word our very few guest speakers uttered.

This felt somehow different: the pupils and parents were all seated. I hardly ever get the 'butterflies' anymore, but I felt them fluttering away wonderfully inside of me. The words of my mother on my first day of school floated back into my mind: "You just be better than that white boy sitting next to you." That same drive possessed me now, as there were hardly any white boys in the audience.

The gathered parents, teachers and students were generous and warm, both with their attention and their applause. I just wished there were more parents in the audience, but in many respects, this was a little glimpse into the underlying problems of inner city education in London.

When I had finished, up stepped Karl; he was in the sixth form and the Head Boy. He was smartly turned out in his crisp uniform. He took a big deep breath; he was clearly nervous and gulping in loads of air. He clasped his hands behind his back and stood up tall and straight as he addressed the audience.

He was remarkably eloquent and really optimistic about his and the school's future. He wanted to be someone and nothing was going to hold him back. He spoke slowly and clearly, with a natural authority. His smile was infectious and he was a wonderful role model for all those younger boys at the school. Geraldine had chosen so well, yet again.

She had found an ambassador and advocate who could connect and engage at levels where her influence might not penetrate.

I sat in the audience feeling really proud of Karl, and the smiles he had put on the faces of the parents and the pupils in the less-than-glamorous old assembly hall. He was so sensitive and empathetic for his young years. He was quietly in control, with an emotional intelligence to match – a powerful combination.

Good leaders create followers; great leaders create leaders.

I had invited my best friend Ray and my brother Louis to the function. Louis was also an old boy from the school, but even in the few years between his school career and mine, the school had started to change for the worse. Louis had never shared my relatively positive and rather 'rose-tinted' view of Cardinal Hinsley School.

By the time I was long gone, the make-up of the school had radically altered, and perhaps not for the better. However, now, standing next to me, even Louis had become more optimistic about the school's future. The values of the school had been transformed towards Geraldine's values.

As we were leaving, with much hope and even more belief in Geraldine and her ability to continue turning around this very challenging project, she thanked me, and Karl appeared with a generous gift from the school.

I asked Geraldine if there was anything I could do for the school. Her instant and probably well-rehearsed response was:

"Work experience. No one is prepared to give these boys a chance. We would do anything for them just to have a taste of work. Most of them hardly know any males who are in employment. Therefore, you especially, can understand just how tough it is for them to see work as an opportunity, and not just a feeling of endless rejection."

How far had I really moved away from the place that I had grown up? I now lived only 5 miles or so away, but it might well have been a different planet. This was a timely reminder: education is never the problem, but it is always an opportunity

MAKING A DIFFERENCE

The old African proverb, "It takes a village to raise a child" came flashing to my mind.

This was my village.

I had been given my mission and I was desperate to help.

On the way out Ray, Louis and I could not stop talking about Karl, and how if he were born in a different place, maybe just a few miles away, he'd probably have been earmarked for great things.

But what were his Spikes? We had a glimpse of his progressive personality and warm disposition. And we knew there was something very special about him, but it would require nurturing and the opportunity to shine. Would he ever get the chance to mobilize them and benefit from them?

I woke up early feeling energized. I composed a careful flyer to go out to all the contacts on our database. I felt it was important that I was very clear and honest about everything. There could be no surprises, or worse still, 'rude awakenings'. The note described the recent difficult background of the school, the challenges of the local environment, but most of all, a plea to help materially change the life chances of some of the hard working and aspirational students.

With my large and comprehensive network, I was confident that we would get support for this relevant and necessary new work experience scheme.

Then, I hesitated. Would my business network really share my passion and goodwill for this initiative?

Answers flew back: some immediately and many within hours. It was thrilling and made me feel that my optimism in our society was fully justified. I received nearly 100 offers of work placements, ranging from banks to retailers to garages.

With the help of the school and my hard working team, we found work placements for twenty of the boys.

We knew the delicacy of the situation and therefore took the time to carefully brief both the boys and employers thoroughly.

It took a few months of careful planning and organization to get everything in place.

The school was buzzing, and their new progressive culture of proactive support and collaboration was first class throughout this painstaking process.

However, literally a few days before it was all due to start, I took an anxious phone call from the school – it's always the seemingly small things that can cause the biggest roadblocks to progress. Despite all our diagnostics and critical path analysis, we had not made any provision at all for the cost of the transportation for the students to and from their prospective places of work.

This was fixable, but really embarrassing for me, as it was yet another reminder that I had moved so far away from my roots. I hadn't appreciated that even bus fares needed to be budgeted for, when a family has so little disposable income.

The only way forward was to pick up the costs of transporting all the boys myself and learn another real lesson.

It all now seemed to go well, and the school dealt with most of the ongoing administration. We felt we had done our bit, by helping establish a much needed and much appreciated tangible opportunity for these disadvantaged pupils, and it felt great.

A few months afterwards, I wandered down to the school to see how things had gone and what lessons we could learn. Overall, the feedback was brilliant, but there were some mixed results. I was especially keen to know how Karl had performed, and I decided to pick this up directly with Louise, whom he had spent his two weeks with.

Louise was an extremely talented design florist, whose shop was based on the trendy (and expensive) Kings Road in Chelsea. She was a florist to the stars, and did so much more than just flowers. She could make any room sparkle with her sharp and deft touch. Stunning floral creations sat alongside sleek ornamental jars, swishes of brightly coloured fabric amongst her unique and innovative arrangements.

I had been mentoring Louise and her business for a couple of years, and she felt she would like to reciprocate, by taking on one of the boys from Cardinal Hinsley School. Louise had always been an extraordinarily generous person.

I had asked all the wonderfully considerate prospective employers to arrange some initial and basic training, and wherever possible, nominate a member of their team to be an ongoing mentor and point of contact for the pupil throughout their two-week stay. Nothing was too much for them.

Louise could never do anything by halves – she had really gone to town in terms of the provision and arrangements, and she was very pleased when she instantly hit it off with Karl.

She'd arranged for Karl to work on the customer service desk for the first week, and then to work on the PC, doing stock control and inventory management for the second week.

Louise and her team were excited and upbeat when Karl showed up. He was charming, keen and obviously bright. But Karl, shockingly, turned up for his first day decked out like he was out for the weekend with his mates.

From the hoody to the baggy jeans and big trainers, it was absolutely the wrong look for upmarket and designer Chelsea!

Louise instantly decided not to put him on the customer service desk for the first day, but she showed him how to use the stock control system on the PC, which was in fact a series of simple Excel spreadsheets. By close of business that day, Karl had redesigned and rewritten all the spreadsheets, simplifying them and making them so much more intelligible. Louise was in awe and really pleased, and told him so.

Just before Karl left for home, Louise very carefully and sensitively asked him if he didn't mind wearing something just a little bit more sober for his next day at work, even if it was his school uniform. She shared with him the exciting week she had arranged for him on the customer service desk.

Karl was not in the least bit put out, and said he completely understood, and looked forward to seeing her in the morning. That was the last they saw of Karl. When she had tried to take down his contact details the previous day, he said he didn't own a mobile, and that there was no telephone at home.

RUDE AWAKENING

I was taken aback, and deeply disappointed. I had to get to the bottom of this. I couldn't shake the feeling of being let down by Karl, but I also could not quite believe it.

It wasn't long before I found myself at the school, and went off to find Karl at the end of the school day. We walked away from his classmates, and he was looking anxious and a little lost. I gently enquired how the work experience had gone. He knew that I knew. He was heavily embarrassed, and instantly asked me not to tell anyone at school. "Things are just not that straightforward," he whispered under his breath. He asked carefully, whether I would be prepared to come down to his home and meet his Mum.

He so needed me to better understand his world.

A week later, I found myself parking up in a grey council housing estate not far from the school, which I hadn't been near for many years now. Many of my old school friends had lived in this very same estate, and I used to happily play football with them after school many years before.

It now looked so different. It felt hostile and unwelcoming. There were abandoned cars, rubbish strewn everywhere and it was intimidating and scary. There was no way I could enter the filthy and malodorous lift; in fact, my stomach churned when the door opened. Walking up the stairs was no better. I found myself holding my breath and going ever faster up the stairs. When I got to Karl's front door, it wasn't properly shut, as the lock had been savagely hacked off.

I rang the bell and the door opened a little more, and I could now hear very loud rap music, and someone singing and chanting along to the music. Karl came to the door and asked me to come in to their tiny and compact apartment. He was looking after his younger sisters and called out to his Mum.

His short and chirpy Mum came bounding down the stairs, still singing at the top of her voice. When she arrived, she was wearing a hoody, big loose jeans and big trainers. Before I could even say hello, she bounced over, gave me a huge kiss and thanked me so much for giving Karl the chance of work experience. She had a huge smile right across her face as she stared with watering eyes at Karl.

She then shared with me just how proud she was of Karl. He was such a help to her, and was always there for her, ready and willing to look after his sisters, as she had three demanding jobs.

I soon worked out that she was a cleaner early in the mornings and worked in a local factory in the evenings, and did something at a local primary school during the day.

The small and tiny flat was spotlessly clean. Here was a woman who was trying her level best, all the time. There was no evidence of any partner around.

She carried on speaking excitedly about Karl. She was close to tears of joy, and shared passionately that as soon as she knew that Karl was actually getting the rare opportunity for some real and relevant work experience, she had volunteered for overtime at all of her places of work.

She then said, beaming proudly: "I went out and bought him the best clothes I could get for his work experience from my overtime money".

By now Karl was looking at the floor with his hands thrust deep in his pockets. I had nothing but admiration for his Mum, but once again I realized just how far I had moved from this place and this life, despite only living a few miles up the road.

WRONG ASSUMPTIONS

As he walked me to my car, Karl apologized for letting Louise and everyone else down, but he didn't know how to tell his Mum that they were just the wrong clothes. He didn't know what else to do, as he felt he had to leave the house wearing them every day, when he was wanting to wear something else.

Karl's mother gave him everything she had and more. Nothing can replace or match that genuine, unconditional love and deep, tender care.

In many respects, we all know many stories just like Karl's. The story of the starfish comes to mind. The story tells of an elderly man, who is walking along a golden beach when he comes across thousands of starfish, washed up on the shore, starting to dry up and surely destined to die. The man stoops to pick up as many as he can and toss them back into the sea. A young fisherman watches him sweating profusely, but still bending over and heaving them over his head for hours. Eventually he gets up and shouts out: "You cannot save them all – there are still thousands of them left dying".

"But I've made a difference to everyone I've touched," he replied.

Every time we assist someone in discovering their Spikes, it's the greatest gift we can ever give. Why wouldn't we give such a free and valuable present?

Soft and less than visible Spikes are always much harder for us to determine or accept. It takes others around you to share their power and ability to influence. Otherwise, they can be misinterpreted as weaknesses.

Sensitivity and care were huge Spikes for Karl, but he required assistance in knowing how to better exploit the keys to unlocking a potential-rich future.

Geraldine found his rich potential because she was looking out for his Spikes, not his limitations.

There are times when we just don't understand things, but we sometimes just get used to them being around us.

Karl's work experience had afforded me insight into life experience. Geraldine's company had reminded me of the art of the possible.

"NOW, HERE, YOU SEE, IT TAKES ALL THE RUNNING YOU CAN DO, TO KEEP IN THE SAME PLACE. IF YOU WANT TO GET SOMEWHERE ELSE, YOU MUST RUN AT LEAST TWICE AS FAST AS THAT!"

LEWIS CARROLL – ALICE THROUGH THE LOOKING GLASS

SPIKE SPARKS

It's far too easy to give up on the 'underperformers' – but they too have Spikes – it is the role of the leader to help them identify their Spikes.

To connect with people in a group, you must relate to them as individuals.

It is no longer feasible to expect the leader to have all the answers. Build the team around the leader's Spikes and the team will deliver the answers.

Never tell your people what to do – instead, tell them what you would like to see happen. If it doesn't happen, don't shout orders; tell them again, making sure you tell them why, and do it with a compelling story of how wonderful the world will be when you all get there. Then, lead by example.

Sharing your vulnerabilities is not a sign of weakness – it is a sign of strength and confidence. It is a powerful way of connecting with those who are important to you.

ON THE SAME PAGE

"Although individuals need not be well-rounded, teams should be."– Tom Rath

"A mentor should be a good listener, observer, and problem solver. While listening, a mentor must not only pay attention to the words but also to the tone, attitude, and body language behind the words." – Armando Rodriguez, an Associate Professor in the Department of Electrical Engineering at Arizona State University in Tempe, who received the Presidential Award for Excellence in Science, Mathematics, and Engineering Mentoring in 1998.[19]

A report generated by PwC[20] states that "a leader's talent is the ability to leverage and maximize the impact of his or her people. To harness the power of their people assets, leaders must be committed to building a supportive culture and effective organizational structures and people processes."

"A mentor is someone who allows you to see the hope inside yourself. A mentor is someone who allows you to know that no matter how dark the night, in the morning joy will come. A mentor is someone who allows you to see the higher part of yourself when sometimes it becomes hidden to your own view... If your actions inspire others to dream more, learn more, do more and become more, you are a leader." – Oprah Winfrey

---

[19] Mohan-Ram, V. (1999) "Mentoring Advice from a Presidential Awardee." (online) Available at: http://www.sciencemag.org/careers/1999/12/mentoring-advice-presidential-awardee [Accessed 05 Apr 2016]

[20] "PwC US Human Capital Effectiveness Report (2007) How leadership must change to meet the future." (online) Available at: https://www.pwc.com/us/en/people-management/assets/future- leadership-change.pdf [Accessed 03 Apr 2016]

CHAPTER VIII
~~WASTE TIME ON FAILURE.~~ SPEND ENERGY ON SOLUTIONS

Nobody wants to work for a pessimist. How much of an optimist or pessimist are you when it comes to rapid change? Ask your loved ones how they view your positivity under pressure.

Sometimes, change creates a culture of complaint. People get mad at the situation. They gripe. They burn up precious energy on frustration and angry feelings.

Some play "poor me", whine about being a victim, and dwell on what they've lost. They wallow around in wishful thinking and long for a return to the 'good old days'.

Still others waste themselves on worry – about the future, what they might lose, or what could go wrong.

None of this negative thinking improves a thing. But it also doesn't make them bad people. In fact, they have Spikes to be capitalized upon. They need the support and direction of those who see the world of change more optimistically.

Change makes a lot of new demands on people, leaving you little time or energy to spare. So instead of getting upset and wasting these precious resources, spend them on solving the new problems.

Buckle down. Channel your thoughts and efforts along productive lines. Get busy instead of getting mad. Crowd out unpleasant emotions by filling your mind with a search for solutions.

Action is better therapy than tears. And doing your part to help the organization adjust will lower your level of emotional stress a lot better than resisting the changes ever would.

But this is rarely achieved alone.

Redirect grief, anger, or worry into a passionate pursuit of results. Work from the heart and you heal the spirit. Put fire into your job habits and you burn off worry and anger.

Spend your energy and time on finding solutions to the problems of change. You can help shape the culture into an energy-efficient system that feeds off the diversity within the Spikes of its people.

Those with little experience or exposure to the 'old way of doing things', will have much less respect for them and have little fear of doing things differently – they should not be frowned upon, but their Spikes must be encouraged and embraced.

"WHEN YOU WIN, NOTHING HURTS."

JOE NAMATH, HALL OF FAME QUARTERBACK

KEITH – WE ARE STRONGER TOGETHER

It was a very full house at Goldman Sachs' River Court offices in Fleet Street. I was the guest keynote speaker for an important Leadership event. Everything had gone very well and I had stayed behind to talk to the extremely smart and driven, young talented employees who were the attendees for the event.

Goldman Sachs always run top-drawer events. On my way out, one of the attendees stopped me in the reception area. He introduced himself. He was tall and impeccably turned out. He said, "Thank you for making the Mentoring Scheme happen at Deptford Green School. It helped me change my horizons. I would never have believed that I could have gone on to university and land this job at Goldman Sachs."

He was to always stick in my mind.

It was my first day of work at IPC Magazines. I've always lived and worked north of the river in London. There is a particular snobbery and competition practised by those who live north of the river, against those who live south of the river. Both sides swear blind that the other side is full of plebs and paupers.

I must admit, I did hesitate when I realised my new place of work was going to be south of the river.

Driving in on my first day was a brave and perhaps foolish move as, predictably, I got lost. I pulled in to the car park of a large school in Deptford, knowing I was close, but having no idea how to get to Stamford Street from here.

I really wasn't ready for what I was about to experience. There was an enclosed area at the front of the school, where passers-by had thrown used syringes, used and burnt out bits of baking foil, and other remnants of what appeared to be the results of communal drug taking. It turned my stomach.

I now hesitated and questioned whether it was a good idea to proceed into the school. Four or five pupils in uniform rushed past me to get into school on time, screaming breathlessly. The sound of their laughter convinced me this was indeed the right place for help.

As I opened the door, there was a charming black man surrounded by kids of every race and colour, with myriad different accents. They were all demanding his attention, and he was dealing with all of them like some latter day Pied Piper.

His golden Spike was obvious for all to see and for the children to experience.

He gently gestured at me, believing I was a parent, and indicated that he would be with me in a moment. I just watched in awe as he doled out dollops of love and attention, whilst managing to bring a calm order to this noisy throng that was outside of his office, the headmaster's office.

I knew it was getting late and it was my first day, but I couldn't move. This was a Master-class in leadership. When he eventually came over, he was soft, welcoming and quite assertive. He asked me for the names of my children, and I told him that they weren't at this school.

He instantly launched into a well-rehearsed speech on the positive aspects of Deptford Green School. His name was Keith and he was the proud Headmaster of this school, with over 1200 pupils; over 70% of them had English as a second or third language. A large number had come from the shelter Britain had offered to the unfortunate victims of the Vietnamese 'boat people' tragedy.

The available local social housing was in high demand, and many communities were fragmenting, as all who could, moved away.

He spoke with such candour, such passion, that it would have been rude to interrupt. This was another of his immense Spikes – he was an outstanding communicator at all levels and to all people, no matter what their background. I eventually confessed to simply being lost, and wanting directions to IPC Magazines.

His eyes lit up and he asked me very directly: "What do you do there? Do you work on one of the magazines for boys or girls?"

I responded: "Not really, I'm just a Board Director." He apologised, but still looked at me disbelievingly, and asked whether as a Director, I could get him some old copies of *Mizz* Magazine for the girls at the school, and perhaps *Shoot* Magazine for the boys? I smiled and responded: "Sure," perhaps a little too nonchalantly to be convincing. I asked him: "How many copies did you want?" He said, "Whatever you can get, as many as you can get – just a few old ones would do".

He was instantly lowering his expectations.

He then walked me to the gates, and we both stared into the enclosed area and looked disappointedly at the detritus of drug taking paraphernalia. He was clearly agitated. "It's a disgrace. No matter how many times we get it cleaned up, the disenfranchised local young people will still always deposit their rubbish in front of our school. They just don't realize or care about the potential damage it can do to these children."

MIKE – GIVE AND YOU WILL RECEIVE

IPC Magazines, at the time, was situated next door to the old headquarters of the supermarket giant, Sainsbury's, and across the road from the Express Newspapers head office. Three big blue chip businesses, just a stone's throw from Deptford Green School.

I couldn't get Keith or his school out of my thoughts as I drove off.

The following week, I arranged for 1000 copies of the current issue of *Mizz* and 1000 copies of the current issue of *Shoot* to be sent to the school.

I received an urgent phone call from Keith: he was worrying that there had perhaps been an expensive mistake, because the school had received copies of the current issue, and not old copies as he had requested.

It gave me a clue into what also needed fixing, and it was the beginning of a brilliant friendship.

I had to explain that there was "no accident," and that there would be "no cost to Deptford Green School." He was gracious and very grateful. Being the opportunist that he clearly was, he instantly asked me, if there was anything else we could do for the school.

Our blossoming friendship, coupled with his boldness, brought many mutual opportunities to bear.

This eventually led to me convincing Mike, the Chief Executive of IPC Magazines, to come and give a special speech at a school assembly, early one morning. Mike came from the humblest of origins and just caught the mood perfectly. He managed to get the packed hall laughing, and shared a few relevant and inspiring stories of his journey to becoming Chief Executive of a large local business.

At work, Mike could be very hard indeed – he had to be. None of us had experienced this far more empathetic and nurturing side of him.

Mike was brilliant; the kids loved him, and this enabled me to develop a long-lasting relationship between Deptford Green School and IPC Magazines.

Keith and Mike were quite similar in what they were trying to achieve and how they went about it through their people. They cared about what they were doing, and brought vision, passion and purpose to all who worked for them. Mike got as much from his experience at Deptford Green School, as the pupils and teachers got from him.

They had very similar Spikes, which were deployed in very different environments, but in actual fact, delivered similar results.

Mike noticed and observed everything. On the way back to the office Mike was in reflective mood. The changing nature of the local neighbourhood had struck him hard.

It wasn't lost on him why I had asked him to attend. He now started asking me what was on my mind.

I carefully explained that what Keith really wanted was some of our people at IPC to take an interest in some of the children at Deptford Green. He wanted visible and positive role models for his students. Many would have had no working adult in their homes or in their lives.

I'd had the massively unique and positive experience of being mentored by some unforgettable people. I'd also had the privilege to have been a mentor for some time at a scheme organized for undergraduates at the recently formed University of East London.

In fact, my mentee from the scheme, Naveed, would join IPC Magazines in the months to come. He had gained the confidence to respond to a job advert. He only let me know after he had been offered a position by the company, that he had fulfilled his goal of joining IPC Magazines. He would play a key role in ensuring our Mentoring Scheme hit the desired spot.

Jill, my long-suffering PA, had been with me at PepsiCo and was my first hire at IPC Magazines. We were the ultimate team.

We had the most complementary of Spikes. She was super organized and efficiency personified. She naturally read all the 'small print' and always had me in the right places at the right time.

She knew I would say 'yes' to everyone who wanted to see me. She managed them all, and no matter how long they had to wait to eventually see me, she made them feel as though they were the most important people in my diary.

We were nearly telepathic. We would argue and disagree, but we always got on, and in many respects, she was the real 'boss'.

At around this time, Mike was invited to be part of a 'Business in the Community' initiative to visit a number of schools in the area alongside a number of Chief Executives of local large businesses. Mike was unfortunately away and asked me to stand in for him. It was a huge and timely privilege.

We visited four or five local schools; and each had their own special charm, and the guests were being 'courted' by the schools to take a long-term interest in the schools and their students. At the end of a long but very productive day, we were all talking loudly and proudly about the insights we had picked up throughout the day. The conversation moved naturally towards the setting up of Mentoring Schemes for the students, potentially by the businesses run by the gathered leaders.

JILL – LEADERS NATURALLY COACH

This was a moment not to be lost. I volunteered to set up and run a Mentoring Scheme for Deptford Green School, which just happened to be the first school we had visited earlier that morning.

On returning to the office, I couldn't contain my enthusiasm, and I gathered my team around me, as I shared the vision of the Mentoring Scheme for Deptford Green School that we would initiate.

There were about eight of us thinking out loud and seeing how we could best make this happen. We soon had an outline of a strategy, and as we did at all our meetings, I then asked for someone to 'own' the actions.

I had learned many years ago that one volunteer is worth a thousand conscripts.

As I paused for a moment, Jill jumped up – she wanted to organize and run the Mentoring Scheme. None of us had expected that. Jill never wanted or looked for the 'limelight'. She would organize all my public speaking commitments and would always say, "I don't know how you do that – I can't think of anything worse."

Jill was now standing and holding some notes in her hand – which was shaking violently – as she tried to contain herself. In an instant, we all had stopped talking and gave her our full and undivided attention. Jill's neck blotched red; she cleared her throat and, without ever glancing at her notes, she launched into her heartfelt desire to make a difference to these students' lives.

Without pausing for breath, she explained how the scheme would look, how it would run, and the varied roles and responsibilities of all of us in the Leadership Team.

It was superb, and there was little that needed adding.

None of us knew that Jill had this inside of her – we knew she was the best organizer in the team, but this was a side of her that was new to all of us. She had the ability to simplify everything that came across her desk. When I had to be in two or three places at the same time, she would be totally unruffled and ensure that everything went to plan. Even those who might be disappointed felt that they were treated with huge respect and a friendly service.

She was usually the first touch point of our 'brand'. She was the most perfect ambassador and advocate for my team, and for me. Jill was always soft and soothing for all who came into contact with her.

Some Spikes are not always obvious, but they are well worth the effort it takes to discover them.

The following morning, Jill came to see me as she had realized that she had taken complete control of the Mentoring Scheme. She was on the point of apologizing for her behaviour, when we talked about organizing being one of her huge Spikes. But this wasn't just about organizing – this was something that was very special and unique to her.

I'd initially imagined giving this task to one of my Leadership team, but Jill had grabbed it, and our job now was to support her and create an environment that would enable her to 'win'.

Just a few months later, we had ten mentors from my team at IPC Magazines. They were building effective relationships with ten of the pupils from the sixth form of Deptford Green School. Naveed, my former mentee, had jumped to be at Jill's side, and he now was in a position to ensure the scheme picked up on all the little things that could make such a difference to the mentees.

I felt very proud. I had developed a mentoring relationship with a few of the teachers at the school and met with them on a regular basis at my office at IPC. They just grew with the confidence from knowing that there was someone out there that they could talk to in private, about anything and everything.

It was going so well that demand was outstripping supply. We needed more mentors. Jill suggested that we opened the scheme up to people from right across IPC Magazines. Not just my team.

With her enthusiasm and know-how, she buzzed around all the PAs of my peers and we soon had more than twenty mentors from across the business.

LEADERS ARE FOUND

By now Jill had become the mentoring maestro. She administered all the training and development for all prospective mentors. She was superb at matching mentors to mentees. Introverts and extroverts were carefully matched; hidden talents were capitalised upon. Not all were instant successes, but Jill was always alert and brave enough to make early interventions and assertive changes as necessary.

Jill had demonstrated to all of us how much more could be achieved when the task at hand was matched to an individual's Spike.

The pupils blossomed, and we collected many human stories of success, and quite a few awards. Business in the Community stayed close to all we did and helped share best practice across all their schemes and clients.

Around the same time, at my daughter's school, which was at the other end of schooling in London, they decided to get rid of their internal Career Counselors. Instead, they replaced them at the school assembly on Friday mornings with a parent, who was invited to talk to the students for 30 minutes about their chosen career.

I had been selected to do this talk in a month, so, I turned up one week to watch one of these sessions from the back of the hall to better understand what was expected of me.

The students were restless and noisy, and giggled playfully as the guest parent was introduced and approached the stage. She had brought along with her what appeared to be a long narrow suitcase and what looked like a suit carrier.

She walked down the hall and stepped confidently on to the stage in front of the gathered students and calmly took off her coat. She first opened out the long case, instantly flipping it into a 'massage' type table. She laid a crisp white sheet over the table. She then opened the suit carrier, took out her uniform and changed into her white gown, gloves, hat and mask. She carried this all out without saying one word.

She had that natural sense of theatre that belongs to all great storytellers.

The noise levels reduced, as many were trying to work out what was going on, but it was still far from quiet. She then brought out a startling array of shiny tools and implements. The members of the audience were now straining their necks to see. Once the hacksaw was placed on the lectern, she had the full and undivided attention of all in the assembly hall.

She was a surgeon and knew how to captivate a young and impressionable audience.

In 30 electrifying minutes, she was able to convince this young audience that the slicing and opening up of human bodies was not just extremely important, requiring great skill, but was also a very fulfilling and satisfying career.

She was extremely knowledgeable, enthusiastic and great fun. You could have heard a mobile phone vibrate; all the students were leaning forward and massively attentive.

Passion, enthusiasm and real knowledge of any career is not easily delegated or simulated.

She went on to share that she had sat in a similar school assembly many years ago and had heard a surgeon speak to the school; she hadn't understood anything he'd said, but she just knew that she wanted to be a surgeon.

She had made the gory and sometimes extreme work of a surgeon appealing to many of the now awestruck students.

Her Spikes of being able to engage and connect with people, coupled with her compelling story telling, were on display throughout this master class.

We soon adopted a very similar initiative for Deptford Green School, with the necessary twist of having our managers as well as the few parents, sharing what they did for a living in front of the school assembly. Many were brilliant, but all were memorable and motivating. It was just as successful.

It opened up whole new horizons and a variety of never-thought-of career possibilities for our talented and now ambitious students.

At the end of the first year of the Deptford Green School Mentoring Scheme, Keith invited Jill and I to one of their open evenings; we were the guests of honour and were privileged to hand out the academic awards for the year.

This was indeed an honour. This time, when I pulled up to the school, the shameful enclosed area had disappeared for good. There was an extra special aura of confidence and optimism about the school. Business in the Community had brought in Ernst & Young, the management consultants, to measure the impact of the Mentoring Scheme with IPC Magazines, and the results were astonishing.

The results shook all of us. Ernst & Young proved that mentoring had a bigger and more positive impact on academic success than teaching!

This was amazing. It was all about taking an active and positive interest in the pupils (and teachers). Everybody benefits from a more caring environment, but so much more can be achieved if someone is taking a special interest in your well-being and success. No matter how good Keith was – and he was very good indeed – he could not do it all on his own.

The climate of success paved the way for further involvement, and the Mentoring Scheme at IPC Magazines had now spread throughout the whole company; at its peak there were some fifty mentoring relationships.

As with all mentoring relationships, the only reason to continue, is if both parties are gaining some tangible benefit.

LEARN, UNLEARN AND RE-LEARN

My leaders and managers at IPC who had thrown themselves into the Mentoring Scheme were also changing. Their once impenetrable 'management speak' had changed, especially those who worked in the IT team.

They had previously been accused of being a bit 'geekish', and perhaps had little in terms of people skills; they spoke a strange language that no one but themselves understood. Having to deal with the keen, but rather sheltered pupils of Deptford Green School, had changed them massively.

One of the most instructive moments happened very early on in the mentoring relationship with Deptford Green. I got a call from the reception desk of our offices at Kings Reach Tower – there were three pupils from Deptford Green School who had arrived to meet three of my managers, but the managers could not be contacted. I soon discovered that the managers were on another site, a few miles away.

I needed to get to the bottom of this rather embarrassing situation.

When I went down to meet the students at reception, it soon became obvious what had happened. The pupils had arrived two hours late for a 3pm appointment.

In trying to explain to them that the managers would always be busy, so they needed to arrive at the agreed time, it became clear that they had NO idea about appointments or time-keeping. They were astonished that their mentors would not be available some two hours later.

Tremendous learning occurred for all concerned. These experiences changed the language and attitude of all the managers who had the pleasure of working with these brilliant children of our local community. We certainly were able to help them, but they also helped us – they taught us humility and humanity.

I am sure if I had brought those same consultants in from Ernst and Young, they would have shown that these managers learned so much more from the students of Deptford Green School than they ever could from me.

Jill and I were politely greeted at the school entrance; we were shown into the auditorium. The academic awards evening had a strong and vibrant Caribbean theme. There was tasty food for all and a steel band playing in the background. The school hall was impressively decorated and it felt like we could have been somewhere in the West Indies.

Everything had been made by willing and creative students. It was a huge pleasure and accolade to be giving out the various certificates to really proud students, with many parents in the audience. We then sat back and enjoyed some excellent virtuoso performances from a number of hugely talented students.

One of the performing students really stuck out in my mind – a young girl who sang a number of Caribbean folk songs with the most amazing voice. I had earlier presented her with a certificate for academic achievement.

I left that evening feeling really proud to be a Director of IPC Magazines. This was really making a difference. We were giving back to our local community – the very community where our future customers and workforce would come from.

Some years later, I was in the Pebble Mill Studios of the BBC, waiting to be interviewed on a programme about the media. There was a band playing in one of the adjacent studios which had its door left open. All of a sudden, the most amazing voice was spreading intoxicatingly all around the studios. Everyone appeared to stop; even the seasoned cameramen and sound technicians were mesmerized by this clear and beautiful voice. She was hitting the most amazing notes, with such clarity and strength.

The applause burst out around the whole building, and we found ourselves applauding, even though we were waiting to do a serious news report.

Just before I was about to go in to my interview a young girl walked past me and said: "Good afternoon Mr. Carayol. You probably won't remember me, but you gave me my academic achievement award at Deptford Green School a few years ago."

She continued: "Martin is still my mentor, even though he has now left IPC Magazines and I have left Deptford Green School. He has helped me get my first recording contract."

We shook hands, she smiled and, with that, she was gone.

What a moment! I was literally speechless and found myself smiling all the way through the serious news interview that followed. If ever there was a moment for me that summed up the beauty and the value of mentoring, then that was it. It brings together the most unlikely of people from the most diverse of backgrounds. There are always people willing to coach and there are always people willing to learn – sharing is everything.

Mentoring is one of the best ways to assist others in identifying their true Spikes. It is through relationships built on trust that conversations around our Spikes are best nurtured and developed.

Those of us who have successfully been doing the same thing very well for years will find it quite challenging to change to something completely new. A strong relationship with a trusted neighbour might well be the best environment to start to explore how can we best adapt and evolve.

The ability to learn, unlearn and relearn will separate the winners from the losers in the future.

"MY BEST FRIEND IS THE ONE THAT BRINGS OUT THE BEST IN ME".

HENRY FONDA

SPIKE SPARKS

Mentoring relationships get better and better – investing the quality time early on will get you the ROI (Return on Involvement) you deserve.

One of life's key requirements is to better understand who you, and those closest to you, REALLY are – the Spike approach helps massively.

It's so much more powerful to 'show rather than tell'. The best leaders are great role models; their actions speak so much louder than words.

One of the most essential legacies of all great leaders – is to have found and nurtured many more leaders.

Difficult concepts and theories need bringing alive. Try telling a personal story to illuminate the point – stories are so much more memorable and much easier to listen to.

ON THE SAME PAGE

Even with the unlimited access to resources at our fingertips, we still benefit from the insight of those who have already walked the path. "A good mentor will give you guidance, but also hold you accountable for your successes and failures. Accountability is the best inspiration because it keeps you working at a higher level – you won't want to disappoint yourself or your mentor. Most importantly, a good mentor will challenge you to become a better version of yourself. They will expose your weaknesses and challenge you to step outside of your comfort zone."[21]

Mentoring improves team productivity by nurturing responsible employees and allowing the mentor to focus on higher-order responsibilities, such as developing new business. When managers feel that mentoring is a waste of time, usually it's because they don't know how to and are choosing comfort over progress. Effective leaders should "determine which of their tasks bring the most value to the business and draft a 'stop doing' list, which includes responsibilities that will be transferred via mentoring. The road to a stagnant firm is paved with the phrase 'It's easier if I just do it myself.'"[22]

A mentor becomes a prized asset within the organization, as mentoring facilitates personal growth by strengthening one's coaching and leadership skills through diversity of mentees. Not only does it help to train and retain talent within the organization, but it also helps create a legacy that has a lasting impact on the mentees, while enjoying the satisfaction of helping develop future management talent.[23]

---

[21] Pierce, S. (2015) "How a mentor helps you find the better version of yourself." (Online) http://fortune. com/2015/06/01/stacia-pierce-importance-of-a-mentor [Accessed 22 Apr 2016]

[22] Thompson, E. (2010) "How to Be a Better Mentor." (online) *Journal of Accountancy*. Available at: http://www.journalofaccountancy.com/issues/2010/nov/20091446.html [Accessed 22 Apr 2016]

[23] Hollister, R. (2001) "The Benefits of Being a Mentor - Mentoring enhances your professional life as well as your protégé's." (online) Available at: https://www.ache. org/newclub/career/MentorArticles/ Benefits.cfm [Accessed 22 Apr 2016]

CHAPTER IX
~~RELY HEAVILY ON YOUR STRENGTHS.~~
DON'T LET STRENGTHS BECOME WEAKNESSES

On occasion, your foremost Spikes may become part of the ongoing problem. When was the last time you just 'stepped out of the way' and allowed others, much better placed, to deal with it?

Put people under positive pressure – like the stress that comes from dealing with change – and they usually turn to their Spikes. It's human nature, and on the surface it makes sense. Rely on what you do best... Fight with your favourite weapons... Stick with well-developed habits, where you really shine. These are your Spikes.

But what if conditions call for new moves? What if doing what you do best no longer works?

When people are doing the wrong things, even if they do them flawlessly, the organization has trouble coping. Even Spikes can become weaknesses, when circumstances change but behaviour doesn't.

A culture of inflexibility develops if people put too much faith in their Spikes alone. So be prepared to abandon your best moves. Show respect for what works. Bring others with different Spikes into play. Go ahead and give the organization what it needs most, even if that's not your strong suit.

Be willing to stumble along whilst others fly. You can get better as you go. If you're doing the right things, you don't have to do them perfectly to get great results.

The key is to keep learning. Develop in new directions. Adapt. Don't get locked into a set of skills or an approach that could become outdated. Be willing to bend, to adjust, because a rapidly changing world requires new competencies.

A diverse and inclusive approach to Spikes within your team will ensure all bases are covered. Do your part to keep the culture from getting stiff, especially, when your Spikes may need to be parked, whilst the team delivers the necessary changes.

"THERE IS NO PERMANENT SOLUTION."

PRICE PRITCHETT

THE WEALTH CREATORS

In a world of increasing scrutiny by many forms of media and the death of 'light touch' regulation, many businesses – especially in regulated industries – appear to be losing their appetite for taking any form of risk whatsoever.

The UK suffered a sharp 12% fall in its productivity figures in late 2015. This came as a bit of a shock to many pundits, who had seen small but steady progress in previous years. When probed further, this was not another drop in manufacturing output, but a significant drop in productivity from the nation's 'golden goose', that is the financial services powerhouse of the City of London.

This fall was due to the burgeoning numbers of new compliance, risk management and audit workers, who have been employed in their thousands to help the banks and insurance companies comply with the new and onerous diktats from various regulatory bodies. They have introduced long-winded bureaucratic systems that have negated all the expensive technological productivity gains of recent years.

Many European banks have changed their CEOs and chairmen in an attempt to shake off the strangling grip of caution and risk-aversion, that had become the norm since the global financial crash in 2008. During the financial crisis, far too many of these financial institutions went for Chief Financial Officers (CFOs) as CEOs, as they feared that the more growth-oriented leadership might well be less controlling. They were so fixated on finding the Spike of 'control' that many of them overlooked the need for Spikes of leadership and inspiration in these turbulent times.

After far too long, these rather controlling types have been jettisoned for the sorely missed Spikes of inspirational leadership and growth.

The regulated industries of pharmaceuticals, telecoms, energy, utilities and financial services are all currently lacking in innovation and are desperately seeking growth. The answer always appears to be to sack the incumbent CEO, without thinking through what Spikes are actually necessary at the top of the business.

When the culture of an organization appears 'broken', it is important to look at the leadership of the organization, but not in isolation. Sometimes the issue or opportunity revolves around the top team and its ability to support, and importantly, challenge the CEO. Teams are at their very best when all the members have the opportunity to capitalize upon their personal Spikes. But these Spikes need to be chosen with the CEO's Spikes firmly in mind.

MATT BARRETT – SMOOTH AS SILK

I have had the privilege of working closely with both Matt Barrett and John Varley during the times that they led Barclays Bank, prior to the global financial crisis. They were both first class leaders. They could not have been more different, with completely different Spikes. Consequently, the leadership team that worked so well together under Matt's tenure had to change, when John took over from Matt.

Matt was affable and personable. He was charm personified and managed to turnaround the bank through the force of his personality, without ever having any major fireworks or serious clashes with his people or the board. He was no 'shrinking violet', and he was one hell of a smart and smooth operator.

Surprisingly, he never changed any of those he inherited on his top team.

His target was to move the culture from an inward-looking and rather risk-adverse banking giant, which had, perhaps, fallen away from any form of innovation and challenge. It was in danger of plodding very carefully towards irrelevance.

Matt mobilised his Spikes of charm and quiet, but forceful determination on his top team. He tolerated their personal rivalries, but fused this energy into a collective and shared ambition. His approach of believing in them and backing them openly and consistently elicited both loyalty and performance.

When the opportunity to communicate with his workforce presented itself, this mild-mannered leader would grow in stature and presence. He was a natural communicator, who used the most colloquial of language, and his Irish-Canadian roots brought the politest, most self-deprecating humour. He laughed at his and his team's expense, instantly making all of them so much more human and accessible.

He was a chain smoker of Dunhill cigarettes. He had the flat burgundy and gold packets stashed everywhere. Despite the recent ban on smoking in all Barclays buildings, he continued to puff away at all the executive committee (ExCo) meetings and in his office. Perhaps not the best role modeling, but interestingly, not challenged or stopped by anyone.

For my first meeting with Matt I had been briefed to take the elevator and that I would be greeted on arrival and taken to the CEO's office. As the lift door opened, to my pleasant surprise, there was Matt – not his assistant or PA. We shook hands warmly, and he was already cracking jokes at both of our expense. He was instantly warm and engaging. Matt was tall and handsome, and boy, did he know it!

He escorted me back into the lift as he suggested we have our chat over lunch. He headed straight to the canteen, which was now emptying out as it was nearly 2pm.

He joined a short queue and handed me a tray as we went around and selected from the delicious-looking and wide variety of dishes on offer. As we approached the checkout, he was locked in conversation with all the members of the smartly turned out catering team. They treated him as a colleague, and he treated them as if they were his peers.

He was clearly in his element. He strode up to a table that had three members of the catering team chatting and having their lunch. Matt asked if we could join them. They were warm and welcoming.

Matt was genuinely curious and interested in them. He gently enquired what they thought of the recently appointed CEO. They all replied that they hadn't met him and were never likely to. "We won't see him having lunch here in the canteen, will we?" They all chuckled together.

He nodded in agreement and started to talk to me about what he had in mind for the session I would be facilitating for him and his team.

In a moment I was 'on his bus'. With the simple gesture of deciding to have our meeting in the staff canteen (as it was called back then), he had enabled me to fully understand what he stood for and have a quick authentic glimpse at his Spikes.

For all his inherent charm and personable nature, I never really got to know him at all. He was such a presence when 'his' people were around. A real showman, but in actual fact, he was quite a private man.

He had many years of experience in the banking industry and no one could ever fool him or 'pull the wool over his eyes'. He always played down his knowledge and expertise, but listened carefully to everything, whilst seeming to be always lost, puffing away on his favourite Dunhill cigarettes.

When he did speak, it was always quite soft, with a friendly tone. Very rarely, he would grab the attention of the room and pause. Sometimes it would seem like everything stood still as he weighed up the room. It was his method of wresting back control from the room, or whoever was speaking.

His silver grey hair, slightly longer than the norm, was always immaculate, and he was always beautifully turned out. He cut a dashing figure, despite the slight whiff of tobacco that never left him.

He could use the most direct and straightforward language to get his point across, but never with any angst or threat. But everyone in his presence knew exactly who was in charge and when he was beyond compromise. I have never heard him raise his voice, but I have seen him less than pleased, and all around reacted positively and immediately.

His enormous Spikes were on constant display, but you had to look for them. They could appear innocuous, but they were what made him such a special and standout leader.

When Matt was appointed the CEO of Barclays Bank, he was not the first choice. The selected candidate, Michael O'Neill, would be the first non-British CEO of Barclays Bank. He was a smart and experienced American banker. He didn't last the week, resigning after one day on health grounds after starting as CEO. It shook the board of the bank. What had he seen? What had caused this sudden about-turn, after nearly six months of positive engagements and many meetings?

They were in danger of looking very stupid and careless indeed. They acted decisively and offered the job to Matt, who was at the time CEO of the Bank of Montreal.

The plan appeared to work beautifully, as Matt accepted the appointment instantly and graciously. It was October 1999.

IF AT FIRST YOU DON'T SUCCEED...

As the announcement was made and his start date agreed, there was a real level of excitement and intrigue across the banking industry. Everyone knew he was the second choice; it just never appeared to bother this hugely self-confident man.

Then suddenly, out of the blue, his luck changed. Canadian tabloids ran lurid front covers of the recently divorced Matt out carousing with a beautiful woman. They were merciless in their condemnation of this high-profile businessman and had hunted down his date and exposed that she was from a high-class escort agency.

There was a feeding frenzy from the paparazzi on both sides of the Atlantic. He kept his head down and never engaged with them at all. Barclays, the venerable and quintessentially British bank, struggled to know what to do. Eventually, it all blew over and they rightly had stuck by their second choice.

Matt joined and instantly started transforming the confidence and pace of the business.

Before long, he was to have his first ever 'town hall' with the top 200 or so leaders in the business at the head office in Lombard Street in the City of London.

The auditorium was packed with far many more than had been invited – all were desperate to catch a glimpse of and hear from this already legendary leader. They had no idea at all what to expect, but were still far from prepared for this very un-British approach to formal proceedings.

As the heavy, chocolate brown velvet curtains eventually drew open, there sat comfortably on a bar stool this calm and dashingly handsome, long legged and dapper man, puffing at a Dunhill cigarette. The image instantly drew loud and audible gasps from this hugely conformist and risk averse audience.

It was show time. For all leaders, every day is show time, but not many were so born to be on the stage, and even fewer could tell stories like Matt could.

As he put the cigarette out in the oversize ashtray, he had placed on a slim table next to him, he turned sideways and now fully faced the audience. He smiled warmly and sincerely, and welcomed them.

There were no notes and no barriers.

This opening drew even louder gasps than the shock of his daring to smoke in the building. He smiled that infectious smile – he knew how powerful he had just become through this unique first impression. He had their full and undivided attention, and they now knew they were in for the ride of a lifetime. This was going to be very different to anything they had dared to even imagine. The excitement was palpable and expectations were ratcheting upwards.

He spoke softly but with an understated strength of character: "Many of you will have read the unfortunate headlines about me in the Canadian and British press. I would just like to confirm… that it was all true."

The gasps were more like screams now. The auditorium was now buzzing like a TV studio with a well-known reality TV star revealing all on the stage.

He paused as the gasps turned to smiles and then to nervous laughter.

After a while he added: "We both had a great time." On came the smiles, relief and even applause.

That was it. Nobody remembers too much else he said that day, but they all felt that they had someone very different and very special in charge of them. Some of the longer-serving members were outraged and angry at his poor attitude and disgraceful behaviour.

For the huge majority, the reign of Matt Barrett was off to a fascinating and exciting start. Well over 100,000 employees were now only talking about one man and what that might mean for their part of the bank.

His time in charge was a unique mixture of huge change

within the business but lots of stability at the top of the business. Matt made an indelible mark, without it ever being about him.

It took under a year for Matt to make what would become his defining move.

His first year had experienced a number of 'bumps,' as he described them. From cash machine charges, branch closures and the potential size of his pay deal, the bank seemed unable to get anything right in the eyes of an expectant public.

He was to learn 'on the job' all about the ferocious and tenacious British media. He was always tanned and immaculately dressed. Matt's trademark good-natured banter was slightly tempered when discussing the critical faltering image Barclays had been accused of during his first 10 months in charge. The critics felt, he should probably have taken a much tougher stance with his direct reports far earlier than he did, to try to nip the succession of gaffes in the bud sooner.

Barclays had been run by its chairman, Sir Peter Middleton – who had appeared very comfortable adding the Chief Executive title to his role – for almost a year before Matt arrived. The City had been calling for action, as the bank appeared to be in danger of losing ground, at a time when NatWest, its closest rival on the high street, was being chased by two Scottish banks half its size. The outcome of the bloody battle propelled the Royal Bank of Scotland above Barclays in terms of its stock market size and left Barclays in real risk of being relegated to fourth place after HSBC, the Royal Bank and Lloyds TSB.

It was time for a very bold move. Barclays announced it had landed the acquisition of the Woolwich Building Society.

"Woolwich is head and shoulders above its peer group in the UK," Matt was quoted as saying. "One studied the competition. From our point of view, they were the number one. We felt great, we got together."

The Woolwich deal was the beginning of a new chapter for Barclays. The recent poor publicity, the insensitive branch closures and the cash machine charges were all consigned to the past. The Woolwich deal was about the future. There was a new injection of management 'folk' from the Woolwich, including John Stewart, its Chief Executive, who became Deputy Chief Executive of Barclays – and a new, more 'radical' strategy approved by the Barclays board.

In one deft move, Barclays had retained its importance and had reenergized itself.

BOB DIAMOND – UPSTAIRS AND DOWNSTAIRS

It was now 2004, and after five years, it was time for Matt to face a new challenge, but the bank was not ready for him to leave just yet. He was offered the role of Non-executive Chairman, despite this move flying in the face of all best practice and good governance.

As soon as it became known that Matt was considering moving 'upstairs', his previously collaborative team now began to flex their competitive muscles. Matt somehow had worked out that it needed a different set of Spikes to lead Barclays through its next stage of development. There was talent galore on the team. They all had very different Spikes, but the betting favourite and the perceived biggest 'hitter' was Bob Diamond.

Bob was by far the most enterprising and perhaps the most obvious leader. He had a near demagogue reputation with his investment bankers, and had worked extremely hard at securing that status.

It wasn't all plain sailing for him. He had been given the opportunity to resurrect BZW, Barclays fading merchant bank. He had it rebranded as Barclays' Capital. He blazed into Russia with huge expectations (and promises) on a tide of hope and goodwill – it would become his trademark buccaneering style.

Martin Taylor, the former Barclays CEO prior to Matt, had resigned after a blazing boardroom row over the future direction of the bank. He was later to reveal how Bob had offered to quit in 1998 after big trading losses in Russia and breaches of the rules that were not made public.

Taylor, who left in the wake of the Russian losses, admitted he regretted not accepting the resignation of Diamond, who was then the new boss of Barclays Capital (BarCap), the rebranded investment bank.

Writing in the *Financial Times*, Taylor said, "I suspect the subsequent history of the business would have been very different had I asked him to go. I deserve blame for being among the first to succumb to the myth of Diamond's indispensability, to which some in Barclays were still in thrall until he left."

He explained how Diamond had hired traders to bolster trading in Russian financial instruments, but that the country soon defaulted on rouble-denominated debt.

"We were clearly in for a serious loss," Taylor wrote. "BarCap turned out to have an exposure, significantly beyond the country limit that had been established. It had falsely marked some Russian banking counterparties as Swiss or American and had blasted through the ceiling. This breach was not made public, although the regulators were fully aware of it. We looked reckless, and our share price suffered serious damage. The traders were fired," explained Taylor.

"[Diamond] maintained that he had known nothing about what was going on. He felt terrible. He loved Barclays. He offered to go. I concluded that the embryonic business that BarCap then was, would fall apart without him, and that he should stay," Taylor continued.

After a protracted and overly long process to identify Matt's successor, the nearly unheard of John Varley, who was then the Group Chief Financial Officer (CFO) of Barclays, was appointed CEO. Matt had clearly not fallen for Bob's indispensability, and perhaps saw beyond his huge Spikes of bold leadership and entrepreneurial 'magic'.

JOHN VARLEY – AMBITION

So, what was it about John that the board had seen and had been so impressed with?

Nothing was ever leaked, and the board and the business gave John a warm but rather subdued welcome.

In a quiet moment, when out with Matt, he shared with me that the deciding factor in a very close run competition was John's scale of ambition for the bank, his selfless nature and the steely determination he would employ when he set about transforming the bank.

He was spot on: these were Spikes that I would be privileged to work closely with in the coming years.

By now, I was working closely with a CEO for the first time since leaving my last executive position at IPC Media. I had sorely missed the camaraderie and team spirit, especially when celebrating the success of months or years concentrated effort on a common goal. Nothing beats winning together.

It was decided that John and I would work together on a series of Leadership sessions called, 'Let's Talk Leadership'. The sessions would cater for a live audience of up to 200 people. It started off as the top 200 in the bank, but word got out at just how open and honest John was at these sessions. The clamour to open the sessions out to more people soon became overwhelming.

Soon, they became a monthly fixture and were run on a 'first come first served' basis. All the sessions were jam-packed and usually filled within an hour of the email announcement of the next session.

We became a tight and 'well-oiled' double act. We had the most complementary of Spikes. He would answer any and all questions directly and honestly. Many in the audience were taken aback by the straightforward nature of the questions and, even more so, by his candid responses. Consequently, the questions became ever more robust and challenging.

We sometimes would not meet between sessions. We would meet at the chosen venue, and his packed schedule meant that I would be there early, gauging the atmosphere and picking up the prevailing vibe. When John would eventually arrive – usually minutes before we were due to start – we would walk on to the stage together, as I quickly briefed him on the evening's focus, which I would have picked up from my conversations with the attendees.

My only question to him would be, "Is there anything you don't want me to ask you about this evening?" He would always smile and respond in his most dutifully polite manner: "Just ask anything you feel is appropriate".

We soon got to know each other very well indeed. The audience also got to know us quite well. Whenever I was in any Barclays building, I was often stopped and asked about what John was really like, and be challenged to ask him about anything and everything. In the main, people wanted to know whether Barclays would remain independent. As mentioned before, under Matt's time, there was still a lot of M&A activity, as consolidation and 'bulking up' was the fad in global banking.

John's simple, effective and consistent response to the question of 'independence' was that he wanted Barclays to be, "a Tier One bank," which meant being one of the top five banks in the world.

This was precisely the ambition and appetite that had got John the CEO's job, and he was fully focused and committed to making this happen.

HEALTHY TENSION

He ran his team and the business very differently to Matt. It felt a lot like the private equity model of running businesses. He would leave the CEO of each of the businesses completely empowered to run their units in the manner they chose, and he would manage them by their subsequent performance. He had been running the legal division prior to becoming CFO. He set stretch targets, fully empowered his direct reports and monitored them closely, mainly by their financial performance.

This was a totally acceptable and, in fact, quite an admired and effective leadership approach, given the transformation that the Bank so desperately required. By enabling his team to focus on delivering their results to the best of their ability, he could, on occasion, appear aloof and distant. To his leadership team, he was all over the financial performance of their business units.

Whilst enabling empowerment, this would inadvertently push the businesses deeper into their 'silos'. There was no sense of collaboration, and it was not even required or demanded.

It's really easy to look back now and feel just how foolhardy these approaches must have been, but they really did not seem so, given the context of the time.

John Varley was extremely mild-mannered and a complete and quintessentially British gentleman in everything he did. He always wore his distinguished, but rather old-fashioned hand-tailored suits, with his brightly coloured braces holding up his very high cut pants.

Even when off duty, he looked exactly the same, with his round spectacles giving him that slight air of an aloof academic. However, those who worked closely with him would recognize his endless energy when chasing targets and a strong determination to deliver, no matter what the odds. Sitting alongside this drive to achieve, was the most incredibly strong and authentic set of values that permeated through everything he touched, all that he did and all that he stood for.

John had this super sense of natural urgency. He was never rushed but always in a hurry.

Whilst being polite and genteel, he would be unforgiving of inappropriate behaviour. At one of our 'Let's Talk Leadership' sessions at the Globe Theatre on the bank of the River Thames,

I was waiting for him to arrive, standing by the stage in my normal business attire: dark suit and white shirt.

He should have arrived some 10 minutes before, but I had been informed that he had been delayed and he would arrive shortly and walk straight on to the stage with me to commence the evening's proceedings.

I had already been 'miked up' and the auditorium was very busy; there was a huge buzz of expectation. Whilst working out in my mind how we would best commence the evening's session, I was approached by one of the attendees, who shouted out that he needed another glass of white wine.

I was extremely surprised by his sheer cheek and total lack of awareness, but I stepped off the stage and walked with him to the refreshments tables, which were in the adjacent room. I politely asked the young man busily serving whether he would be kind enough to serve my colleague another glass of white wine.

The events team and those serving the drinks were a little taken aback but ensured he was served, and one of the events team came over and escorted him back to the auditorium.

I returned to the stage and continued to wait for John to arrive.

Some 10 minutes later, the same man returned and this time was complaining that there was no more chilled white wine.

I had just seen John approaching the entrance to The Globe and I gestured to one of the events team to come over and tend to my unreasonable friend. At this stage, he became quite irate and insisted that I personally found some chilled white wine for him and that I served him.

Still trying to be diplomatic, I shared with him that I was a little busy and it might be better if he was looked after by our friendly and smiling events team manager. He was not having any of it, and stepped up to me and started speaking loudly and directly in my face.

At this moment, I heard someone say, "Why don't I get you your chilled white wine?" We both looked behind me and there stood John Varley, Group Chief Executive, Barclays Bank.

My pushy friend just stood there, staring at John and staring back at me and said nothing. He eventually muttered, "I am sorry, that won't be necessary".

John and I then stepped on to the stage and commenced a fabulous and interactive evening. As luck would have it, our friend was sitting in the very front row and now, recognizing that I was the compere and host for the evening, he continued to squirm and seemed to shrink as the evening continued.

FEELING ABANDONED

On my way out of the Barclay's offices at Churchill Place in Canary Wharf late one evening, my mobile phone went off; it was the chairman's office. Matt wanted a private chat. That always meant 'now'.

I made my way back into the building and up to the 31st floor. Matt came out to meet me at the lift in his usual laid back style. He stood up and shook my hand warmly and we moved to the sofa and chairs in his smart and large office. Matt always appeared to have time on his side and at his behest. He was never hassled or anxious; it was all so calm.

I noticed that he seemed curiously nervous, but instantly fell into his charming and humorous banter. He teased me and joked about recent important events at the bank. He was brilliant at probing me for information whilst seemingly just 'shooting the breeze'. But something was definitely up with him.

I thought I knew him well enough by now to be a little forward. I asked him what was on his mind. He shot back with that smile of his: "I'm so pleased that you asked".

He leant back in his chair, and closing his eyes, started talking about the role of the chairman. He certainly liked it, but missed having a real 'executive' team to lead and interact with. He could do this 'non- executive' thing, but in actual fact, he was at his best and with all his Spikes firing when he was the Chief Executive. I certainly shared his view, but I was not at all prepared for my next mission.

Matt shared with me some of his growing vulnerability. He had done everything not to try and 'drive the car'. He had given John all the space and time to find his feet and make the show his own. Matt had been incredibly good at not 'marching all over John's parade'. He didn't want John wasting time second-guessing what his chairman would do, or worse still, what his chairman wanted doing.

Inadvertently, Matt had become isolated from his former team, and by not wanting to interfere in any way, he had become a near recluse on the 31st floor.

By now I had guessed my task. He wanted me to have a careful whisper with John, and try and fix his isolation, ensuring John did not misconstrue his motives.

"I'm sure John has told his team to leave me alone so that I can get to grips with my new responsibilities. I would do the same if I were in his shoes. But I miss the coaching element of working with the team. I can still offer advice and sound counsel. But no-one has been to see me or has even called me."

This titan of corporate leadership was hugely honest and so vulnerable. It was a huge responsibility (and honour) that he had entrusted me with this delicate task. It needed incisive action, but there was so much that could go awry here.

I left his office and went home to think about how to approach this.

The following afternoon, I was in John's office. Meeting with John rarely took long, but one always left absolutely clear on precisely what was agreed and when it would be delivered.

We sat down, with him behind his desk, and with me in front of it. We knew each other well enough that I didn't pull any punches. I told him exactly what had happened and nearly verbatim I repeated what Matt had shared with me.

John was very quiet and deep in thought. He smiled and said a little sheepishly: "I was so desperate for him never to feel that I couldn't cope, so I have soldiered through without ever seeking his view about anything to do with my job… I have also perhaps prevented the team from going to him with their problems and issues, as I've completely misunderstood and misread Matt's needs."

The following day, John went to see Matt. I received a call from Matt, and went up to see him. The swagger had returned and the smile was filling the room. He was now back with his Spikes to the fore.

They were such different leaders, but I thrived working with both of them: two really special and outstanding leaders.

PASSIONATE ABOUT PENSIONS

Whilst John was not necessarily a natural, 'people person', he had the trust and respect of all who worked at Barclays Bank.

When Barclays eventually decided to change the rules and provisions of its Pension Scheme, far later than most of its rivals, it went down very badly indeed. After the initial announcement, many of those who had worked loyally and professionally for the bank for many years felt betrayed and let down.

John decided that he would handle this tough situation personally. Many of his close advisors felt this was a poor idea, as some of the feedback had turned quite nasty and ugly.

John had decided that he would hold a 'live' session at Barclays HQ at Churchill Place in Canary Wharf; it would also be filmed and beamed out to all Barclays locations, where there would be the capability to address questions directly at him.

The atmosphere in the room was electric and many had turned up in order to hear directly from the CEO, but also to share their anger and frustration directly with the boss.

When John entered, it was to the most muted and barely

polite applause. With little small talk, he got straight down to business and explained in no-nonsense terms why Barclays Bank could no longer afford such generous pension provisions.

There were some gasps and some shifting of seats as he spoke so clearly and crisply. There was no sugar coating and he was dead honest, if a little earnest.

The first salvo of questions took no prisoners whatsoever. By now, John was standing and he addressed every question as forthrightly as it was delivered.

It soon became clear that whilst he stuck to the overall message, he clearly felt the passion and shared the pain of some of his hardest working and loyal employees.

At the end of what could have been a very rowdy and heated session (which had become quite emotional, but never got out of hand) he strayed off script and promised to personally review the scheme and personally come back to his colleagues.

A few weeks later, he announced some softening of the rules of the scheme and proved to all, that he had not only listened but had acted decisively. The scheme was still considerably less generous than the one it was replacing, but it was now, in the main, grudgingly accepted.

Whilst John changed nearly all his direct reports during his tenure, it is worth noting that those that left went on to become the Non-Executive Chairman of the Nationwide Building Society, Chief Executive of Northern Rock, Chief Executive of JP Morgan Cazenove and also one of those who stayed, Bob, went on to succeed him as CEO of Barclays Bank.

Good leaders create followers – great leaders create leaders.

SPIKE SPARKS

When people respect someone as a person, they tend to admire them. When they respect them as a friend, they tend to love them. When they respect them as a leader, they tend to follow them.

Self-belief and humility are the two outstanding traits of our great contemporary leaders.

Blame is still far too popular today. Blame never ever adds value. Look for solutions and build trust. It takes longer than blame, but leaves less damage.

Leadership means setting an example and becoming a role model. Become the leader you would love to follow – your people always follow your every move.

When we say leadership – we now must ALWAYS mean the leadership team, and the bigger the organization the more leaders it needs in the team to succeed.

ON THE SAME PAGE

In a Harvard Business Review article, Michael Watkins states, "Leaders in transition rely on the skills and strategies that worked for them in the past. That's a mistake. Executives in transition must gain a deep understanding of the situation at hand and adapt to that reality. Otherwise, to paraphrase Mark Twain, people with hammers will treat everything like a nail, even when the job at hand may be better accomplished with a drill or a saw."[24]

"True leadership lies in guiding others to success. In ensuring that everyone is performing at their best, doing the work they are pledged to do and doing it well." – Bill Owens

"Change doesn't really happen at a company; it happens with people, so in order to lead change, you have to know how to lead people," says Pamela Rucker, Chairwoman of the CIO Executive Council's Executive Women in IT.

To bring about a transformation within a company, Suren Dutia states, "Determine the strategy for the company and identify CEO candidates' experience executing a similar strategy. The right replacement CEO will complement the existing leadership team's skill sets and have experience in scaling and managing a company through the upcoming stages of growth."[25]

---

[24] Watkins, M. (2009) Picking the Right Transition Strategy. *Harvard Business Review*

[25] Dutia, S. (2016) How to Bring in a New CEO for Your Startup. *Harvard Business Review*

PART THREE

SPIKE FOR CHANGE

CHAPTER X
~~PANIC.~~
STAY COOL

When struggling with your lack of experience, find a mentor who has done everything you hope to do and more. Aim as high as you can. Who would you choose as the perfect mentor for yourself today?

Change scares a lot of people. Facing the unknown gets spooky. Even knowing what's coming can rattle your nerves. A sense of helplessness can hit if you get the idea that you have no control over your destiny. Sometimes these feelings get so intense they produce a culture of panic.

When fear leads to frenzy, the result is lousy judgment, poorly conceived plans, and too much wasted motion. Panic kills your concentration, causes you to jump to conclusions and leads to reckless behaviour – all this at the very time when the organization needs you to be at your best. Having differing Spikes within the team ensures that we don't all freak out at the same time.

When change shakes the organization, some know how to hold steady. A level-headed way of looking at the situation keeps them from going off half-cocked. Action is important, but acting impulsively will probably only make things worse.

Change should get your attention – it always gets theirs. In fact, they go all out looking for places that love change or have been forced to change. It gives them an emotional charge and they take it very seriously.

The secret is having those around whose Spikes are knowing how to strive and struggle without losing focus, and understanding how to be more intense, while still remaining in control.

These people use the energy that change generates to give the culture a greater sense of urgency. But they can stay focused. Rather than bouncing around like a pinball, haphazardly ricocheting from one worry to the next, they discover what counts the most. Then they stick with that.

For some of us, frantic activity creates stress, making people emotionally drained – and eventually burned out – without much of true importance being accomplished.

Success under these conditions comes from cool-headed thinking, clear focus and well-aimed action. Those whose Spikes enable them to thrive in these fluid and volatile conditions are all around us, but perhaps we've never discovered them, because we've never asked the question: "What are you great at?"

Enlist these individuals now, as they help create a culture that is steady under fire.

SOMETIMES I THINK THE WORLD HAS GONE COMPLETELY MAD. AND THEN I THINK, "AW, WHO CARES?"AND THEN I THINK, "HEY, WHAT'S FOR SUPPER?"

JACK HANDEY, "DEEP THOUGHTS" FROM SATURDAY NIGHT LIVE

DONALD – SOMEONE WHO BELIEVED IN ME

This particular board meeting was one of my toughest ever, and probably my most valuable. It was the first time I would be on the receiving end of a hugely personal assault by the Chief Executive, with my peers launching in as well; all onslaught stemmed from the fact that I had missed a deadline.

Was it an exaggerated reaction and deeply unfair? If only that were true – I had worked very hard to earn and deserve the unrelenting beating they had administered.

In retrospect, my behaviour had merited this treatment, but it was still shocking and painful. In a strange way, it was a pivotal moment for my future: hurtfully memorable and instructive. I was determined it was never going to happen again… And it never has.

In many respects, it was the necessary kick up the butt that was to change my life and career forever.

The PepsiCo culture was a tough and hard driving one. I was by now on the board of Pizza Hut UK. We were a quite unique gathering of executives at the time, with most from PepsiCo, a few from Whitbread and a couple of recent additions.

PepsiCo was extending two of its star fast-food restaurant brands rapidly across Europe, KFC and Pizza Hut, with stunning success. PepsiCo had designed and fuelled a culture that was constantly dissatisfied, no matter how successful it became – and it was undeniably very successful indeed. However, it never allowed itself to even taste satisfaction.

At its heart and core sat the iconic Pepsi Cola brand and business – the ultimate in challenger brands. The company had bounced back from bankruptcy twice in its long history, and had institutionalized the survivor's entrepreneurial zeal into its hard driving culture.

In order to accelerate the introduction of Pizza Hut into the UK, PepsiCo entered into a bold partnership with the quintessentially British company, Whitbread, the large, but rather benign traditional beer brewer and pub owner. Whitbread was just embarking on what would become a radical and successful transformation. Whitbread is nowadays unrecognizable from the rather sleepy, risk-averse and slow beer-centric business it was back then in the early 90s.

It is now a fast moving and hugely profitable brand-based business, with the likes of Costa Coffee and Premier Inn as part of its fast growing empire. This is a very different business and culture from the one that PepsiCo chose to partner with. Whitbread had a number of aged pubs and restaurants in prime high street locations, that were now looking tired and 'off the pace'. PepsiCo had a vibrant and young brand in Pizza Hut, which needed high street locations in a hurry.

On paper, this made perfect sense, but how would these very different cultures work together? The tenacious and highly enterprising PepsiCo culture simply overwhelmed the rather polite, homely and bureaucratic Whitbread approach. Make no mistake: this was a Pepsi fueled business.

Our board was made up of executives from both businesses, but it soon became a 'full on' PepsiCo culture and business – no matter what the 50/50 respective shareholding implied.

PepsiCo knew how to remain a consumer fixated challenger brand, and recruited brilliantly to keep this attitude energised and fully focused. They used a smart approach regarding both rewards and recognition, which kept their hungry and ambitious well-chosen talent 'fleet of foot' and fearless.

I had never been in a bonus-driven environment – this both thrilled and motivated me like nothing I had experienced before.

This felt like the meritocracy I had been searching for – the stretch targets were deeply embedded in my mind and I never lost sight of them for a moment. I built a team that was as hungry and fixated on tangible success as I was, but vitally, they could do the things that I was not so good at. It was the Spike philosophy, but without yet really understanding the true power of the method.

We were like a military unit that was constantly behind enemy lines. I kept the volume pumped up, and we were a tight-knit and interdependent group that took no prisoners. I had no time for cynics, and had built a 'band of believers' who shared a common purpose of a desperate need for recognition.

We felt like the 'A' team, and unbeknownst to us, acted as wantonly as the 'A' team. We had developed a swagger and a smugness from our continued success and myopic focus on delivery.

We never missed a bonus opportunity. We worked extremely hard and played even harder and louder. Hey, but we were the untouchables – or so we thought.

We felt invincible: we were a 'band of brothers', and it was certainly 'all for one and one for all', but whilst we were a team, we were also deeply elitist. Our success was precisely that: 'our' success. Our colleagues felt excluded and disconnected.

My colleagues on the board were waiting, quietly and patiently, for the first mishap. I was to gift them all they were waiting for, and more.

The CEO got us all together to share the exciting news that we had won the bidding for a very prominent site, slap bang in the centre of London's thrusting West End, in the prime entertainment location of Leicester Square. It was a huge site and would become the largest Pizza Hut restaurant in Europe.

This was a huge profile project, and because it came somewhat 'out of the blue', it was not in the very full and already very aggressive PepsiCo 'openings' plan.

The boss needed a volunteer to take this on – the trap had been laid, and I walked into it. I couldn't bear the silence as he asked who would take on overseeing and project managing the opening. I didn't notice the seasoned veterans in the room hanging back and saying little. I obviously knew just how tough an assignment this really was. I was under no illusions that it would be a huge stretch, as my team was already at its limits, but I just couldn't resist the potential kudos and the glory of delivering against the odds.

I played my role in this gathering Shakespearean tragedy to perfection. Larry, the CEO, wavered a little, and challenged me: we could really take this on as well? By now, I felt I could not back down.

He calmly challenged me again, repeating that "failure was not an option" – the eyes of PepsiCo were all on this "grandstand opening."

As I breathlessly shared my excitement with the team, they fed off my passion, confidence and exuberance. They would follow me into battle anywhere and at any time. We were off.

Part of the problem was that we lacked the necessary 'naysayer'. I'd removed the two I'd inherited in the team who were just too painstakingly risk-averse and cautious. They wanted to check and double check everything. I was after speed and a spirit of enterprise – as a result, we were all far too similar in our sense of urgency and action orientation.

We had 16 weeks before the grand opening event.

After six weeks, we were at least a week ahead of schedule. Things were getting fraught, and for the first time we were arguing with each other as the pace increased and the tension grew.

I kept pushing, harder and harder. We were working all hours and getting ratty and bad tempered with each other. The warning signs of stress were everywhere.

Paul, my second in command, was the super project manager, meticulous and thorough. He came to see me late one evening and shared that we were going way too fast, and that we were bound to fall over. I listened without hearing him. He was persistent and convincing, but I didn't (couldn't) hear him.

I gave him the perfunctory pep talk and ushered him out of the office and back to work.

Later I was returning to the office having visited the site in Leicester Square, and as I parked my car, Paul was coming out of the building.

I tried to avoid him, as I knew he would try to convince me to slow down. He confronted me and we had heated words, but no more so than before – we were still very close.

Paul started shaking. His voice was breaking and he had started to well up. I now stopped pushing and walked over to him and we sat down on a wall next to his car and had a far more reasonable conversation.

He left his very large mobile phone on the roof of his car, and we both calmed down: I realised that I had to listen to him properly and honestly.

We shook hands and agreed we would have a total review of

our progress and adopt a more risk-managed approach to the completion of the project. There were just far too many moving parts – and we were not experts in this field, despite having many of the normal implementation team on hand.

Eventually, we both stood and hugged each other, knowing common sense had prevailed.

Paul got in his car and drove off and I went inside to pause and reflect on his strong advice and caution.

Within ten minutes, Paul was back; his car screeched into the car park and he was screaming my name. I looked out of the window and rushed out to meet him. He looked terrible: his eyes were bulging and he was running around the car. I grabbed him and got him to just stop. He was by now hyper-ventilating – he'd left his mobile phone on the roof of the car and had driven off.

"I've lost the phone!" he cried out desperately. I tried to console him: "We can buy another". Back then, mobile phones were still relatively new, and were large, ugly and very expensive.

Paul was desolate and inconsolable. He soon burst into tears and knelt down, sobbing loudly. Within the hour, he was in an ambulance and I was by his side.

He never came back to work, and never spoke to me again. I tried calling, writing but to no avail. I'd become a part of his past that he just didn't want to associate himself with, or be reminded of anymore.

It hurt like hell. Many of life's most important and vital lessons are born out of pain.

I will never forget Paul's meltdown. How could I? It was my fault.

THERE IS NO 'SMALL CHANGE'

As if to really rub the salt in my wounds, the following day, I took an urgent phone call from the building site foreman at Leicester Square. All work had been shut down, as a swinging pickaxe had accidentally chopped through a couple of power cables.

In an instant, the mad dash was over. There was no way we would now deliver in time. This was the first time my team would have tasted failure, and it was to be as public as if the entire world had stopped to stare. There was a subsequent buzz around the offices, as it became clear that the so-called 'A' team had failed in the most transparent fashion possible.

We gathered in my office to think about Paul, and lick our wounds and salve our shattered egos. No one else seemed to care, but everyone seemed to notice.

For the first time since joining, I was not looking forward to the next board meeting.

I was right to have been apprehensive, as the gates of hell were laid open for me by my colleagues and Larry.

We shot through the agenda – the final item was an 'Update on Leicester Square'. Everyone in the business had known about the accident, but Larry wanted me to talk through my "abject failure to deliver."

My throat was instantly dry, and I broke out into a fit of involuntary coughing. My hands were sweating and my colleagues enjoyed every shattering moment of my discomfort.

There was no mercy on offer and I soon realised that I didn't deserve any.

It is true that everybody deserves feedback, but this was torture, and it would never be forgotten.

Their questions were unforgiving and brutal: "Why didn't you ask for any help?", "What made you think you could do this on your own?", "Anyone with an ounce of sense could see that it needed more resources and experience than you had at your disposal."

They were enjoying themselves far too much to relent, or even care about how I was feeling.

They were letting me know, in no uncertain terms, that this was how I usually behaved in the board meetings. It was humbling and hurtful.

Larry eventually hauled them off me. He could see that I was battered and had learned a lesson the toughest way possible. I would never ever forget this most valuable life message.

On leaving the meeting, we all knew the rules, and as we walked through the door we were 'together' as a team again, despite my heavy mauling by my board colleagues. They all knew that, once we were outside the boardroom we had to become a tight unit, bear no grudges and never mention it again. They never had to mention it again – it was scarred indelibly on my mind and I would wear that badge of shame for many years to come. But at that moment it felt like little or no consolation. I was in pieces; even worse, they had enjoyed it!

I was limping and hurting. There was a horrible burning feeling inside of me; my fingers were tingling and my ears were popping. My emotions were running out of control. "Everybody deserves feedback" kept ringing in my head, but I've yet to meet anyone who really appreciates it under the glare of their colleagues' anger and in the middle of a board meeting.

It felt like a management appraisal delivered by people who seemed rather too keen to administer some brutal and crushingly negative feedback. They seemed galvanized by the fact that, up until that point, I had been the master of the art of feedback, but had yet to be on the receiving end of a negative response.

A huge lesson in humility and hubris would linger way beyond the battering and bruising I received in that fateful board meeting.

It was with my heart still beating loudly that I rushed down to my office, avoiding eye contact and not speaking to anyone. Jill, my PA, could sense what had happened, and tried to comfort me. I just had to get out.

Stopping only to collect my sports bag and ignoring the elevator, I disappeared down the stairs at a gallop.

Across the road there was a leisure centre, which I found myself running towards at speed. I needed to get rid of the burning sensation and get out of these clothes that were making me feel claustrophobic. Before I knew it, I had changed and dived into the pool and was swimming furiously. No one could see me cry whilst I was swimming.

After a few lengths the heat started to dissipate, but the pace didn't. Sucking in huge gulps of air and pulling my battered body through the water, I suddenly collided head on with an elderly gentleman who was casually floating on his back.

He stood up and, rubbing his head, exclaimed, "You must work for Pepsi," and turned around angrily and walked straight out of the pool and into the changing rooms. Talk about being shocked out of my introspection! But I was intrigued, so I too headed for the changing rooms and couldn't help but ask him, "How did you know I work for Pepsi?"

"Easy," was his casual response. I insisted that he told me more. Incredulously, he responded that he would, but that I would need to send a car to pick him up at his house, take him to a restaurant of his choice AND pay the bill!

Then, and only then, would all be revealed. He left me staring at him in disbelief, at his sheer brazen impertinence. He continued dressing and, just as he was leaving, he wandered over to leave me his personal business card before going. I smiled at his 'front' and confidence, and his charm.

But he had already helped me.

I was no longer as angry with myself, and I had that feeling again, of being in the presence of someone really special. Little did I know just how special he was going to be for me.

The following day I found myself compulsively dialing his number, and thoroughly enjoying his conversation and somewhat involuntarily agreeing to send a car the following week and also to book his restaurant of choice, Le Gavroche.

Le Gavroche was the home of the world-renowned master chefs, the Roux Brothers, and was reassuringly expensive. I had never been to or even heard of Le Gavroche or anywhere near that plush or pricey. This was to be the first of many (costly) lunches I was to have the pleasure of experiencing with Donald.

The dining rooms of Marks and Spencer had taught me the basics of table etiquette, but I was a real amateur when it came to polite conversation, small talk and 'sign posting' particular messages en route.

Donald was a class apart. He made me feel so comfortable, whilst providing me with strong but captivating feedback – he made everything feel palatable and pleasant, no matter how wrong or gauche I was.

He was entertaining, hugely well informed and he somehow managed to get me speaking about myself and sharing things in a manner that I had never done before to anyone – even myself.

He showed me how to carry myself in such a splendid place (and many others like it), without ever allowing me to feel that I was a novice or didn't belong.

Many lessons were delivered, but none more powerful than 'showing as opposed to telling'. He spoke and behaved in a manner that enthralled me. Learning was great fun with Donald, and he could correct me just with the raise of an eyebrow or a short glance over his glasses.

It was really difficult to work out why he was so generous with his wisdom and time. He was brilliant at making me feel fabulous and hugely confident. My self-belief just soared, and my behaviour and aspirations moved onwards and upwards.

With Donald on my side, I somehow felt protected. Nobody could intimidate me anymore and I gradually lost my inferiority complex, which was a prerequisite for most of us from the disadvantaged landscape of Harlesden.

He somehow managed to keep me talking for what seemed like ages and he created a climate of comfort that made me reveal more and more and more. His taste in wine was impeccable, his knowledge of the menu was alarming, but none of this mattered when he managed to be both charming and so challenging without ever offending.

Eventually, my persistence paid off and he at last shared with me how he knew I worked for Pepsi: "All of you guys act as though you own the swimming pool."

FLYING COLOURS

As we left, it seemed natural and easy for me to agree a further date the following month. Over the next year or so, we toured the fine eateries of London, at my personal expense, but this was all a huge and necessary investment in myself. These lessons were never forgotten; they changed my vocabulary, developed my sensitivity and gave me a love for excellent Bordeaux. It was money seriously well spent.

I was to learn that he had served on the boards of some of the UK's top retailers in the 1960s and '70s. It appeared that there was nothing about business that he had not seen or experienced. That alone would have made it worthwhile meeting with Donald, but frankly that was just a fraction of what he had to offer.

The real benefit was something very different. Perhaps it was wisdom; it was certainly powerful and changed me forever. It's all very well having years of experience, but it's what you learn from it that matters. And he was better than any MBA course and certainly any corporate development programme I'd ever been sent on.

I'm not really sure how long we met for; there was nothing to count – this is the mark of a special relationship. Time just shot by in his company. This wasn't about hours, days or weeks or effort; it was about desire, memorable experiences and life changing feedback. Feedback, when delivered well can be wonderfully uplifting, especially when shortcomings are pointed out with positive language and potential solutions.

I could not wait for my lunches with Donald – they were always the highlight of my month.

One of the most magical things that Donald did for me was to call me one month telling me that I should expect a phone call the following day, and to take the offer seriously and respond positively. It was right out of the blue for me.

He said it was time. I hadn't a clue what he was talking about, but if there was anything that I felt that I had already learned, it's that I should be taking his insights very seriously.

At times like these when I had nerves or doubts, Donald would always say, "Don't worry René. You'll pass with flying colours, flying colours my friend."

This became our very personal mantra: "Flying colours, flying colours!" Flying colours is an old navy expression, meaning conspicuous success or triumph. Ships would raise their most colourful flags after victory in battle or a race into port.

With this saying, the worry and concern left me, and I had a huge injection of confidence: I felt a million dollars.

The following day a head-hunter called and mentioned IPC Magazines, who I had heard of, but knew very little about. He was confident that I had the right profile and, more importantly, was the right 'fit' for a media business, despite the fact that my background was nearly all retail and FMCG.

The head-hunter was right, and more importantly, Donald was right. This was an opportunity that would play to all my Spikes.

Despite seven interviews with various members of the Board at IPC Magazines, the effort did not put me off. It just felt right. The final meeting was with Mike, the Chief Executive. It was April 1995 and I was pleasantly surprised when I was greeted outside of Mike's office by his charming and professional PA. Loretta was ultra-professional and an ambassador and advocate for Mike and IPC Magazines. She was also black. In actual fact, we were both a little surprised at each other (being black) but perhaps too shy or embarrassed to mention the obvious.

Political correctness was alive and kicking.

After probing her for all the information I could get, I eventually broached the subject: were there any executives or directors of colour at IPC Magazines?

And she replied: "Not yet," with a professional twinkle in her eye.

Her closing comments were, "You and Mike will get along fine." What prophetic words!

He was just the sort of boss I was looking to work for; direct, straight-talking and demanding. He wanted to win and was looking for a team of like-minded individuals who could work together. He was focused upon diversity long before the word had become fashionable. There were three women on the board and now he was considering me!

This was 1995 – not so long ago – but the world was very different then.

Having now left PepsiCo, I started seeing less and less of Donald: a new phase of my career had started, and somehow (shamefully) I just got busy and I let our relationship disappear. I still deeply regret having done so, to this day.

He was both generous and harsh; he was supportive and deeply challenging, but he was always there, no matter how trivial or momentous my personal challenge was.

He taught me so much just by being himself. He behaved and spoke in a manner that I thought was the way one should behave and speak. Just by being with him, my behaviour changed. Little did I know that he was laying down the foundations and honing the Spikes that would guide my career and my life from this point onwards.

Many years later, a phone call from a newsagent I'd never met before shook my world. He was informing me that Donald had passed away, and that he had wanted me to know when that happened. The newsagent didn't stay long on the phone; my knees buckled. He spoke as though he knew me really well. Donald had spoken about me a lot to him.

I had no idea that Donald was a lonely man. Or that he had lived only with his mother until she passed away.

I couldn't breathe and just wandered around in a daze.

I attended the funeral service on a bright and sunny morning. There were not many of us there. It was now obvious just how different we were and just how generous and kind he had really been to me. He was Jewish. He was gay. But most of all, he was my mentor, friend and confidante. He was my rock.

All I could hear was Donald's voice, praising me and encouraging me: "Flying colours René, you'll pass with flying colours."

It hurt. I felt I had abandoned him, when he had always been there for me.

We were so different. We lived differently, loved differently, worshipped differently, but we were as close as two people could get.

Are these things important? Well, yes and no. No, they're not important, because there is nothing particularly unique about these aspects of his life. But they uncovered something far more revealing: Donald and I were in some ways nearly opposites – we were worlds apart. And yet, he proved to be the perfect mentor.

The very fact that I didn't know about these aspects of his life made for yet another uncomfortable truth; it showed that I hadn't asked HIM enough questions over the years and had failed to find out more about the real Donald. I had not taken the time to discover his Spikes.

Maybe he didn't want to reveal much about his life; maybe he just wanted to pass on his knowledge. But I should have found this out, instead of remaining ignorant about someone who knew so much about me.

The best listeners are the best communicators.

This was such a tough moment for me and he was again teaching me so much, in his gentle but unforgettable manner, which was a formidable Spike of his.

On leaving the service, I wondered, for the first time if this intelligent and influential man had found the relationship as important to him as it was to me? It was a relationship that had given me so much. How had he ever found the time to invest so much in me?

When looking for a mentor, don't always look for people who are exactly the same as you. Rather look for the person who is the very best, regardless of race, religion and outlook. And search for someone with different Spikes to you.

The more similar you are, the less space you are leaving for learning. We had completely different Spikes, yet he made all my Spikes Spikier.

Every time I find myself at a loss or in a tight corner I think of Donald and what he would say, and it all becomes so much clearer for me.

He always passed with flying colours.

SPIKE SPARKS

There was a time when you did not quite believe in yourself, when someone, somewhere took the time to believe in you. Who are you taking the time to believe in today?

True partnerships have trust, transparency and the willingness to share risks. True partnerships survive when they hit torrid times. How many 'true' partnerships do you honestly have? Now build the necessary ones with this in mind.

Make bold promises and deliver them.

The real leader is the one who will confront the fact that they have led the team in the wrong direction. Their honesty and humility in confronting their errors will be repaid by the team's increased loyalty.

Take full responsibility and ownership for the friends you keep – and those you decide to walk away from.

ON THE SAME PAGE

"Leaders don't create followers – they create more Leaders." – Tom Peters

It can take someone a substantial number of years to achieve the success they want; some may never even get that far. Though they can shorten the learning curve – even drastically curtail it – with the guidance of a Mentor.[26] With advice and support, one can realize one's Spikes, while avoiding the most common mistakes, as well as opening up new opportunities through personal contacts and foresight.

"A mentor empowers a person to see a possible future, and to believe it can be obtained."– Shawn Hitchcock

In a Case Study[27] published for Aviva, "One director realized she had focused on fixing what was 'wrong', resulting in her losing confidence, rather than playing to the strengths she had been hired for. She introduced the approach to her team, who found they could become more effective and motivated by reallocating staff to different tasks." The evaluation conducted by Graham Borley from the Talent Management Academy found that the Strengths-based coaching programme showed an ROI ratio of greater than 14:1.

"If your actions inspire others to dream more, learn more, do more and become more, you are a leader." – Chris Guillebeau.[28]

---

[26] Masterson, M. (2011) *The Pledge: Your Master Plan for an Abundant Life.* John Wiley & Sons

[27] MacIndoe, G. "Something inside, So Strong." [online] Available at: http://www.perfectmanage.eu/userfiles/2350/files/StrengthscoachingAviva.pdf [Accessed 02 Apr 2016]

[28] Guillebeau, C. (2010) "Get Excited and Change Things." (online) Available at: http://chrisguillebeau. com/get-excited-and-change-things/ [Accessed 03 Apr 2016]

CHAPTER XI
~~TRY HARDER.~~
TRY EASIER

There's just too much information, so you will need to clear some space. How many old and rather obsolescent routines can you stop today, that would simplify and streamline your life with little lost?

People commonly respond to the stress of change by putting out more effort. The greater the change (that is, the bigger the adjustment they need to make) the harder they try. But they stick with the same old habits. They bet the future on "more of the same." Their heart is in the right place, their intentions are good, but they fail to realize that many solutions of the past don't fit the problems of the future.

In fact, a lot of today's problems are actually caused by yesterday's solutions.

You can't handle change very well if you don't change – no matter how determined you are, and regardless of how hard you try. Really, how much faster or better can you do things, if you essentially keep doing them the same old way? Just how much more effort is it possible to give? Sooner or later, you reach your limit.

Trying harder, while using the same old tools, techniques and thinking patterns, creates a culture of desperation.

The secret is to simplify. Search for different solutions, easier ones. Look for shortcuts, ways to save time and money and effort without sacrificing high standards. Eliminate unnecessary steps. Ask, "Why are we doing that?" Get rid of things that get in the way.

Find a better approach. Innovate. Bust out of your old routines. Be willing to make a radical change. If the organization expects you to do more with less, do it better and quicker. Your only hope is to find an easier approach. Easier starts with difference, so be honest about your Spikes – they may not lend themselves to rapid and constant change. Now, start to embrace those with Spikes that simply feed off rapid change, or if you're the risk-embracing change agent, look for those who can help prevent an overindulgence of instability.

Try easier. Build a culture that believes in simplicity and difference. You no longer have to be good at everything – that's the team's job.

Your job is to positively embrace difference – it's the most powerful route to success.

"THE LESS EFFORT, THE FASTER AND MORE POWERFUL YOU WILL BE."

BRUCE LEE, EXPERT IN MARTIAL ARTS

GOING BACK TO MY ROOTS

It was going to be my first trip back to Gambia since arriving in the UK in the early 1960s. It was 1982 and Mum had been back in Gambia for well over a year now. She was only meant to go for four weeks. My parents had only been back to Gambia once in the mid-70s, and none of us had realized just how much Gambia meant to her. We had often heard Mum and Dad arguing loud and late into the night about the merits of returning to Gambia for good.

It frightened all of us. They would always end up both grudgingly agreeing, that, "for the children's sake," London was a better solution, but that we would all return to Gambia at some stage.

None of us agreed with them. London was our home, not Gambia.

Big changes were taking place in my life all at once; I was at university, my son was a year old, and now, out of the blue, my Mother had decided that she was going back to Gambia on holiday.

It was October 1981, and Mum came into my room to talk to me. She rarely ever did this; it was far more usual for her to scream my name from downstairs, and I would drop everything and go sprinting down. But this time, something was clearly up; her voice was uncommonly soft and solemn, and there was obviously something important playing on her mind.

She paused, which wasn't like her at all. She went on to ask me very quietly to look after my two younger brothers, whilst she took a well-needed break to Gambia for four weeks. I knew my Mum had not had a holiday or a break for years. "Of course!" I replied, without considering or realising what I was really signing up for!

In retrospect, I don't know how she continued for so long. There were no family holidays, and I can only ever remember her working. By this point, Mum was working as the head chef in a large industrial kitchen, serving hundreds of people every day in the west of London.

She had the huge Spike of being able to switch off her emotions, and just persevere through life, doing whatever was necessary, no matter how painful or demeaning.

By this time, I rarely heard her laugh, as my Father was no longer around. He had been the only one with the care and presence of mind to make her giggle, and sometimes she would laugh until tears rolled down her cheeks. She missed him badly, but would never admit it – she would not survive if she acknowledged this to herself, but I knew.

She could not afford to confess her obvious unhappiness, and the fact that she missed him severely. Her children needed her. They were all far too young to really understand what this brave woman was trying to achieve in a strange and unwelcoming land, which she did not want to be in.

Their very special partnership had come to a sad and untimely end, mainly due to the fact, that my father's very African 'manhood', had been undermined by his inability to provide a solid economic foundation for his wife and his five children. She had wanted to go back home to Gambia, but he could not face the shame of returning home 'empty handed'.

Mum had lost any outward sign of shame within a year of arriving in London, but inside, she was still a very proud African woman, and her home was calling for her ever louder.

If only we had been able to feel or understand what Mum was going through.

Mum became very hard and unforgiving, subject to huge mood swings. When she felt really low, we all suffered. Beatings increased in frequency and intensity. With each strike, resentment grew. Every thrashing would fuel the growing divide between all of us and our increasingly depressed Mother.

My sisters found it intolerable and, before long, they had both left home to live with their partners, who they would eventually marry. I too, became seriously frustrated with Mum: she would 'fly off the handle' at any moment. I was seriously tempted to leave, but I could never abandon Mum. But staying was not easy.

Mum said she would be back in four weeks, and she was entrusting me with running the house and ensuring my brothers were well fed and attended school every day.

So I found myself with my son, my two brothers and a house to run and the exciting world of university before me. It was really easy for me to understand that Mum needed a break. At first, I was really pleased with the confidence she had in me – that I could keep this ship afloat whilst the captain was away, for the very first time.

This was my first real insight into my love of responsibility – and being in charge. If only I had known this would become a rich and vital Spike for me in later life.

As the four weeks drew to a close, my phone calls with Mum were becoming very strained.

It was obvious to me that she had something to say, but wasn't saying it; at last, Mum shared with me that she was going to be away for another month. Too young to hold my emotions in, I was angry; I had no time to study… I found myself cooking every day and my brothers were a real handful. My son was a baby, and whilst he was beautiful and straightforward, he still took time and attention.

Eight weeks had now become three months, with no sign of Mum coming back. By now, I was missing an increasing number of lectures. I had been hauled in by my tutors, who agreed to give me the rest of the first year off, enabling me to start all over again after Mum had returned.

Mum never returned.

ON OUR OWN

I found myself with a ready-made family. My brothers were to live with me for some five years; life was never going to be easy, but none of us knew quite how tough it would become. I'd seen and felt the effects of poverty, and there was no way I was going to live in that world. But I could no longer afford to keep a large, four-bedroom home going, so we moved into a small, two-bedroom flat that I rented, with my brothers, sharing a cosy and very compact bedroom.

My father had moved to a miniscule room, in an even more decrepit part of Harlesden than the one we had first lived in. Without Mum's Spikes of budgeting and improvisation, he was lost. Most of all, he missed Mum and his children. His strong sense of African pride never enabled him to contemplate returning home with nothing.

I just could not understand this stubborn and self-defeating approach, especially as he was suffering badly. As far as I was concerned, pride was a very challenging Spike to have. At times it was his huge strength, but now it was serving to hurt him very badly indeed.

I had to go out and find work. My father had always wanted me to be an accountant (an idea which I had always quietly resisted).

Before long, I found myself in what was then called the 'Labour Exchange', the government's vehicle for finding work for the many unemployed across the nation. It was situated next to the grand, but ageing national football arena, Wembley Stadium.

It felt odd and demeaning. This was not what my parents had sacrificed so much for. All the untidy hand written cards clipped on to the bare walls, were for menial or factory work. Eventually, I found the only card that was for office work. There was a vacancy very close by for a trainee accountant.

The girl at the desk handling the selected cards was clearly bored and not enjoying having to reject most applicants, who were all trying to land the best paid job available.

It was my turn, and her expectations of everyone had become crushingly low. I was wearing a suit, which was somewhat the worse for wear, but with my shirt and tie, I looked terribly out of place, with nearly everyone else in casual clothes and trainers.

My throat was very dry, and my discomfort was obvious.

My friends from the tough local estate, where we grew up together had all left their respective schools as soon as they could. Many were unemployed. The UK was in the grip of an unrelenting recession, and the high unemployment rate (17.5%) would soon lay the ground for Margaret Thatcher's domination of the British political landscape.

This was a much harsher Britain for those who had come so optimistically from the colonies.

Those of my black friends who had found work rarely had the luxury of choice. Far too many of them worked in the tough and dirty conditions of the local 'glass' factories, down the road from the Labour Exchange.

The wages were far below what we would today describe as the 'minimum wage'. My friends would last just about a year, usually leaving because of the many cuts and lacerations to their fingers and hands. They usually couldn't play cricket with the rest of us during the summer months, due to their badly cut and painful fingers.

I could see no reason for wanting to join them, but they were much better off financially than I was, or so I thought back then.

At weekends they sported the latest and trendiest clothes. They could buy cigarettes and alcohol, when we all went to the jam-packed local youth and community centres.

They played loud reggae music for the young black kids in all the disadvantaged areas of London. For a few hours, together we were somebodies. We found an identity that bonded us.

TOUGH LOVE

Shared adversity can build trust very quickly.

What I had not quite fathomed or realised, was the misery and lack of recognition that most of my friends suffered from Monday morning, through to Friday afternoon.

No one ever appeared to be interested in them, let alone their Spikes. They were part of the UK workforce, but nobody seemed to care.

A few of my friends had managed to get apprenticeships, mainly through the 'careers offices' of their schools. They were paid even less than those working in the factories at the start of their working lives, but if they had the determination, there was a career to be had. Some of them are still with these employers to this day, some 35 years later.

The girl at the desk did all she could to convince me not to waste everybody's time, and just go for the factory work. She was inadvertently playing to one of my Spikes – I would never, ever give up. The more difficult and impossible the mission, the more motivated and fearless I became. I had locked my sights on the trainee accountant job and I was out to get it.

Just over an hour later, I sailed through the formality of the most cursory of interviews. I was now proudly working in an office in Wembley for the Road Transport Industry Training Board – a government quango – as a trainee accountant.

I was being paid the princely sum of £2,000 a year! This meant that I was earning far less than all of my friends who had left school early and who had no intention of going into further education – at this stage their logic was increasingly hard to fault. I could not even begin to think that this was an investment in my future – we lived from week to week. There were no grand plans or strategies – just survival.

Somehow the world did not appear fair. When it came to the weekends, they could afford to buy a round of drinks, they were dressed in the latest fashions and, most of all, they could buy decent football boots – and they bought new ones every season!

At about this time, the only role models for young black men in the inner city came from two distinct groups. First and definitely foremost, were the villains. They appeared to have the best of everything, but in actual fact, if we took the time to look a little closer, we found they had very little indeed.

Their lifestyles were attractively compelling to those who despaired over their current circumstances – and despair seemed a far more accessible emotion than hope, which demanded huge self-belief and drive.

Some of the villains would have smart cars; most would have sharp suits and even though this was long before 'bling', they would have all their jewellery on full display. They never worked, and never wanted to work, and were proud of it. And oh yes, most importantly: the girls loved them!

The second group, were working really hard and were made to feel ashamed by those who weren't working, who smeared them as 'sell outs'. We had not yet realized the multiplying and positive power of a supportive environment at 'home'. So these men were hardly seen: our vital role models were forced into hiding. They would get up early and return home late. They were made to appear as foolish 'slaves to the system'.

The local 'community' we grew up in was beginning to make having a job and hard work unfashionable and totally un-cool. Dangerous times indeed.

It didn't bother me that I was seen as totally unfashionable and un-cool. I needed to work. It was not even a debate in my mind. Without being consciously aware of it, I was driven by an overwhelming desire to make Dad proud. I wanted to right the painful and obvious wrong of him not having a chance to succeed, but instead, having to face abject failure every day, with no understanding of the real 'rules of engagement'. He believed that his beloved Britain would eventually give him the break for which he had worked so tirelessly and blindly.

This, of course, never came to pass.

I was determined this sort of ignominy would never happen to me. I needed to succeed, no matter what the cost. But locally, it was so easy and acceptable to become cynical, disenchanted and disenfranchised.

Now that my Mother was away, it was doubly important that I worked. It was becoming a hell of a challenge to try to convince my younger brothers that a job and hard work were definitely the way forward. They found it hard to believe that there was a direct link between academic qualifications and the quality of jobs that were open to them.

My youngest brother was 14 when Mum left and he definitely missed her. He became a little withdrawn and very moody; he blamed Mum for any of his underachievement and lack of drive. This was really unfortunate, but understandable at the time, and the attitude would stay with him for many years to come.

I disliked the mechanical nature of accountancy and the myopic planning and attention to detail it demanded, and although I was passing my accountancy exams, I desperately wanted to get back to university.

Eventually I couldn't hide the fact that I was completely and utterly disinterested in accountancy. The atmosphere in the office was one of quiet diligence, and sometimes I felt the urge to scream or shout – just to wake everybody up.

This was not playing to my Spikes at all.

TOUGH CALLS

Before long I found myself in my Manager's office, handing in my resignation, despite needing the money. I could feel myself vegetating and I was desperate to grow and learn.

He couldn't understand why I wanted to leave a job with relatively good future prospects, when unemployment was so high at the time. I could be very bold indeed, and sometimes a little reckless about the risks associated with any move.

He asked me what I really wanted to do. I then suddenly realized that I hadn't considered this at all. It was simply very clear to me that I didn't want to be there anymore. Thinking on my feet, and noticing the picture of a huge new computer on the wall behind him, I muttered, "Computing."

Computing was new and 'all the rage'. Computers were fresh, sexy and unknown. He instantly and helpfully told me that they were about to open up their own Data Processing department, and were looking for a trainee Computer Programmer.

Within three days, I was one of 10 internal candidates sitting an IQ test. The following morning, I was offered the job and commenced on a salary of £2,500 a year. This was still far less than all my colleagues who had left school early. But for the first time in my life I had some true recognition, and this really mattered to me.

This need for acknowledgement would never leave me.

Not for the last time in my life, there was no one to share my success with. Mum and Dad weren't around and my brothers were too young to understand, but I felt fantastic. I also learned that there was little point in sharing the news with my friends at the time, as it would just serve to alienate them from me that little bit more.

I kept my little success my big secret.

This was a feeling that I now wanted again and again. Mum's absence had certainly provided me with extra motivation and drive, but it seemed, at times, a negative fuel of anger and desperation. But an appointment to a new position, having passed the entrance test at work, was a new-found positive fuel. I just couldn't wait to re-fuel again. This was the true power of a meritocracy. I was someone.

At the start, I was a terrible programmer, but a very good learner. I exasperated the Chief Programmer, who was a brilliant coach. He would spend hours with me, trying to prevent me from simply doing the task, and to spend more time thinking through the elegance of the solution.

He convinced me I wasn't just writing computer programs, but we were actually changing the way the organization behaved forever. I had a purpose. Now, that excited me; I gave him, and the job, everything I had.

He had vitally given me 'someone to believe in' and 'something to belong to'.

Nobody at the office knew that I was dropping off my son on the way to the office, working the full day and sprinting back to pick him up on my way back home, prior to preparing dinner for my brothers.

To be honest, I wasn't aware this was unusual or exceptional: I just did it, because it needed to be done and, consequently, the next year flew by. I cut my teeth at work and struggled to 'play mum' to my brothers, and be both mum and dad to my son, whilst just about managing to pay all the bills.

By now both my sisters were married, and had their first children and they were experiencing challenges of their own.

Geoff, the Chief Programmer, and my first ever coach and mentor, had disappointingly decided to go back to his previous employer. It was the first time in my career that I realized just how important the relationship with your boss is in terms of affecting how you feel about the company at large.

Geoff was the best coach I have ever had. His huge Spikes were his patience and optimism, whilst teaching, with a sense of humour that made even the most major chastisement bearable. He was a perfectionist with pragmatic standards.

We got on famously, and I admired all he stood for. I willingly jumped at every task he set me, and felt awful when I let him down. Because of this passion and effort, he always persevered with me. He had seen a Spike.

I hadn't yet grasped just how valuable a complementary Spike could be in terms of enhancing and safeguarding my own Spikes.

A world without Geoff was not where I wanted to be, but I knew nothing about the outside world. I told him that I wanted to leave as well. Geoff advised me to get the Yellow Pages out and start making phone calls to all the companies within walking distance of our office. It sounded a little absurd, but I phoned all the local companies and asked if they needed a 'junior' programmer.

MAKING ENDS MEET

Looking back, it was amazing that anyone listened at all, as I continuously talked myself down: in good old British fashion I spent the first five minutes explaining all the things I could not do. I made a point of explaining how inexperienced I was, and that there was no way I could be left alone to do anything.

Not really the Spike approach at all!

After this marvelous piece of salesmanship, it was no surprise that after 25 phone calls, no-one was interested. My next call was to a building company, Kyle Stewart, directly opposite to where we worked and, to my shock, they wanted to see me immediately.

Geoff allowed me to dash across the road at lunchtime, and I breathlessly entered their offices. I had never seen a computer terminal before. We were still working on what was called 'punched cards' back then.

Rob, the Chief Programmer, showed me around for about 10 minutes. I asked many stupid questions, which beautifully showcased my lack of experience and lack of knowledge.

Just as he was showing me off the premises, he offered me the job. I couldn't believe it. When I asked him why (another piece of dynamic salesmanship), he said, "You're more enthusiastic than all of my people put together and you really want this job. I can train you to do the rest."

This is a a good approach: hire for attitude and train for skills.

A Spike he recognized in minutes would now last a lifetime.

Another big piece of learning for me was that, in the main, most of us spend our years at work with our 'heads down', never really understanding what our true market worth is or could be.

The only true way of finding out how much you are worth in the marketplace is to go on an external interview. Rob offered me £4,000 a year, to start more or less immediately.

This was an unbelievable sum of money.

By now I had met Yvonne. She had joined the Road Transport Industry Training Board, also as a trainee. We were instantly attracted to each other. We came from quite similar backgrounds and shared a similar determination to change our circumstances.

We had completely different Spikes.

Yvonne was patient, quiet and really careful. She was slow to open herself up to those she did not know. She was always humble and cared for everyone close to her.

Life was very tough indeed, but we were very happy together. She instantly fell in love with my son. For the first time in his life he had a 'mother'.

My new job had come at the near perfect time.

Our lives instantly changed. I was to spend ten months in a very male-dominated environment and, for the first time in my career, I was to experience 'overtime'. The construction industry had historically been forced by the trade unions to use additional overtime payments to incentivize and reward its employees for having to work very long hours.

The concept of overtime had started to disappear in many white-collar environments, as the more challenging economic outlook enabled many employers to move towards long hours becoming the norm.

Overtime, to me, was the manifestation of the direct relationship between hard work and reward, and would motivate me during these tough times.

It was a mid-sized building company that was desperately trying to compete in an aggressive marketplace, and, unlike most other UK based businesses, was converting from an IBM mainframe to an ICL mainframe. They were going from 'Big Blue', which was at the forefront of computing, to ICL, a relatively small, but confident UK computer company.

This was a huge 'conversion', as all the company's existing computer systems needed converting from the IBM format to the ICL format. They had loads of work and needed it completing urgently. So not only did I benefit from a relatively large increase in salary, but I could also work all night and all weekend, if I wanted to.

What a break, and what an opportunity!

For me and my family this changed the game. I discovered stamina and an appetite for work that was to hold me in good stead for many years to come. We had just got used to shopping in the cheapest places, buying the worst cuts of meat and making every penny count.

I volunteered to work most evenings and most weekends. For the first time since my Mum had left, we had some financial breathing space. This felt so good, that almost instantaneously, I knew I would never (voluntarily) allow myself to fall back to those most difficult and empty of times.

The methodology and working practices that Geoff had indoctrinated into me, were now beginning to make perfect sense. Because of these, I was now easily the best, and more importantly, the fastest programmer in the company.

With the modular approach that Geoff had beaten into me, I was by now hugely more accurate. I churned out programs far quicker than any of my peers. Everything seemed to be going well, but I didn't realise that perhaps the number of hours I was working – and consequently, the amount I was taking home – was starting to 'raise eyebrows' amongst some of my peers.

That might have been bearable to them, if I hadn't been quite so prolific with the programs I was producing. I never knew my colleagues well enough to share with them my situation at home, which might have helped explain my extra drive. It just did not seem appropriate to do so, in what was such a competitive male culture.

BEHIND EVERY CLOUD

After about 10 months, the business had been acquired and was being merged into the new parent company, and many duplicate roles within our side of the business were being cut or 'rationalised'.

We were still under enormous pressure to deliver, so we never thought there would be any redundancies in our department. But I was soon stunned to discover that the only two who were selected to go, were the Chief Programmer, Rob, and myself.

It was a huge shock to Rob, and a shock to me as well, but again, I learned a huge lesson.

Rob had spent a lot of time providing the team with management 'air cover', and he was relatively outspoken in defending us from some of the negative changes that were taking place in the company.

It seemed totally illogical and so unfair. Rob was philosophical and pragmatic, and left the same day as the announcement.

He advised me to 'get out, and quick'. I knew he was right, but I needed the money.

I was even further shocked to be asked to stay around to assist with the workload, and my colleagues were a little embarrassed that I was still turning up, and fully committed, working long evenings and all weekends.

I had financial responsibilities, and I had tasted unemployment – it didn't matter to me that they had rejected me and wanted me out. I had a purpose that was way beyond what they could affect.

From my own point of view, it took me some time to fully realise that I hadn't built rock solid relationships with my peers, and, more importantly, the management. I had naively thought that just doing a good job was more than enough.

This really hurt; I now had to face having no source of income, again. I was given a month's salary, and in those days there was absolutely no help offered by the company in finding another position.

In a matter of weeks, emotionally, I'd gone from being on top of the world to the darkest and deepest despair. At least I could still come into the office in the evenings and at weekends – I was quietly told to use the normal office hours to "look for a job"!

I was clearly needed but, hurtfully, not wanted.

It was time to find another job, despite feeling really low, and having had my confidence 'shot to pieces'. Again, I naively headed for what I knew: the Yellow Pages.

But things had changed hugely by now: computing was becoming more established and many companies were playing 'catch up'. There were certainly many, many jobs being advertised, but I was clueless as to where to look and how to capitalise upon my experience.

I didn't have any form of professional network and I hadn't cultivated an informal network that could have helped me identify any openings or career advice. I was dead keen to finish off my university degree, but that seemed a million miles away from where I now found myself.

I knew nothing of the many fast-growing recruitment firms who were specializing in identifying the talent necessary for the fledgling computer industry.

Not knowing where to look or whom to ask, and suffering from the embarrassment of being unemployed, I resolutely stuck to the Yellow Pages. My process was very simple: the job just had to be close by. Having my son around meant that I was unable to travel really far, and I needed to be at home to prepare the evening meals for him and my brothers.

With the building company being so close to home, I'd been able to dash home, prepare dinner, get him to bed, leave him in with my brothers, and then dash back to work.

This complex approach to finding the right job would make me empathetic towards working mothers forever, and perhaps helped me better understand why so many women were torn between their family and career.

The Yellow Pages led me to the high street retailer, Dixon's, whose head office was in Edgware, a 20-minute drive from where I lived (but at that stage I couldn't afford a car). It was by chance and real coincidence that I called just as they were placing adverts for programmers and analyst programmers.

Somehow, I managed to convince the friendly voice on the end of the telephone that I could go for an interview that very day.

Within the hour I was sitting in the reception at Dixon House, and two hours later they had offered me a job as an analyst programmer. They, like Rob and Geoff before them, had identified that, whilst I might not have had the right experience, my Spikes of enthusiasm and passion were huge and impressive positives.

The interview was with Terry, the head of Store Systems (whatever that was). He soon realised that I could code and was not afraid of hard work and long hours; in fact, I thrived in that environment. They were installing ICL systems and I had (limited) experience at these.

Terry took a calculated risk on my experience, but he just knew that I would learn quickly, due to my overwhelming need for recognition, and he also offered to support me through finishing the rest of my university degree course. I would now give everything and more.

The feeling of joy was incredible; I rushed out, caught the tube back home and found myself babbling incoherently to my younger brothers, who listened politely, but were far more interested in getting outside and playing football.

I soon realised that (yet again) I hadn't asked about the package, and frankly, didn't care. I just needed to be back in work and desperately needed the self-esteem that being in employment would afford me.

A letter confirming my employment arrived the following day, and I nearly lost my voice from running around the house cheering. They had offered me a starting salary of £8,500!

For the first time in my short career, I was now earning way more than all my friends, who had left school at the age of 16. I could afford a car and I could send my son to the expensive up-market nursery that had just opened around the corner from where we lived.

Especially given my very low expectations, life could not have been better.

My mother was still in Gambia and it had become clear to me that she wasn't coming back. Ever.

My anger had subsided, as I realized this was something that she had to do. Her twenty years in the UK had been an awful trial; she'd been homesick from the first day and had never really settled.

The breakdown of her marriage had left her desolate and empty, and as I was growing up very quickly – perhaps a little quicker than my brothers and sisters – she had grasped the opportunity to return home. She had sacrificed everything and more for us.

It was 1982 and I could now afford to go and visit my mum. Yvonne would look after my son, brothers and our home. She was irreplaceable and brilliant.

It seemed a journey into the unknown, as I had no real idea what Gambia entailed, or how it would look or feel to me. I just had this tremendous calling to see Mum and let her know that everything was fine, as I could sense that the guilt of absence was driving her mad.

GOING HOME – ALONE

I decided to just book my air tickets and go. I hadn't had any time off since she left and was really excited about seeing her again.

Gambia had just experienced an attempted coup d'état, whilst the President was out of the country. The airport was closed, and a curfew had been imposed. The British Foreign Office had recommended that it was unsafe for tourists to travel to Gambia. But the Foreign Office had no idea or understanding of just how much I needed to see my mum.

The internet was not yet in existence, and I was spending every spare moment in the office trying to find a route to Gambia. Eventually, I planned to fly to Paris and then from Paris to Dakar, the capital of Senegal, and then somehow make my way to Gambia.

My school geography had taught me absolutely nothing about Africa whatsoever. I shamefully knew nothing of Senegal and Gambia's shared heritage, culture and language.

Mum said that Dakar was about 120 miles from Banjul, and I stupidly assumed (as that was roughly the distance from London to Birmingham) I could probably hire a car or get a train. With my London mindset, I was sure it wouldn't be difficult.

My mother's younger sister lived in Dakar. I had never met her, but Mum gave me her details and I excitedly contacted her. She arranged for my cousins to pick me up from the airport.

This was a big adventure for me, but my overriding desire

was just to see my mum again.

My flight from Paris was delayed for hours by a huge snowstorm. By the time I arrived at Yoff airport, it was very late at night and I couldn't find my cousins anywhere. I now felt very out of place. Everyone spoke French. My inadequate schoolboy French was just about holding up, as I desperately tried to find a public telephone.

Miraculously, I heard someone shouting in Wolof. I assumed they must be Gambian, and headed straight for this very busy but friendly man. As I started speaking a very Gambian version of Wolof, with an unmistakable English accent, he laughed out loud and then broke into fluent English.

His name was Bassirou, and his father was one of the wealthiest men in Senegal. Miraculously, he knew my aunt and uncle very well indeed.

As we drove to their home together in his car, he gave me a whistle stop history of Gambia and Senegal. We would become very good friends over the years to come.

My aunt was relieved to see me, as she had no way of knowing what had happened to me and didn't know if the flight had left Paris at all. My mum had been on the phone constantly. When I eventually spoke with her, she just could not stop crying. She sounded really close on the crackly telephone line.

Dakar was incredible. It was very French, with some stunning historical buildings and a fast-growing middle class elite, that I was instantly rubbing shoulders with because of Bassirou.

I was now perhaps beginning to understand why Mum so wanted to return, and why my Father couldn't go back empty handed.

I was soon to learn that I was actually moving in very privileged circles and most of Dakar was nothing like this at all.

I started venturing out on my own and made a few local friends of my own age. They lived not far away from the pleasant residential district where my aunt lived. But it might as well have been a different universe. I soon realised just how fortunate our 'hard' life in London really was.

They had to hustle every day to make ends meet. They were all streetwise and fearless. They constantly exposed and capitalised upon their differing Spikes, all the time. They were always on the look-out for opportunities to earn small amounts of money for doing all kinds of tasks or errands.

They had become a loose federation of hustlers, who worked as a team and shared their earnings. Some headed each day to the thriving port of Dakar and helped the many fishermen to bring in their daily haul of fish. Others headed to the tourist hotels, to act as guides to the well-heeled travellers.

The tour guides were amazing linguists, without much – if any – formal education. I heard them speak many European languages. They knew that the ability to communicate with strangers in their own language soon established a level of trust, which they could quickly turn into fee earning opportunities. I watched and learned.

I spent a couple of weeks at my aunt's place hoping that things would stabilize in Gambia. It soon became really clear that travelling to Gambia at this time was going to be risky.

There were no further flights from Dakar to Banjul airport, as the airport was now officially closed, as were all border-crossing points. My aunt insisted I stay in Dakar until all had settled down, but I didn't have enough time off work for that level of patience. I could not come all this way, only to return home without seeing my mother.

I was going to see Mum, no matter what.

Eventually, I convinced my aunt and uncle to let me take a taxi from Dakar to Banjul. Not many of the taxi drivers were prepared to take the risk of trying to enter Gambia whilst it was under a strict nighttime curfew, especially with many reports of fighting in the streets of the capital being broadcast on the radio.

There were strong rumours that the beleaguered President Jawara of Gambia, had asked his friendly (and much larger and more powerful) neighbour, Senegal, for help in quelling the rebellion. The Senegalese had, for many years, had the most impressive and active militia in the region. The French armed forces were present all around Dakar, and they were investing hugely in training and developing the Senegalese forces.

This was starting to become even more tense and scary.

DOES ANYONE KNOW MY MUM?

There is always someone around with that risk-embracing Spike when you need it. This particular taxi driver was Gambian and confident that he could get through to Banjul, having only returned from there that very morning. He played the lack of readily available transport to his huge advantage. My cousins were busy trying to negotiate his 'outrageous' price down.

I just wanted to see my mum.

It took six long and dusty hours to get to the Gambian border in the back of an old Peugeot taxi, which seated eight passengers a little too snugly. I was crushed between two large Senegalese women, who talked continuously in Wolof.

Something amazing began to happen. When Dad had been at home, Mum insisted on speaking Wolof to all of us, even though we answered in English. I hadn't heard Wolof being spoken for many years before coming out to Senegal, but now, all of a sudden, it all came flooding back.

Despite not being able to speak fluently, I understood everything, and it gave me a strange bond with these Senegalese women, who responded so positively when I took a gamble with a bit of Wolof in my strong English accent. I was learning from my hustler friends.

We got to the border at 10pm and it was very dark and foreboding. The ancient ferry that had been criss-crossing the

River Gambia non-stop for the previous 30 years, had been moored up for the first time ever because of the attempted coup and the curfew.

Most of my fellow passengers trudged wearily into the unwelcoming police station, which had no doors or glass in the windows. It was unbelievably hot and sticky, with only hard stone benches, but they made themselves as comfortable as they could and resigned themselves to sleep until morning.

This was totally unacceptable for me, as I was on a mission and had to get to my mum's, that night! I found myself walking up and down the jetty with my suitcases, speaking to the fishermen who had their wooden boats moored up for the night.

I somewhat comically, but earnestly, asked the fishermen if they knew my mum, and unsurprisingly, none of them did. I started trying to negotiate with them to take me across water, which was now dark. They all declined and tried to convince me to wait until the morning.

Maybe I should have listened to the pragmatic common sense, but I was not in the least bit afraid or concerned about any danger – I just needed to see my mum.

Eventually, one of the much older fishermen approached me whilst I was sitting on my suitcase with my head in my hands. He spoke softly and quietly in English. He didn't want anyone to hear what he had to say. He knew a hidden mooring point where we could safely dock on the other side of the river, and he could then get me to safety. As I started to gather my belongings, he said I would have to pay a ridiculously expensive fee, in advance.

He quietly lifted both my heavy suitcases and walked back along the jetty to his boat.

I was well past caring about safety by now. It was pitch black as he threw my suitcases onto the floor of the boat. It seemed to take a long time for them to hit the bottom of the boat. Before I could dither about preparing to jump, he just pushed me into the boat; I seemed to fall for quite some time before hitting one of the suitcases. He leapt like a cat from the shore, bouncing past me and before I knew it, he'd started up the small outboard motor and we were on our way.

I could see nothing at all around me, apart from the distant lights of the small city of Banjul in the distance. I was getting soaked with the spray from the water and the boat stank of fish. The once-friendly fisherman now, strangely, spoke no more English.

When we eventually got to the other side, he threw my suitcases onto the pier and then pushed me out after them, and, in a flash, he was gone. He had disappeared back into the darkness, and was well on his way back to the safety of the other side of the river.

I was soaked, it was dark, and I had two huge suitcases and didn't have a clue where I was or where I was going.

It now began to dawn on me just how foolhardy I had been. There was no one on the deserted streets; for the first time it felt unsafe and I was a little scared and smelt of fish.

I wandered away from the port, slowly and cautiously, and made my way up one of the main streets. Many stray dogs kept me alert, growling menacingly as I approached.

A police car came tearing down the road with bright search lights beaming around the quiet houses and parked cars. I hid in a shop doorway as the lights lit up the suitcase I had dropped and left behind in the street.

The police stopped and shouted out: "Is anyone there with that suitcase?" I held my breath and sweated in the hot and humid night. When I dared to look, there were rifles being pointed from the back windows of the police car.

I now felt very alone and isolated, but my overriding fear was that I would not see my mum. I just kept reminding myself of the purpose of the trip – this made me feel brave and emboldened. After what seemed an eternity, the police car drove off very slowly.

For some reason I didn't – or maybe couldn't – move. The police car soon returned and stopped by the suitcase again. I couldn't look. They now pulled off for good.

After an hour or so, a car driving slowly with no lights on pulled up, seeing me fed up and sitting on my suitcase at the side of the road. The driver asked me if I was mad. He said there was a curfew in place and the police were arresting anyone who was on the streets after midnight.

He jumped out of the car, threw my suitcases in the back, hurled me inside and we continued to drive with no lights. Every now and again he would pull up the car, and switch off the engine and we would both lie flat, as police and army vehicles went by.

I knew my mum lived in Serrekunda, but there were no postal addresses, and street numbers were not yet fashionable. It was a five-mile drive and we needed to get out of the city and take the main highway up the Atlantic coast.

He looked me up and down, and asked, when was the last time I had seen my mother? That did it. I was babbling and blubbing at the same time. The tears just would not stop.

He never said a word, but just carefully and quietly started up the car and turned it around and we were off. Where we were going, I had no idea.

We drove very slowly in the pitch black. We stopped at a bar; there were lots of people inside, and none were going to leave until 6am in the morning when the curfew was over.

The driver parked silently in an adjacent street and took me inside. I again asked if anyone knew my mum; I was getting used to this now, nobody did. He took me outside, and we began driving with no lights again, stopping and starting as any vehicle approached.

After another few miles he stopped on the corner of a street, where a man was desperately trying to get his dog back into the house before the police came by. I stepped out carefully, and asked him whether he knew my mum. Unbelievably, he said: "Yes." She was living next door.

I thrust a large bunch of notes into the hand of my more-than-generous driver and hugged him hard.

I ran up the stairs with my suitcases and hammered on the door. When Mum opened the door we both just hugged each other tight and burst into tears of complete joy.

Within minutes we were inside, and the wonderful aroma of Mum's magnificent cooking meant that I suddenly remembered just how hungry I was.

As we ate together, she wanted to know every single detail about my brothers and sisters.

It was the first time I'd heard her laugh out loud in years.

My Mum, Yvonne, Geoff and Rob were all completely different to me, and they were equally different from each other. Yet their Spikes complemented mine in their own ways brilliantly.

Hmmm … I was learning the hard way about Spikes and that having different Spikes around me always brought out the best in me.

"NOW THIS IS NOT THE END.
IT IS NOT EVEN THE BEGINNING OF THE END.
BUT IT IS, THE END OF THE BEGINNING."

SIR WINSTON CHURCHILL

SPIKE SPARKS

Do everything you can to better understand and then break down those 'soft' barriers that disadvantage women in our families and relationships. Value their difference, because they are worth it!

Take risks with young talent and promote early.

There is nothing like the feeling of success to fuel further success.

Everyone deserves help at some point.

Build straightforward meritocracies – no matter what the apparent downsides might seem to be.

ON THE SAME PAGE

Leaders lead, inspire and motivate people. Managers plan, organize and manage tasks. The main difference is that leaders have people who follow them while managers have people who work for them. A successful business owner needs to be both a strong leader and a good manager to get their team on board to follow them towards their vision of success.[29]

"Building an exceptional team or institution starts with a founder. But being a founder doesn't mean starting a new company. It is within anyone's grasp to be the founder and culture-creator of their own team, whether you are the first employee, or joining a company that has existed for decades."[30]

"Bad managers play checkers. Good managers play chess. The good manager knows that not all employees work the same way. They know if they are to achieve success, they must put their employees in a position where they will be able to use their strengths." – Marcus Buckingham.

"Truly effective managers are able to recognize the unique strengths of each team member and optimize all those natural gifts. If you're in a leadership position, it might sound like a daunting task, but it's not. The first step is paying attention, identifying each person's strength and then managing around those essential skills. The results include increased productivity, improved performance and higher employee engagement and retention."[31]

---

29 "Understanding the differences: Leadership vs. Management" (online) *go2HR*. Available at: https://www.go2hr.ca/articles/understanding-differences-leadership-vs-management [Accessed 21 Apr 2016]

30 Bock, L. (2015) *Work Rules! Insights From Inside Google That Will Transform How You Live and Lead.* 1st ed, London: John Murray.

31 Clark, T. (2014) "11 Ways to Build the Strengths of Your Team Members" (online) Available at: https://www.liquidplanner.com/blog/11-ways-build-strengths-team-members [Accessed 21 Apr 2016]

CHAPTER XII
~~PLAY IT SAFE.~~
TAKE MORE RISKS

Learn to escape the pull of the past. Try changing environments to where most are not as fortunate as you are. This will encourage you to take more risks, as those with so much less are so much more risk-embracing. When was the last time you were surrounded by people much less well off than you are? It's a necessary and constant learning curve – stay in touch.

Change redefines where the biggest gambles lie. No longer is there safety in the status quo, in trying to conduct business as usual, or in sticking with what brought success in the past.

The so-called conservative approach has become the biggest crapshoot of all.

The surest security in today's world comes from a willingness to take risks. You need nerve, and if it's not your strongest suit, then start looking for those with Spikes that lend themselves to taking calculated risks, no matter how much they may not be your natural 'cup of tea'.

Guts give the best odds for success because the organization's future depends on its ability to find better ways to do business. A culture unwilling to experiment has little chance to innovate. It gets stuck in its own history. Without the courage to risk, it can't expect to crack the code for breakthroughs. It has to learn to embrace difference.

Unless employees give themselves permission to be pioneers – to explore, to go forward without guarantees, to move toward the future without road maps, the organization will always trail behind the competition. In this fiercely competitive world of ours, that's not playing safe – that's taking reckless chances, which threaten the organization's very survival.

You need to use your imagination, and better still, the imaginations of those who think and see the world differently to you. Try out some of their seemingly wild ideas. Break out of these old routines and dare to do something different. Extend yourself and each other – see how far you can reach. Put some adventure into your approach, instead of handling work in the common, conventional manner.

Doing things the same old way may seem a lot safer, but it actually hurts the organization's chances for success. A culture where people won't stick their necks out won't find it easy to win, but a culture that thrives on the Spikes of its diverse workforce might well achieve what was once thought impossible with the linear and cautious thinking of yesterday.

"MAKE A BET EVERY DAY, OTHERWISE YOU MIGHT WALK AROUND LUCKY AND NEVER KNOW IT."

JIMMY JONES

ERNEST – THE CITY OF HOPE

Ernest had been allocated to be my driver (and would soon become my confidante) for my very first week ever in Johannesburg, South Africa. He was careful, cautious and extremely helpful throughout my stay. He played his cards very close to his chest. It was instantly obvious that we were very different. But what was his Spike?

In a very short space of time we had managed to build a level of trust, friendship and mutual respect, despite Ernest being ultra-careful about how he engaged with me in the early days. Simply by spending so much time together we came to know each other quite well. I had soon come to realise that he possessed an openness and friendliness, which made him very special, as this is, unfortunately, not the usual South African way. Recent history has made them far too wary of strangers.

This tension with anyone different, especially with their brothers and sisters from their neighbouring states, would eventually explode into full-blown xenophobia, with tragic results.

After we met for the first time at the Arrivals Hall at Johannesburg airport, we talked as we walked over to his car. He opened the back door for me, which I then closed and said I wanted to sit in the front next to him. He was a little taken aback. He insisted that it would be much nicer for me to sit in the back, but I wasn't having it. I settled in the front seat next to Ernest as we proceeded out of the airport.

We were stopped by two security guards at the exit of the car park. One was pointing a shotgun right at us, whilst his colleague demanded that we stop the car and take the key out of the ignition. He was shouting at the top of his voice. Ernest was calmness personified. Totally unruffled, he removed the key, waved it in the air and then restarted the engine. Both of the guards' demeanour instantly changed, and they now talked and engaged warmly with Ernest. He spoke many different languages and was charming and soft with both of them.

This was a telling insight into what made Ernest tick. He was an extraordinary diplomat. He spoke seven languages or dialects. He could navigate just about any situation with his calm and understated personality. This was an excellent Spike to have, given his work meant engaging with just about anyone and everyone.

As we drove out of the car park, he noticed that I had been startled by having a shotgun locked, loaded and pointed directly at me. He said in his soft tone, "They knew you were not a 'car-jacker'. But we have had a large spate of robberies and car-jackings in and around the airport. The authorities want to be seen to be confronting these robbers, especially in the high-profile surroundings of the international airport."

He continued: "But they do not yet realise that the armed guards, with guns at the ready, create just as much anxiety as the robbers do."

He was by now a little less anxious and tentative with me. He was obviously not used to having in-depth conversations with his passengers. But I wanted to know everything about his country and him, and more.

Ernest was born in Soweto, and coincidentally, on exactly the same day in the same year, as I was born in Banjul, Gambia some 4000 miles north. This gave us an instant and authentic bond, and he appeared to relax a little and start to open up.

He repeated, his voice ringing with pride: "I was born in Soweto and I will die in Soweto." He said this while putting his right hand over his heart. He was obviously hugely proud to be from Soweto and had trusted me with that knowledge.

For the short time that I spent in Johannesburg on this trip, Ernest had already become far more than a driver; he had become a friend and a 'brother'.

After a couple of days of taking me from meeting to meeting, and only speaking in a very quiet and deferential voice, he eventually and carefully chose his moment to ask something of me. He asked me whether I would pay him the honour of visiting him and his family in Soweto.

Honour for him? This was an unbelievable honour for me.

When I turned up at his small, but very tidy house in Soweto, there were well over 100 people standing outside, waiting to greet me. I could not work this out at all. I thought there must be an event that Ernest wanted me to attend with him. I soon realised that I was, in actual fact, the 'event'.

They were welcoming and authentic. They were thirsty for knowledge. Ernest had shared my story with them all. We had loads in common, with some telling differences.

I could see the questions in their eyes: who was this man, who was allegedly born in Africa, but spoke and behaved so differently to anyone they had ever met before?

Ernest introduced me, and the way he did soon led me to understand why they were so keen to meet me. They had only recently been given the ability to travel, but not many yet had the means to do so. They were beginning to have real access to the world outside of Soweto. They were gulping in the oxygen of freedom and liberation and were hungry to learn and mix with this exciting and completely new world. I soon realised that I was a real, living and accessible symbol of this this new world.

Ernest shared with me excitedly that two Nobel Peace Prize winners lived on the road next to his. At one end, was the house of the Arch-bishop Desmond Tutu and at the other end, the house of their former President, Nelson Mandela.

I was as impressed and as proud as he clearly was, and wanted me to be.

Whilst joining in the loud and friendly conversation with his friends and relatives, I was asked by a couple of the braver ones: “Where is Gambia? Which part of the Caribbean is it in?” This innocent question said everything about the necessary development of the people of Soweto that lay in front of them. Apartheid had robbed them of much more than their freedom.

The emancipation of all of South Africa’s people would, unfortunately, take more than a generation, but they would remain understandably impatient for the huge and seismic changes their ‘young’ nation required.

I didn’t look or feel very African to them. Throughout the apartheid years, they had all been starved of information, especially about themselves and their heritage. There was next to no access to the outside world, and they obviously (just like me) had never been taught the history of Africa.

I invited Ernest to have dinner with me on my last evening before returning to London, not realising just how groundbreaking an offer this would be for him.

I planned for us to go to one of the modern eateries in Melrose Arch, one of the trendiest and most upmarket parts of Johannesburg.

Ernest was very smartly turned out. Having parked the car,

Ernest and I found ourselves walking side by side, lost in deep conversation on a warm and balmy Friday night. Laughing together and totally immersed in our conversation, we never noticed that three young white South African men were heading towards us, occupying the entire sidewalk. They were also lost in deep conversation and laughter.

As we drew quite close to them, Ernest and I were so busy talking, that I never noticed him instantly step into the road, to allow them to pass. His Spike of diplomacy sat next to his hard-learned deferential behaviour. I continued walking and came face to face with them, still speaking to Ernest, who by now was some five metres behind me – and standing in the road.

I suddenly looked up and I was in touching distance of the three guys, and politely said, "Excuse me," just as I would have done in a street in London. They looked very surprised, but smiled and immediately moved to one side.

It now dawned on me that Ernest was no longer next to me. I turned around and saw that he was a good few metres behind and still standing in the road, off the pavement. He just stood there with his jaw on the ground, wondering how I had kept on walking, and even more stunned that they had let me pass.

In turn I stood, with my jaw on the ground, not able to believe that he had felt compelled to step off the sidewalk and stand in the road.

This taught me a massive lesson. South Africa is definitely changing for the better, but some of the cultural shifts necessary are probably going to take more than a generation to become institutionalized.

MARCELLUS – THE CITY OF DREAMS

On a subsequent trip to Johannesburg, Ernest had picked us up at the hotel as I had planned to spend Saturday morning taking my son, on his first visit, to see the many special sights of this great city.

The car drew up to the contemporary architectural masterpiece that is the Apartheid Museum, on the outskirts of Johannesburg. We were expectant but unsure of what to expect. I somehow knew that this would be emotionally grueling.

As we walked up to the entrance, Ernest enquired how long we would be inside. We had been advised by our friendly hotel concierge to allow 4 hours to go around the museum. But we are, of course, Londoners, and were confident we could whizz around within an hour. Ernest looked very dubious, but he was far too polite to correct us.

I bought two tickets for the stunning-looking museum. When I was given the first admission ticket, it said 'Whites Only'. The second ticket said 'Blacks Only', but even this shock hardly prepared us for the startling and perhaps necessarily harsh journey into the museum.

One entrance was made to feel as foreboding as many had for non-whites in Apartheid South Africa. It was demeaning and inhuman.

I happened to take the 'Whites Only' ticket and entered through the door marked 'Whites'. It was a smart and tidy entrance. As I was politely shown through, there were black and white TV monitors everywhere. They were playing continuous newsreels from the 1960s.

As I walked slowly along, I felt confident that I was well versed about the history of Apartheid, or at least a version of it. On the first screen, John F. Kennedy, the President of the USA at the time, was at his most eloquent and damning about the odious Apartheid regime.

I hadn't realized that the US were quite so outspoken about the situation in South Africa. I stopped and hung on his every word.

The next TV was playing Martin Luther King. He was compellingly powerful in his unflinching condemnation of the Apartheid regime, I was mesmerized. Then I moved on to Muhammad Ali who spoke with solemn grandeur. I'd never heard him so articulate and forceful. My feet were firmly planted to the floor as I listened and was moved by their passion and powerful monologues. Why had I not known more about this before?

The museum had chosen three icons of recent American history, all with the amazing Spike of being outstanding communicators. They had chosen superbly; their words resonated right through me. It was unforgettable.

My son, Marcellus, had disappeared through the 'Blacks Only' entrance. I had taken far longer getting through the entrance walk-way than I'd anticipated spending in the whole museum. Nothing could have prepared me for that assault on all my senses. My hands were shaking and I couldn't stand still.

I stood up straight at the end of the walkway and waited for my son. I could not see or find him. For a moment I thought he might have gone on ahead of me.

He was very young when Mandela was released. I now started to realize that he and his generation had not lived through the harrowing, but limited news coverage of Apartheid the way I had.

Sharpeville and Steve Biko were but names and moments in history for them.

Eventually he came out. He was on his haunches and crying his eyes out. Nothing could have prepared him for what he had just experienced. Going through the 'Blacks Only' entrance must have been a sad and poignant reminder of just how tough and terrible things had been.

Marcellus was traumatised. I tried to console him, but he just kept crying and pointing back at the entrance. He gave me his ticket and I walked back outside and came back through the 'Blacks Only' entrance myself.

There were a couple of burly men in the intimidating uniform of the old South Africa Defence Force. They instantly grabbed me and man-handled me into the museum. Just in time, I realised that they were re-enacting what it might have been like during Apartheid.

Again there were black and white TV monitors showing some of the major protagonists of that time, including some of the black leaders of the day: Steve Biko, Walter Sisulu, Nelson Mandela and many more. Their moving and angry speeches were interspersed with sickening footage of an out of control police force and army, savagely beating children and their parents.

The visual experience of the brutality and injustice of the Apartheid era was overwhelming. Had I forgotten? Was I just hardened to all this or had I just subconsciously so wanted to move on that I had forgotten it?

We had, unfortunately, lived through the carnage and brutality as witnesses, and could never forget the terrifying images and news reports. Most South Africans had never seen any news coverage or footage of this explosive and hurtful period in our planet's history. Many would suffer an anguish similar to Marcellus' on their graphic discovery of the truth.

It would take the majority of people to believe in Mandela's dream for the nation's fabulous potential to be realized.

It was a draining and brutal experience – despite knowing that this was not currently occurring, it seemed all too real.

The brilliant and must-see museum, eloquently told the story from the beginnings of Apartheid, until it finally ended with the election of Nelson Mandela in 1994.

It was not an uplifting experience, but we somehow felt better for actually understanding more than had previously been available to us about those awful times. We left listless but better informed and extremely moved by the experience and exposure.

We spent over 4 hours at the museum, and could have spent much longer.

Marcellus is blessed with the Spike of incredible people skills. He loves being loved and gives everything to his relationships with people. But this experience had sucked all of the positive emotion out of him.

We drove to Soweto in silence. It was still hard to understand how humans could treat other humans in such a manner. For someone wired the way Marcellus is, this more than unsettled him.

Fortuitously, Soweto brought out completely different emotions. Having last visited it a couple of years before, this was the most pleasant of surprises. It had been decidedly good previously – now, it was fabulous.

Many of the old sprawling and filthy 'dormitories', that had housed the men who had been forcefully transplanted here from their 'home' townships and villages, had been bulldozed and replaced with new and clean apartment blocks. These were some of the millions of workers who had fueled the wealth of South Africa. The lack of sanitation and horrendous living conditions had made my blood boil with anger and regret. The buildings were now quickly, and thankfully, disappearing and being replaced by apartment blocks, which were admittedly squat and utilitarian looking, but signified progress, all the same.

Much more had changed. There were now so many more new houses and some beautiful homes belonging to the new and growing black working class – the beginnings of a new middle class. It is worth noting, that whilst this growth is admirable, it has still to make a tangible difference to the huge number of those who are still unemployed.

The infrastructure of Soweto had moved on immeasurably, but not many were satisfied that the government had kept its promises. There was growing anger at the perceived slow pace of change, and fury at the apparent nepotism. We instantly understood the people's impatience and disappointment.

Perhaps because I did not live there, I could maybe better see and embrace the changes that had actually taken place. I remember feeling that Soweto looked and felt chaotic and out of date, just like the Banjul I was born in. Now, Soweto had flown past Banjul by every measure imaginable: from electrification to the new roads, from many new cars and buses to new schools and hospitals.

There was an unmistakable air of confidence, but perhaps the locals didn't really feel the 'transformation'. They felt they had few reasons to feel grateful – they wanted more and now. The big retail brands were moving quickly into Soweto: this was no longer a township – it had become a teeming and vibrant city of some four million people.

Eleven brand new train stations ferried large numbers of Johannesburg's workforce to and from the area. There was a real and tangible buzz, despite Soweto still having many issues remaining on its path to self-actualisation.

Again, Marcellus had no visual history of Soweto, or the '76 student uprisings or the squalor and wretched conditions under Apartheid to call upon. In front of him, he saw and experienced a thriving and colourful African metropolis.

We had travelled Africa quite a bit together, and Soweto easily held its own with many of the African capitals we had visited in the past, in terms of infrastructure, energy and confidence.

Previously, as darkness fell, there had been an unmistakable and foreboding atmosphere of hostility and danger in Soweto. This had now totally disappeared. It had been exchanged for an air of hope and togetherness.

Soweto had started to become much more 'self-policing' as its citizens no longer wanted to go to sleep to the sound of gunshots. It now had the largest hospital on the African continent, a university, municipal parks and, most of all, proud residents. Change can happen: this was living proof that progress is always best begun at home and that development cannot be reversed.

There was a growing sense of pride and identity. Cities themselves can have Spikes. Soweto was enterprising and entrepreneurial. It had a sense of collective belief, borne out of the hard times. It was no longer the poor workhouse of Johannesburg. Soweto was now providing many jobs and careers for its inhabitants. Large businesses were moving their offices and factories to where the emerging talent lived.

We left uplifted. We went on to visit a new development called Cosmo City in Johannesburg. We stopped at a collection of old and more recent apartment blocks that had been smartened and refurbished. This was an untidy and bland suburb of Johannesburg.

The well-intentioned government, with supportive construction companies, was desperately trying to live up to its election promises of better housing for all. Those living in the townships and squatter camps, assisted by the emerging black media platforms, were vocally holding the government to account.

Cosmo City was initially targeting the educated and potentially more affluent young Africans from the townships. They needed to be given the real opportunity to get on the property ladder in Johannesburg. For far too many, despite being employed, the financial stretch of home ownership was simply not plausible in the nation's commercial capital of Johannesburg.

The government was innovative and bold. They sought like-minded partners and moved relatively quickly. Affordable mortgages were made available. The intention was to have an inclusive approach, with the dream that many from different walks of life and backgrounds could live together.

But many young white couples had also been priced out of Johannesburg's booming housing market. They soon also turned to schemes like Cosmo City.

Marcellus jumped out of the car and wandered freely around. He had lived in Gambia for some six years when he was younger and had consequently become instantly very comfortable here, in urban South Africa.

When we returned from parking the car, at first we couldn't find him. I heard his blast of a finger whistle and looked up. He was on a balcony with a young white couple, sharing a bottle of white wine. His Spike of getting on with people was on full display again.

When he eventually came back down, he was lost in conversation with people of all races and backgrounds. They all appeared to have a unique tie, perhaps it was because they were not old enough to be riven by having fully witnessed the ravages of Apartheid. They all joked and somehow looked forward to the rest of their lives with optimism and little remembered pain.

Marcellus was instantly at home and enthralled at the prospect of mixed communities; he had immediately caught the positive vibe of a young new nation. This was such a different stance and outlook to those, both black and white, who had lived through the Apartheid era.

The split in the outlook of South Africa's generations is perhaps marked by the name many of the older blacks use to refer pejoratively to the younger generation: 'Born Frees'.

Maybe that is exactly what the struggle was all about?

Circumstances can be made more positive by seeking out and embracing the benefits, rather than becoming depressed by focusing on the failures alone.

IF YOU LOOK, YOU WILL FIND

My continuing work with Barclays Africa was by far the most important and meaningful work I had ever been involved in.

My initial involvement was in helping identify a new generation of indigenous Managing Directors (MDs) for all the 11 countries across Africa that they operated in at the time. Up until then, most of the MDs had been expats from the UK.

I never thought that I would ever have the opportunity to work in the land of my forefathers. I would have paid for myself, in order to have this incredible learning experience.

We soon found out that it was highly unlikely that we would find the perfect banking leadership experience, readily available in the countries where Barclays had their businesses. We challenged ourselves on the way forward. We changed tack, and started looking for the Spike of leadership. It was clear that we had more than enough banking technicians, but woefully few leaders.

As we started looking for leaders, we found many potential candidates, but very few with any banking experience. As soon as you start looking for Spikes, believe me, you quickly realise that you are surrounded by them, but usually the individuals concerned have been previously written off because of their limitations.

We knew that we had to set them up for success. Just throwing them straight into a culture that was obsessed with skills and formal education would result in great difficulties, if not failure. Unfortunately, many of the existing African management had been institutionalized into subservience and deference.

I had built strong and trusting relationships with all of the recently appointed MDs and acted as their coach and confidante. They were all very different and had come from a variety of backgrounds: management consulting, telecoms, insurance, among others.

What they did have in common, was the Spike of being strong and inspiring leaders. We arranged an ongoing programme of induction and 'on-boarding' for them.

At one of the on-boarding sessions, having spent the whole day listening to a reiteration how integral first class customer service was to banking, and how substandard it had become across Barclays Africa's businesses, many of the indigenous African leaders in the room were becoming uncomfortable with the rather stark and unforgiving message that was being delivered.

After sharing some 'vox pop' videos of existing Barclays Africa customers, either berating the service or having become immune to a desperately low standard, the atmosphere was getting a little fraught.

It was only after noticing the seriously uncomfortable body language on display across the auditorium that I realized that my audience was not used to this very direct approach. It was a little frustrating, but I had to learn that, whilst they intellectually understood and accepted the messages, the overriding culture found this criticism very difficult. I had to learn to better 'walk in the shoes of my audience'.

We soon started learning from each other and began enjoying it thoroughly. They accepted that I had to be quite direct, but I became a little more sensitive to their perspective and feelings. It can take time for any ingrained cultural attitude to be fixed, especially when it necessitates gradually confronting real and immediate issues.

As an inspiring but tough and draining day drew to its close, many of the audience left quickly and quietly. About half a dozen remained and now were heading purposefully towards the stage. It was only at this moment that I realized that these were the most senior of the leaders in the room and they came from many different parts of Africa.

They approached the stage as one solid unit; Isaac, who was the longest serving of them, and a veteran of leadership in

Zimbabwe, was at their helm.

Realizing that they wanted to speak to me, I approached them a little nervously. Isaac stood in front of them and stared directly at me. He cut an imposing figure: he was well over 6ft tall and barrel chested. He stepped over to me and, with his arms outstretched, he hugged me hard. With a beaming smile he said, "We are all really proud of you." He then paused and said, proudly: "Son of our Fathers."

It left me speechless and delirious with pride.

This was yet another memorable part of my working experience in South Africa, and it was the most moving of tributes from the most generous of men.

Whilst they may not have yet conquered the art of customer service, they knew all about humility and authenticity. I was the one receiving the lesson.

ELLA

This was an unforgettable experience that taught me so much. The lessons I learned were to embolden all my subsequent business trips to all parts of Africa. In the main, I found them to be the most authentic of people, who were always genuinely grateful, even for the smallest positive contribution.

The following day at the lunch break, one of the other business leaders at the bank, Andy, approached me with a large smile and asked me, rather nonchalantly, whether I enjoyed coming to Africa and having to stay in a hotel.

I told him it was not my preference. He immediately declared, "Well, next time come and stay with me and my wife, and meet my daughter".

I was pleasantly surprised that this Yorkshireman, whom I had only recently met, with his shock of short blond hair, would be so friendly and so welcoming. I really appreciated the gesture, but thought he was just being hospitable. I valued the fact that he'd gone out of his way to make me feel even more welcomed.

Andy had quickly become one of the best and most popular leaders across the bank. He had a Spike of a highly tuned emotional intelligence. He had a sixth sense for judging situations. No matter what the cultural backdrop of the branches he visited across the continent, he was able to deliver strong messages of change, which were all well received and embraced.

This was on yet another trip to Johannesburg, a good few years after my initial one. I was a bit of a veteran by now, and really looked forward to the overnight flight. For half of the year there was no time difference between London and Johannesburg. I donned a grey tracksuit and some trainers, hoping to gain some sleep on the 10-hour flight.

However, arriving at Johannesburg airport, I was tired, having been up for most of the flight. I felt disheveled and felt a bit of a mess, and was in desperate need of a shave and a shower.

Having cleared the never-ending and onerous queues at immigration, I was very keen to get to the hotel for a much needed 'buff and polish'.

I was pushing an empty baggage trolley to the carousel to pick up my heavy bags when I noticed a man waving vigorously in the far corner, surrounded by his family. He whistled in my general direction. Not for one moment did I think he was addressing me. I continued pushing the trolley. Suddenly, he yelled at me to bring the trolley over to him. I felt the rage rising within me. I just clenched my teeth and just about managed to ignore him. He now took a few paces towards me, gesticulating and shouting for me to hurry up and get the trolley over to him. I instantly abandoned the trolley and marched over to confront this outrage.

On hearing my English accent, he apologized immediately. We both stood there staring at each other. He pointed at a number of black men in grey outfits collecting trolleys and delivering them to waiting customers for a few Rand. He couldn't apologize enough; I also felt a tinge of British guilt. We shook hands and nervously went our separate ways. Once again wrong assumptions had presented a clear lesson for all involved.

I rushed away from the embarrassment of getting so angry and heated in this land that had been through so much. I was desperate to get out of the airport.

I strode over to my usual meeting point to find Ernest. He wasn't in his customary place. There was a large huddle of drivers holding white placards with the names of their prospective passengers on.

I searched and searched but couldn't find my name anywhere. I was about to call Ernest when suddenly, there was a tap on my shoulder from behind. I turned around, and there stood Andy with a huge smile on his face. He smiled and said, "I gave Ernest the day off."

He grabbed the trolley from me, welcomed me to Johannesburg and off we went to his car. My whole demeanour had shifted from anger to pleasure. Andy was gregarious, charming and very, very proud of South Africa. He took me on a bit of a sightseeing tour on the way to his home, and the running commentary (from another 'outsider') was brilliant. His enthusiasm was infectious.

We instantly hit it off.

We pulled up at his stunning house in the northern suburb of Dainfern. It was in one of the most upmarket 'gated' communities in Johannesburg. There were 1800 tasteful homes, all unique, and all built to the highest specification. In the centre of this spacious and manicured complex, was a championship class golf course with a huge clubhouse, around which Dainfern life revolved.

These gated complexes were becoming increasingly popular across South Africa. They provided high profile 24/7 security and a feeling of safety, and had become especially popular with the large expat community. Everyone could appreciate why they were so admired, but along with the extremely high and impenetrable walls that blocked the view of the many beautiful homes and buildings in Johannesburg, they gave a negative feeling of apprehension and misgiving.

This was nothing like the Africa I had become accustomed to. This was more Geneva or Zurich. It had all the luxuries and conveniences of any modern European suburb. Andy parked the car in his treble garage, alongside the obligatory golf cart. Clean and safe, but a little clinical, and perhaps lacking the 'soul' that Johannesburg specialized in.

As we came into the beautiful modern lounge, I met Kathy for the first time. She was just as welcoming and charming as Andy. From the corner of my eye, I spied a beautiful young girl, hiding behind the sofa.

It was Ella. She stared at me and I stared back. She was just over a year old, and had the strong and striking features of many of those of the Zulu tribe. I smiled warmly at Andy and Kathy, who were waiting for my reaction. Ella was stunning and, as I picked her up, she laughed and smiled. Our relationship blossomed from that moment. She never stopped smiling and trying to speak to me.

She was to become my special symbol of the new South Africa.

Andy and Kathy had both worked for Barclays Bank in the UK. They married soon after Andy had accepted a Pan-African leadership role based out of Johannesburg.

They were struggling to have the children they so desperately wanted. They had explored adopting from the UK, but for anyone over 40, it's a lengthy and difficult process, made far more challenging for anyone living abroad.

They explored adoption in South Africa, which is equally as difficult when you're over 40 years old. They discovered that they could qualify for adoption if they were prepared to consider the children of HIV/AIDS victims. Many of these children are orphans, as the HIV/AIDS pandemic had ravaged families and lives right across South Africa.

Most of these children have little hope and negligible chance of success. Andy and Kathy had thought long and hard. They were very brave and resolute, having visited one of the local orphanages and experienced the lack of hope that surrounded so many of these young orphans.

They decided that they would apply for the adoption of an HIV/AIDS orphan.

This is a courageous move at the best of times, but in a different country, with a different culture and crossing the racial divide – these factors made them very special people indeed.

They were given the option of choosing the gender and the age of the child they wanted to adopt, but the only thing they were insistent upon was that the child was not HIV/AIDS positive.

Quite understandably, they couldn't spend years loving someone, knowing that they would eventually have to arrange the funeral of the child they had so longed for. They decided that they wanted the process to be as natural as possible, and so they wanted no preconceived views on what gender their child would be. In this way, their experience was as near to nature as they could have it, but in other ways, it was far away from what society had prescribed.

Andy and Kathy always got on like a house on fire, and since marrying they had never had a serious argument. Andy was so easy going and they were far too much in love for that to ever happen. Kathy had the complementary Spike to Andy's creativity, of being super-organized and ultra-efficient.

Eventually the agreed date for going to the orphanage to collect their new child had been set. The week before, uncharacteristically, Andy and Kathy had bickered all the time. Two days before going to the orphanage, they had a blazing row and neither of them could remember why.

They hardly spoke at all for 48 hours. They drove to the orphanage in complete silence.

On arrival, the matron came out to meet them and give them one last chance to withdraw, or perhaps to make an informed choice on which child they wanted. They looked warmly at each other and asked her to proceed as planned. The only condition they had requested was to have the last child brought into the orphanage before they arrived.

The matron returned holding a tiny bundle wrapped in white. Andy and Kathy were quiet, anxious and very much united. She handed the small bundle to Andy. When Kathy opened up the bundle, there was gorgeous Ella, smiling and laughing – as she would continue to do for all the time I've had the joy of knowing her.

When Andy held Ella, he and Kathy had tears of joy streaming down their faces. He whispered that from that moment, he knew that the life in that small bundle would be more important than his own, and somehow he felt that he would now sacrifice everything he had for their new child.

All three of their lives have changed immeasurably for the better. They have since also adopted Jack, who's a couple of years younger than Ella.

I'm privileged to be Ella's godfather and have remained close to her and the family after they moved to Sydney, Australia, a few years after. They were truly emblematic of both Johannesburg and the new South Africa.

"OUR FRIENDS SHOULD BE COMPANIONS WHO INSPIRE US, WHO HELP US RISE TO OUR BEST."

JOSEPH B. WIRTHLIN

MAGNIFICENT MADIBA

We had all been asked to arrive early by our hosts, BP, for the grand opening of the BP Lecture Theatre, at the newly refurbished and magnificent British Museum in central London in November 2000.

Uniquely for an evening seminar in Central London, everybody had arrived before 6.30pm, despite the lecture commencing at 8pm. Seated in the auditorium I turned to my best friend, Ray, and whispered, "Why are we whispering?" We were not the only ones: all of the 200 guests were whispering. It was eerie, but it somehow felt the right thing to do; we were all on the same page – proud to be in the presence of greatness.

How appropriate that David Attenborough, the master of gravitas, was the well-chosen host for the evening. He masterfully prepared us for the presence of someone so unique and special.

At 8pm sharp, in walked Nelson Mandela: he had his hands outstretched on the shoulders of his granddaughter. She guided the frail but strikingly tall and handsome 'Madiba' into the expectant auditorium.

We were spellbound. He exuded a powerful aura of both peace and authenticity. The great man spoke for some 40 minutes. He was honest, authoritative and wonderfully engaging. It felt impossible and wrong to argue with anything such a forgiving and optimistic force for good had to say. He used every part of his being to communicate: his voice, hands and eyes. He was a master of rhetoric, taking deep breaths, leaving long pauses, giving smiles and exuding that 'aura'. This was mega-Spike territory.

Mandela had positive magic for everyone.

He had the ability to praise and admonish, without ever patronising or scolding. He avoided the complex, keeping his ideas simple and compelling – another Spike.

When the Q&A session started, we felt the true power of Mandela. He was asked, "Mr. Mandela, my daughter of 22 and my son of 23 are going out into the wide world on their own for the first time. What advice would you give them?"

Mandela thanked him politely for the question, and then paused and thought – we all appeared to be thinking with him. He spoke slowly and instructively: "The worst advice in the world is unsolicited advice. Just be patient; they will come to you for advice in time. That is the advice they will listen to and respect."

I can't remember anything else he said but I'll never forget how he made all of us feel.

Having been released in 1990 after 27 years of incarceration, he was elected President of the Republic of South Africa in May 1994. Unlike far too many of his fellow African leaders, at the peak of his power and popularity, he stood down. He passed power peacefully and democratically to his successor.

It is still far too rare for even the best leaders to know when to move on, especially in Africa.

A SWIMMING LESSON

Whilst working in the offices of Barclays in Johannesburg, Andy came in very excited to share a special story with us: Nelson Mandela had been in the nearby swimming baths in Houghton.

Whilst Mandela was out walking on a Saturday morning (he lived close to Houghton in Johannesburg), he popped into the swimming baths. He just sat quietly on his own at the back. He watched a highly competitive game of water polo between some rather overweight middle-aged men.

When the game was over, one of the players went up to Mandela and bid him good day and asked what he was doing at the centre. He said that he had heard all of the shouting and encouragement from outside and had stepped in to see what was going on.

Mandela enquired what game they had been playing and he was told that it was water polo. The men divulged that they were all long-term friends, who had played water polo together since their college days. They now played in this pool every Saturday for many years.

Mandela smiled and enquired politely why they had no black players in their teams. He was told that it was, "a sport that black people did not appear to want to participate in."

He asked whether, if he came next week, they would teach him how to play?

Mandela has a few extraordinary Spikes, and like all of us, many limitations. But it's his Spikes that we will all rightly remember. So many people have benefitted and been transformed by them.

ROBBEN ISLAND

It was on my necessary trip to Robben Island off the coast of Cape Town that I really started to understand and appreciate the true power and legacy of Mandela.

We had just arrived in the plush comfort of the state-of-the-art cruiser, which carried us from Cape Town harbour to Robben Island. There were about 40 of us on the trip – we were from all over the world, but this was no sightseeing excursion.

This was always going to be deep and meaningful, and no doubt, emotionally painful. This was a visit I had wanted to make for many years. This was to be a colossal lesson in contemporary leadership and transformational change.

The island was ugly and threadbare, but nothing prepared us for the isolation and harshness of the cells and the 'living' conditions. The prison cells had been left untouched since they had been occupied by Mandela and his contemporaries for far too many unforgiving years.

We were greeted by our softly spoken and welcoming guide for the tour around Robben Island. He had also been a prisoner here for many years alongside Mandela.

He was a sharp and powerful reminder of what their rock-solid belief and conviction had led them to. The power of these values is impossible to forget, once seen and touched. Our guide was still 'young at heart', articulate and humble; he had been taught to read and write whilst in prison. He had gone on to complete a degree by correspondence by the time they were freed. He was taught by Mandela and his leadership team.

The conditions were desperate and harsh, but their spirits were never dampened, let alone broken.

At the end of a heart-rending but uniquely uplifting visit, our guide shared with us his final thoughts. He was amazingly optimistic and hopeful about the future and, despite everything, there was no bitterness or anger. His Spike of tolerance and forgiveness touched all of us.

He lit up the room when he spoke about his dream of a "Rainbow Nation where ALL South Africans, no matter what race, religion or tribe, would live and work together to build a nation that the rest of the continent could look to for peace, progress and prosperity."

This was lasting leadership in action – even when Mandela was not around, we still felt aligned and empowered by this unique and enduring force for good.

FINAL APPEARANCE

I was lucky enough to be invited to the World Football Cup Final to be held in the impressive, brand new Soccer City stadium in Soweto in June 2010. The tournament favourites, Spain, were due to play the Netherlands in the final.

It was blisteringly cold in the stadium, and most had blankets over their legs as they withstood the chill winds swirling around the jam-packed stadium. As kick-off time drew nearer, it was announced that the former President, Nelson Mandela, would be making an appearance. He sat in a golf cart that slowly took him all around the perimeter of the stadium.

Everybody stood and everybody cheered.

He was in a black leather hat, which covered his ears. He waved and smiled that million-dollar smile. The applause continued long after he had been gently driven off.

Little did we know then, as we settled down to watch the final, that he would never be seen at a public event again.

South Africa is still Africa's most advanced economy; despite this, it still has to transform itself. The past is important, but it cannot constrain or determine its future. It will require bold and inclusive mindsets, very different from those of the recent past, to capitalize upon Mandela's exceptional legacy.

"TRUST EACH OTHER AGAIN AND AGAIN. WHEN THE TRUST LEVEL GETS HIGH ENOUGH, PEOPLE TRANSCEND APPARENT LIMITS, DISCOVERING NEW AND AWESOME ABILITIES, OF WHICH THEY WERE PREVIOUSLY UNAWARE."

DAVID AMISTEAD

SPIKE SPARKS

Vision can be the remarkable ability to see what is beyond everyone's grasp and being bold enough to articulate it. Think Mandela and peace in South Africa!

When facing a 'burning platform', it is essential to have a 'band of believers'. There is no room for cynics.

Don't waste time building complex and expensive defenses to second-guess the attacks your competitors MIGHT make against you. Creating a competitive advantage is always more difficult, but the results are so much more fulfilling than building defensive walls. Let THEM worry about defending against YOUR attacks.

Inspired leaders are great storytellers. Graphs, charts, matrices and bullet points are for accountants. No-one remembers complex abstracts, theories and algorithms, but we all remember David and Goliath. What are your stories?

Reward successful risk-taking.

ON THE SAME PAGE

"The secret to my success is that I bit off more than I could chew and chewed as fast as I could." – Paul Hogan

"People will rise to meet seemingly insurmountable obstacles and challenges if they understand the worthiness of the personal sacrifices and effort. Supporting that understanding must be mentors who provide leadership; without both ingredients, a cause will go unrealized and a mission is likely to fail."– Glenn R. Jones (Creating a Leadership Organization with a Learning Mission in the Organization of the Future)

"If you don't risk big, you can't win big." Minda Zetlin shares that, "taking risks, and being willing to fail, are considered so important these days that leaders at even large companies puzzle over how to make their employees into bigger risk-takers, and having started a business that went under is considered a badge of honor."[32]

"A good leader leads the people from above them. A great leader leads the people from within them." – M. D. Arnold

---

[32] Zetlin, M. (2015) "5 Things the Smartest Leaders Know About Risk-Taking." (online) Inc.com Available at: http://www.inc.com/minda-zetlin/5-things-the-smartest-leaders-know-about-risk-taking. html [Accessed 24 Apr 2016]

PART FOUR

SPIKE IS PERSISTENCE

CHAPTER XIII
~~TRY NOT TO BREAK THINGS.~~
WELCOME DESTRUCTION

Playing too safe benefits no one. Never underestimate what can be achieved when you back yourself and believe in the future.

How often do you persevere when all around keep saying, "it can't be done"?

Change, by its very nature, is destructive. It gets messy. It causes confusion. That bothers a lot of people. They warn against change, or argue for taking it slow and easy, so nothing gets broken.

If they get their way, the organization has to tiptoe around, trying to be orderly, and attempting to avoid hurting anybody or upsetting people. Eventually, such a culture gets the organization into big trouble.

A culture that's unwilling to break things can't move fast. If it tries to salvage everything, it ends up carrying a lot of old baggage. Bureaucratic practices and all kinds of other bad habits build up over time.

Even beloved tradition can anchor the organization to its past, making it tough to respond to the pull of the future. Protecting what 'is' often sabotages what 'could be.'

It may sound strange, but destruction is one of today's conditions for survival. Just as a snake sheds the skin it has outgrown, the culture needs to rid itself of habits that have outlived their usefulness.

This usually demands a different set of Spikes at the helm, driving the necessary transformation.

Help to do away with the bureaucratic practices that get in the way. Break with tradition when it becomes an obstacle. Don't be afraid to butcher the sacred cows. Instead of blindly protecting old beliefs, throw them against the rocks of reality to see if they bounce or shatter. Be willing to smash some glass.

Sure, all this gets messy. It makes a lot of noise. Some people will get upset. But organizations, and individuals, always must make certain sacrifices if they want to stay strong.

There is room for a whole array of diverse Spikes, but in the right roles at the right times.

Help create a culture where people are rewarded for disturbing the peace.

"IF EVOLUTION WAS WORTH ITS SALT, BY NOW IT SHOULD'VE EVOLVED SOMETHING BETTER THAN SURVIVAL OF THE FITTEST."

JANE WAGNER

RISK READY

Every now and again, an assignment turns up that demands a completely different approach, and as long as it plays to my Spikes, I usually find it irresistible. So it was, that when the call came from the BBC in 2003 to play a part in its ground breaking TV series Mind of a Millionaire, I was overwhelmingly tempted.

They had tracked that I had worked with both corporations and entrepreneurs and wanted someone who understood the differing challenges and pressures of the two environments. I was to meet many incredible entrepreneurs, and some of them are still friends of mine to this day. They are a compelling but odd bunch. There is nothing uniform about them, and there are a few of them who are always there when they need you!

During the lengthy austere times brought on by the prolonged global financial crisis in 2007, there have been many occasions where companies which I have been involved with have had to take some calculated risks. The corporate hesitation is palpable. Whole departments and functions collectively hold their breath. The merry-go-round of meetings just never stops happening. The number of attendees at each meeting increases, as no-one wants to be left out of avoiding responsibility.

This overly cautious mindset can quickly paralyse any form of positive thought, let alone action.

It is not realistic to believe that risks can be totally avoided or completely managed out. In fact, those who move first and decisively can gain themselves a significant competitive advantage. Just think about how Apple continues to scare the pants off its rival phone makers – and the rest of the now comparatively tired-looking phone industry – with every subsequent release of the iPhone.

Sometimes you have to bet the business. It feels scary and it might be the 'last throw of the dice', but on occasion, it must be done. It might be the right thing to do, remain aware of the huge risk involved in betting the business.

In the recent past, we have seen a few major players 'betting the business' without realizing that they were doing so. And if you are going to potentially sacrifice everything, do so for a really substantive reason.

Dick Fuld at Lehman Bros, Bob Diamond at Barclays Bank, Fred Goodwin at The Royal Bank of Scotland, Peter Sands at Standard Chartered Bank – these are just a few bankers who never saw the world of risk change forever. The mercurial serial British entrepreneur, Sir Philip Green, may have gone too far with his sale of the venerable retail chain BHS for just £1, appearing to having milked it for all the advantage he possibly could, before quickly jettisoning it prior to its obvious demise.

There are as many contemporary examples of those who have gambled and won, and some quite spectacularly, like Nelson Mandela, Jeff Bezos at Amazon, and of course, Mark Zuckerberg at Facebook. They all laid huge bets and they won.

An old Ashanti proverb tells us, "No-one tests the depths of a river with both feet."

Very true, unless you are one of those rare businessmen or women: an entrepreneur.

Whilst filming the BBC2 TV series, we had the somewhat mixed pleasure of rubbing shoulders with a whole batch of entrepreneurs.

I had the huge privilege of working closely with the quite brilliant business psychologist, Dr Adrian Atkinson, and his team from HFI, who shared with me their great insights into the psychology of the entrepreneur. Our job was to try and identify the traits that combined to produce a great entrepreneur.

BACK YOURSELF

Fifteen of these massively focused individuals were mixed with 15 non-entrepreneurs, and all thirty were put through a battery of tests, games and psychometrics. We were asked the tough but exciting question, "Was it possible to sort the natural risk-takers from the risk-averse in this group of thirty?"

You'd better believe it was! After a few intense days, 13 out of 15 were identified. Having worked with and learned so much from the sharp and ever alert Adrian, looking back, it now seems so obvious and relatively straightforward to spot these entrepreneurs on my travels.

On the first morning of filming, we were at the splendid Edstone Hall, a grand old stately home in Warwickshire, in the middle of England. Adrian Atkinson and I had just met and he was off: "What are we going to do for so many days of filming?"

I answered that we were going to put all of the thirty people in the large dining room having breakfast through a battery of tests, in order to find out who were the genuine entrepreneurs.

He grabbed me by the arm and said, "Come on, I'll tell you who they are right now." I just did as I was told, convinced that this impatient arrogance would soon come crashing down. As we walked down the aisle, the room was boisterous and noisy. Four of them were playing a friendly game of cards. Adrian stopped and said: "Those two are real entrepreneurs." I looked hard and tried to spot what he had observed.

I stared hard, but obviously at the wrong things. Adrian, clearly losing patience with my inability to see the 'obvious', whispered, "The two of them are cheating." I looked again, and saw one of these smiling men sneakily pull a card hidden up his shirt-sleeve. His partner in the card game was peering over the shoulder of one of the other players and squinting at the hand his opponent held. Not even a friendly game of cards at breakfast, for no money, with people they didn't know, was beyond their huge desire to win at nearly any cost.

Adrian went on to identify his chosen 15 entrepreneurs; as he often reminded me, he got 14 of the 15 right, using his powers of observation and the tell-tale signs of a 'risk-ready' appetite.

The first and perhaps biggest challenge was to define what we meant by 'entrepreneur'. We decided on a rather crude but very helpful approach: our working definition would be 'self-made millionaire'.

As a precursor to the series, a BBC survey of the 70,000 self-made millionaires across the UK revealed some striking results. Over 49% of them were dyslexic! Some 59% of them came from deprived or dysfunctional backgrounds.

To my mind, this went a long way to explaining their quite amazing desire to succeed. It was like they spent their lives trying to prove to someone really important to them that they were good enough and that they were not 'damaged goods'. Because of their backgrounds, many had faced either rejection or a complete lack of recognition when they were much younger.

Adrian was very convincing about the importance of the formative years from 7-11 years old. His research had shown that major negative events could colour the rest of our lives. For many of our entrepreneurs, being dyslexic at school was a huge burden of rejection. Many didn't know they suffered from dyslexia until they were much older; but simply being sent to sit at the back of the class was a debilitating experience that would help stimulate their need to be recognized as 'fit for purpose'.

If this was not enough petrol for an already fast car, the judge they tended to choose to impress was… themselves. An unrelenting task-master who would never ever be satisfied. This need for recognition would never leave them.

There were many huge risk-embracing Spikes on display, but all our gathered entrepreneurs still had very differing Spikes, and consequently, different approaches.

The most obvious standout Spike of our gathered potential wealth creators was an all-encompassing desire to win, at just about everything and anything they did. I'm not simply describing a competitive spirit – I am talking about a total obsession with winning and coming first. For the entrepreneurs in the group, second place was no more than first of the losers. They not only took no prisoners; they bayoneted the wounded!

In retrospect, the real entrepreneurs could not even begin to hide their irrepressible desire to win and, consequently, their appetites for huge and sometimes alarming risks.

In the more even-tempered and hierarchy-driven world of corporate UK plc, there, unfortunately, thrives a very different culture of 'not wanting to lose'. A near palpable fear of failure pervades amongst the senior executives of the private sector and is even more pronounced in the public sector.

Consequently, the prevailing attitude amongst large (including surprisingly successful) organizations is to avoid mistakes at all costs. And this 'more haste, less speed' approach has become endemic. This cautious approach to business has paralysed pace and removed hunger.

Such an ultra-deliberate attitude leaves an enormous gap for the entrepreneurs where first-mover advantage is their key competitive edge. Speed and courage is everything. These entrepreneurs do not do 'failure'. They have redefined failure and see mistakes as a necessary step in learning.

We could all learn from their mantra: "If you have not made any mistakes, then you have not really been stretching yourself".

And you had better believe that these rare people are perpetually at a constant stretch, and they know no other way to operate. Full on and all-out assault is business as normal, always.

Nearly all of the entrepreneurs in question had tasted failure, and usually more than once; in fact, some of them had made it into an art form. But they were indefatigable, never having to bounce back because they were never knocked off their feet in the first place.

There was another common Spike amongst them, but manifesting itself quite differently from each of the individuals in our disparate gathering – they could never be a team. They all had to be in charge.

For all the courage, dynamism, cheating, fortitude and resilience – and there was an excess of these skills – I never really witnessed any real innovation. What was on display was 'heavy duty' push and determination. The individual variations could easily become masked by the HUGE Spike of being 'risk ready', all the time!

Whenever we 'normal' people have a bad experience with a product or service, we might complain, switch our allegiance to an alternative product or service or, more likely, being British, do nothing. The Brits are more likely to demonstrate our great British reserve, the 'stiff upper lip', thereby getting the service we deserve and unwittingly creating the gap for the entrepreneurs.

FIND THE GAP

Our gathered entrepreneurs were very different. A bad experience would make their eyes sparkle and instead of depressing them, it excited them.

This potentially means a gap in the market; hypothetically a business opportunity. They would rapidly switch into 'overdrive'.

Another revelation for me was that, in the main, our survey informed us that women tended to become entrepreneurs a lot later than men. Women tended to be in their late thirties or early forties by the time they started a business, and only built businesses in areas where they had expertise or knowledge. Rarely would they be the serial entrepreneurs who would chase any new opportunity with gusto. This chasing of any seemingly viable opportunity, whether they had experience or knowledge or not, was generally a male preserve.

When a possible gap has been identified, an entrepreneur brings their forceful side into play and just pushes at the opportunity, making it or breaking it.

Yet, another obvious trait was the ability to fail fast. This is so different from the way corporations tend to think and act today. It might take many months (or years) for a large business to realize that despite all the testing, steering committees and risk managers, the initiative has failure written all over it. The now standard RAG (Red, Amber and Green) progress reports may well be screaming out, with Red splashed all over, but the project continues, facing small incremental failures, and no one dares to call a halt.

This overly indulgent approach to failure wastes resources and tends to kill belief.

Our entrepreneurs are quick and nimble, especially when it is clear that they are wasting their scarce resources and attention. The initiative is usually unceremoniously dropped and they have the ability to cut all emotional and physical ties and reposition their efforts.

Once on the chase, they would lose all sense of fair play and ignore the normal rules of engagement. This was where their creative spirit would emerge, but it would be far more likely to be an approach of 'trial and error', as opposed to a flash of genius or a painstaking experiment in laboratory conditions. Most entrepreneurs, when asked the secret of their success, would say it was all down to hard work and luck. They were able to work extremely long hours whilst still being energized and full of hope and zeal. 60 hours a week was standard practice.

Around the same time, I was approached by the telecoms company, Orange, to lead an in depth survey of the UK's entrepreneurial readiness, titled 'Entreprenation'. This survey showed the total number of working adults who had started their own businesses across different countries: in North America it was 1 in 10, in Australia 1 in 12 and in the UK 1 in 34! Why? A lot of this is to do with how we treat success and failure in the UK (and in 'old' Europe).

The 'newer' European nations like Latvia, Lithuania and Estonia, had very different risk appetites when compared to the older and more cautious stalwarts like France, Italy, Germany, and of course the UK. Dominant here are the old perceptions about 'incumbents', who as soon as they reach number one in their served markets, through risk embracing and fast moving cultures, then suddenly forget their daring and drive. They move to protecting their new-found status, and inadvertently crush that maverick behaviour that has won them the prize in the first place.

Incumbents are generally quite unforgiving of failure. Let's take our minds back to the once famous Freddie Laker, who initiated the budget airline phenomenon here in Europe, and that was back in September 1977. His ground-breaking 'Skytrain' initiative was to offer prices for the golden transatlantic route of London to New York that many could not believe. Despite the huge benefits this would bring for the potential customers, the whole of the European aviation industry collaborated to eventually push the fledgling airline to bankruptcy some five years later.

Southwest Airlines, the 'daddy' of low cost airlines, started out in 1967 as Air Southwest. Its original plan was to stay within the confines of the state of Texas, thereby avoiding federal regulators and the big international airlines. This smart move still incurred the wrath of the incumbents and their supporting cast of national bodies.

The now-legendary entrepreneur, Herb Kelleher, and his co-founder, Rollin King, refused to buckle under the collective pressure.

Some of the incumbent airlines of the time (Braniff, Aloha Airlines, United Airlines, Trans-Texas, and Continental Airlines) initiated legal action, and thus began a three-year legal battle to keep Air Southwest (as it was originally called) on the ground. Air Southwest eventually prevailed in the Texas Supreme Court, which ultimately upheld Air Southwest's right to fly in Texas. The decision became final on December 7, 1970, when the U.S. Supreme Court declined to review the case without comment.

The huge and relentless determination of the founders eventually paid off. The rest, as they say, is history. The Southwest Airlines model has now been much copied all over the world, and with huge success, by companies such as Ryanair and EasyJet across Europe. But without the likes of the pioneering Freddie Laker, maybe these companies would not have happened.

However, just like with many other pioneers, some have to fail, in order for those coming later to learn from the mistakes and resolve them, prior to making it work. Laker was pilloried and ridiculed both by the media and business at large.

On the other hand, when there are brilliant successes, we tend to wait for them to fail; at times it even feels as if we are WILLING them to fail. This does not make for a great environment to take large risks and it is even less conducive to winners being celebrated.

We in the UK and Europe, still do not admire those who have taken all the risks and have eventually delivered and won. There is still no 'European dream' that sits alongside the ubiquitous American dream.

A couple of the stars of the Mind of a Millionaire TV series were David Gold and Sir Ghulam Noon, both brilliant entrepreneurs with quite different approaches but, tellingly, quite similar backgrounds.

David Gold, today one of the UK's most successful businessmen, was born into extreme poverty. This never held him back despite many setbacks, which would have knocked many others out of the race forever.

David started out at a very young age by helping his mother sell buttons from a stall outside their house in East London. Moving indoors, they then converted their front room into a card and sweet shop. From there, he went on to run a bookstore in Charing Cross and, before long, branched out into publishing, printing, and later, distribution.

David Gold is 186th on the 2010 Sunday Times Rich List, and is currently valued at approximately £350 million. The name of his holding company is Gold Group International. Core businesses include Gold Star Publications, Gold Air International, Ann Summers, Knickerbox, a number of property companies and, of course, West Ham United Football Club.

The facts are one thing, but meeting him said everything about this driven man.

A brown Bentley pulled up; out stepped a slim man in his early sixties who walked towards the studios with a purpose. He was carrying a small bag and was extremely charming and polite to everyone he met on his way in.

We decided to take David back to where he was born in the East End of London, more or less opposite Upton Park, the home of his revered West Ham United Football Club. At the time he was the joint owner of Birmingham City Football Club – his dream was to one day acquire his beloved West Ham FC. I felt that it was only a matter of time.

DAVID GOLD – NEVER FORGET

The house he had grown up in was small, dark and dingy: a two-up-two-down, on a non-descript road, where, even now, all the houses looked and felt the same. The house had been converted into a small independent grocer's store and all of upstairs was utilised as a haphazard storeroom. My guess was that the rooms upstairs had hardly changed since David lived here.

As we were upstairs getting the cameras, sound and lighting ready, David came up and stared out of the bedroom window. He had brought his own lunch of homemade sandwiches and a Thermos flask of tea. The bedroom was miniscule, grey and drab. The garden, if it could be called that, was a concrete slab.

As we were setting up I asked David: "What memories does this bring back?" David hardly stirred; when he eventually did turn around there were tears streaming down his face. I managed to get the crew to leave quickly whilst David started talking. He said the only memories that came to mind were of "abject poverty."

He'd shared this room with his brother; their father had left them when David was very young, never to return. "Mum brought us up on her own. She appeared always to be at work, but somehow always made it home for our evening meal. I never realized how poor we were, but I do remember having to go to bed with our clothes on, as there was nothing to put on the fire, and also having only one meal a day.

"Our mother was an optimist, she always said that tomorrow everything would be brilliant and we would have loads to eat. 'You just see,' she would say."

He was by now really sobbing and I noticed that he was wearing a belt which had DG inscribed on it, DG diamond cufflinks and a diamond encrusted lapel pin with, DG on it. At first we thought Dolce and Gabbana. No, it could not be, it was obviously DG for David Gold. A sign of that need for recognition.

I asked him: with all his fabulous riches, all the companies that he owned and with all of his continued success, why was he still working as hard as he had ever done? He turned around, looked at me and said in a rather surprised tone: "You really don't get it, do you? I'm just never going to be poor again."

Two of his companies, Knickerbox and Ann Summers, have his daughters as CEOs. But what of his dear mother? Well, she was the chair of all his businesses at the time!

Another of our entrepreneurs, Sir Ghulam Noon, moved to England with very little and started out his business in 1988 armed with little more than a small kitchen, a delivery van and a vision.

From very humble origins in Bombay, he was now running a £150-million-a-year business. This success, coupled with his commitment to a number of charities, gained Noon a knighthood as well as wide-spread recognition.

He is supplying pre-cooked Indian meals to many of the UK's top supermarket chains, including Sainsbury's, Morrison's and Spar. British Airways is another large customer.

On seeing the huge public appetite for Indian food in restaurants, he started manufacturing authentic Indian dishes for the supermarket shelves. After a disastrous fire at his factory in 1994, which might have put many people off, he started again and built up his business to where it is now, making more than a quarter of a million curries a day.

His biggest seller, not surprisingly, is Chicken Tikka Masala, the unofficial national dish of the UK.

As with most entrepreneurs, David Gold and Sir Ghulam Noon have been knocked down on more than one occasion and were both from very ordinary and impoverished backgrounds. But just like the other self-made millionaires who appeared on the TV series, they have bags of desire. This is not just 'fire in the belly' – more like a raging inferno.

All the entrepreneurs on the set of Mind of a Millionaire taught me many things, but the major lesson was that the only difference between a failed entrepreneur and a successful one, is that the successful ones never ever give up.

David and I have built a friendship since the TV series, and I have had the pleasure of meeting and interviewing David a number of times. He is hugely charming and polite, but there is a steely and outspoken edge to him. I've learned that if I ask him a question, he will answer it, no matter how politically incorrect the answer maybe.

I memorably once asked him in front of a packed and fully engaged audience, to share some highlights about growing up with nothing. He shared many humorous and poignant anecdotes.

I eventually asked him: "If you could have dinner tomorrow evening with any three people from history, who would they be?" He paused momentarily, and then said "Jesus Christ, Julius Caesar…and Mrs Green."

I obviously responded: "I get Jesus Christ and Julius Caesar, but who is Mrs Green?"

"She was my form teacher at school. On my last day of school, the last thing she said to me in front of the class was: 'Gold, you will achieve nothing in your life.'"

On this occasion David was awaiting his judgment day, but like most of the extraordinary people who appeared on the series, for them, every day was a judgment day.

SPIKE SPARKS

Do not too readily accept that because something was true in the past, it will still be true today.

If you don't make a difference, you don't matter!

The greatest leaders have equal measures of humility and self-belief. On their own, these attributes are important – in equal measures they are immense and transformative.

Establish winning principles but be prepared to fail.

Take a moment to check whether you have become just a little cynical. Think positive, talk positive, act positive and become more positive.

ON THE SAME PAGE

"One key to successful leadership is continuous personal change. Personal change is a reflection of our inner growth and empowerment."– Robert E. Quinn

Frances Hesselbein aptly stated that, "Culture does not change because we desire to change it. Culture changes when the organization is transformed; the culture reflects the realities of people working together every day."[33]

"Culture was long thought to be merely a 'soft' resource in the corporate equation. However, more and more business leaders are beginning to recognize the necessity of culture when it comes to creating and sustaining long-term growth and change. What is the key to creating a strong business culture? Leadership. The best cultures start with CEOs who set the tone for the rest of the company, guiding others through the often difficult process of corporate transformation."[34]

Organizational transformation begins with the personal transformation of the leaders. Organizations do not transform; people do![35]

"The key to successful leadership today is influence, not authority."– Ken Blanchard

---

[33] Hesselbein, F. (1999) "The Key to Cultural Transformation." *Leader to Leader*, Volume 1999, Issue 12, pages 1–7

[34] Mattone, J. and Vaidya, N. (2016) *Cultural Transformations: Lessons of Leadership and Corporate Reinvention*. 1st edition. Hoboken, New Jersey: John Wiley & Sons

[35] Barrett, R. (2006) *Building a Values-Driven Organization: A Whole System Approach to Cultural Transformation*. Oxford: Elsevier

CHAPTER XIV
~~AVOID MISTAKES.~~
MAKE MORE MISTAKES

Change often leaves people feeling exposed, vulnerable, insecure. They get jumpy about doing anything that might make them look bad. Fear of foul-ups causes them to freeze up. Productivity nosedives. It's a common problem when the organization makes it safer to do nothing rather than do wrong...

Cultures that don't tolerate failure also have trouble developing new competencies. People can't afford to experiment. They have to stick with what they know, and fixing problems gets tough when folks are reluctant to use trial and error to find out what works.

Fear of mistakes locks learning out of your work. It limits your repertoire. Failure, on the other hand, is the master educator. Rapid innovation, in particular, almost always grows out of a high error rate: more attempts, quicker insight, and faster solutions.

Obviously, this does not give you a license to get careless or do dumb things. Sloppy, half-hearted effort can never benefit the culture. Honest mistakes, though, are life's main schoolroom. Usually success is a direct by-product of screw-ups.

On the surface, it sounds irresponsible, but to flourish in a rapidly changing world you actually need to make more mistakes. Fail quickly. Fail often. If you do something and it doesn't work, just recover in a hurry and try something else.

Look at your job as a laboratory. Try things. Experiment. Know, going in that many of the things you attempt won't pan out, but that those mistakes can still light the way to success.

Attract the Spikes of courage and curiosity – they will help develop a culture that is willing to fail its way to the future.

"YOU MISS 100% OF THE SHOTS YOU NEVER TAKE."

WAYNE GRETSKY, HOCKEY STAR

MUTUAL MENTORING

As you have read in previous chapters, I've been very fortunate to have benefitted from some very special mentors; those wonderful leaders who have the Spikes of generosity, wisdom and expert insight – from Donald, Larry, Geoff and Mike to many, many more.

We all benefit from active role models, and as I was to find out, mentoring is a two-way street. The mentor is just as enriched by the ongoing relationship as the mentee.

The next three chapters will share some of my richest and most rewarding mentoring relationships. I know each one of these very special people taught me as much as I was able to ever share with them.

Mentoring only works when both parties are getting something meaningful out of the relationship. Otherwise, why would you continue to meet up?

Back in 2004, I was invited to be part of an eclectic group of people, brought together from a variety of industries and backgrounds, to assist the Royal Navy down at the HMS Nelson Naval Base in Portsmouth on the south coast of England.

The Royal Navy, like all of the UK Armed Forces, was struggling to attract new recruits, and was also looking to attract more diverse ones. The more than 20 odd different 'brands' or sections within the Navy were perhaps serving to confuse or dilute their messages.

At the time, Paul was a Major in the Royal Marines. We instantly hit it off after I had argued with an Admiral, who was the Second Sea Lord, and the most senior naval officer at the two-day Leadership Retreat. We had been briefed that there would be NO rank or hierarchy at the Retreat (despite all the naval staff being in uniform). It became very clear that the naval hierarchy was so enshrined by all who worked there, that dissent was just not an option.

We had a full-throttle exchange in front of all at the Retreat. After a few minutes of what I thought was a good-natured but very passionate exchange, he ordered me to stop, and stated that the discussion was now over. I'd never heard anything so ridiculous in my life, but then I wasn't an officer in the Royal Navy. I just ignored the order and carried on.

By now, most were watching this exchange with some interest and some others with a little fear for what might happen to me.

Adrian, the Admiral, was beginning to lose his composure; I could see and sense this, so I also backed off and sat down.

Paul approached me and engaged me in a lively conversation, which took all the heat out of what was becoming a very difficult situation. We had loads in common, and we have been close friends and confidantes ever since.

The following morning, Adrian found me at breakfast and sat next to me; he apologized for the difficult exchange the night before, but I was not in the least bit put-out or offended in any way whatsoever. He obviously had not enjoyed being challenged in front of his more junior officers.

He was a much bigger man for our conversation over breakfast, and we were to also stay in touch over the coming years.

Paul and I had so much in common and just trusted each other's judgment on all things; although we have lived on different sides of the world for the most of our friendship, we have remained very close and hugely capitalised on each other's Spikes.

Despite being an officer, Paul, somewhat paradoxically, had a visceral concern and disrespect for 'privilege' and was the most ardent believer in meritocracy. He would teach me and show me so much about 'looking beyond the rank' and searching for the nascent talent. Paul himself was living proof that leaders are neither born nor made, but are found – and usually in the most unexpected places, if you look hard enough.

He has told me on several occasions that he was never comfortable being an officer, but he loved being in the Marines and simply wanted to be in charge!

Before setting out to write Spike, I spoke to Paul and a few other of my mutual mentors, in order to capture their stories and their journeys of discovery.

It soon became clear, that given the inherent humility they all shared (something that all new-age leaders should aspire to), it might be far easier if they told their stories, and we looked to identify their Spikes together afterwards.

I've had the privilege of both mentoring Paul and working with him. His language is born of who he actually is and shaped by the searing focus to uncompromisingly save lives.

"WAR IS CRUEL AND YOU CANNOT REFINE IT."

WILLIAM TECUMSEH SHERMAN

PAUL'S STORY

Paul kicked things off by his rich reminiscence (in his very own words) of his initial arrival in Afghanistan and the time he served under a quite brilliant and inspired leader when he was a Lieutenant Colonel in the Royal Marines.

By now, Paul and I had engaged in the 'hire for attitude and train for skills' approach, which we constantly discussed and debated. As ever, Paul was the quickest learner I have ever had the pleasure of working with. He never, ever needed a second explanation.

He was always embracing risk, despite the huge danger he constantly faced. He continually shared the decision making to mitigate the risk, but always took the overall responsibility.

More Spikes are always better than just one, no matter how strong or outstanding that one may be.

This is Paul's story:

HELMAND, AFGHANISTAN

We had been operating all day in searing heat amongst the close confines and small deserted villages of the Green Zone next to the River Helmand; the fighting had been sporadic and the atmosphere was tense.

Although we had only suffered one injury – mercifully a non-fatal gunshot wound – our Afghan allies were clearly rattled and we all knew the Taleban were close and awaiting their moment. As last light approached, we were ordered to withdraw, although it was clear to me that we would need to return the next day.

Our operation was to divert the Taleban and prevent their reinforcements moving up north to where the Brigade assault was being conducted. We had seen enough 'combat indicators' throughout the day to know that a sizeable Taleban force was close. My instinct was to stay in place and defend our position, rather than cede ground to an enemy adept at placing booby traps. However, orders are orders, and the military is nothing without discipline, particularly in a combat zone.

There is however, always room for 'tactical interpretation', and so, whilst the Sergeant Major was organizing the withdrawal, I risked his anger by jumping in a Jackal All-Terrain Vehicle (ATV) and quickly did a tour of the battlefield.

My aim was not high-risk tourism, but rather to find my junior commanders whilst they still had 'eyes on the target' and get them thinking about the next day's probable mission.

Despite the stories you may have read about inferior military equipment, some of it was fabulous, and the Jackal ATV allowed me to spin around our position viewing the target from several angles.

As we say in the military, "Time spent in reconnaissance is seldom wasted", and by the time I got back, the Sergeant Major was seriously upset with me, because I had disrupted and risked a complicated manoeuvre, but I had achieved my aim.

I knew the next day would demand a complicated operation planned overnight, and I did not think that the traditional NATO planning and orders process was 'fit for this particular purpose'.

The problem with any process, however well designed, is that it is designed for today and nobody can know what tomorrow will bring. As the situation changes, the process falls increasingly out of date, and the 'manager' focused on delivering the process becomes increasingly isolated from the team.

The unintended consequence of modern technology is paradoxically greater complexity as, regardless of the sector, we all have more information to consider in ever shorter timeframes. The result for many managers, when faced with this information overload, is an inability to reach decisive conclusions, often referred to as 'paralysis through (over) analysis.' If I have a Spike, it is one that I have learned through working across multiple industries including the medical sector, the military, government, the media, the construction industry and marketing. The one common fact I have learned is that the people on the ground always know far better than the middle managers what is actually happening – in the military we call it 'Ground Truth'.

Therefore, the natural solution for a leader under pressure and starved of actionable intelligence, is to simply ask them – isn't it?

Unfortunately, most are not programmed to think this way.

The first barrier to overcome is entirely psychological, as we have been brainwashed into thinking that if we are in charge, then we need to maintain the myth that we know everything and can do anything. The Spike that I have developed is to simply accept my own limitations and to invest myself in nurturing a relationship with the 'talent on the shop floor.'

Aloof managers are often portrayed as arrogant; in actual fact I believe that aloofness is more to do with personal insecurity, as these managers simply do not have the confidence to engage with people who are not like them. Building a more personal rapport with the team on the ground is a long-term project. Good leaders invest time in breaking down institutional barriers allowing a free and frank flow of opinions. However, good leaders also know that this is a delicate balance, as over-familiarity quickly erodes respect, and so the trick is to encourage opinions whilst maintaining authority.

Spike is also about identifying the strengths in others and a leader's job is maximizing the strengths that they have 'positively identified' in their team members. Our society has embedded in our psychology some quite illogical ideas – none more so than the concept that senior management are the most intelligent people in an organization. The self-evident truth is that the cleverest people are rarely at the top of an organization, as even in modern Britain, employment opportunities are still more a function of opportunity and upbringing, rather than raw intelligence.

The unavoidable consequence is that, at the tactical level there is always a rich supply of informed and intelligent people, with opinions well worth garnering.

Returning to Afghanistan.

With no thanks to me, we extracted smoothly from the battlefield and moved to a tactical rendezvous in the desert, whilst awaiting our Brigade orders.

Exactly as I had anticipated, we were ordered to return to the same location, find the Taleban and immediately become decisively engaged. Our objective was to ensure that they could not move up north and flank the main Brigade assault. I immediately brought my junior commanders in and explained the outline task and then asked them to give me their opinions as to how they felt their individual sub-units could be used to best effect.

The sniper commander advised me on how he could best deploy his sniper pairs; the heavy machine gun and MILAN missile teams suggested the optimum fire base positions, and the Jackal Commanders explained how they could use their mobility to create a mobile firebase and tactical reserve. The artillery and ground attack aircraft controllers also suggested Fire Support plans as the whole team offered options to support the Close Combat teams. The Close Combat teams were the main effort, as they were going to penetrate deep into the treacherously close country alongside the Helmand River. We knew that this was where the Taleban would be waiting.

Once I had gathered everyone's opinions I sent them away and wrote my orders. Although they individually understood their part of the tactical situation better than me, it was my responsibility to weave these part plans into a single coherent whole. Through years of working together my Spike had become knowing what parts to take from whom.

Ultimately, you can delegate everything except responsibility, and it was my responsibility to 'de-conflict' the various mini plans and deliver a single set of executive orders.

The challenge was two-fold. Firstly, we needed to keep track of the forward line of my close combat troops amongst the foliage of the Green Zone, and then bring our superior firepower to bear without risking a friendly fire incident.

The second challenge was that the Taleban held the close terrain, and that it would be booby-trapped and planned for ambush. The further we progressed into the Green Zone, the greater the probability of casualties.

The reality of the complex modern world is that nobody can be 100% up to date, and therefore, as a leader, you have to become comfortable working on limited information and taking calculated risks.

We have all seen people lose control as they are put under pressure to make decisions, whilst waiting for vital information that will never arrive. That type of 'manager' wants to make the 'perfect decision', but the complexity of the modern world rarely allows for 'perfect decisions' to be made in an effective timescale. 'Finished' always beats 'perfect'.

This type of manager has no role in a complex, fast moving environment, because in these environments opportunities are fleeting, and time is the most important variable of all. There is no fool-proof technique for taking calculated risks – it is all about instinct and judgment.

Modern leaders are effectively judged on their track record for taking calculated risks, and the best source of advice for them is always going to be the junior leaders who are closest to the tactical issues.

If you have built your team well, you will have placed intelligent and trustworthy individuals in key positions – the role of the leader is then to collate these opinions and build them into the bigger picture.

Like everything in life, the best combat plans are the simplest, and so we decided to only infiltrate about 500m into the Green Zone, with the intention of setting up a fixed defensive line acting as a 'come on' to the Taleban. Although the Taleban had proven themselves to be brave and highly resourceful, I doubted they would have the discipline to resist the temptation of attacking the fixed line.

My assumption proved to be correct and we were engaged in heavy fighting for over six hours. Despite the fact that we rarely laid eyes on our colleagues through the undergrowth, we managed to suppress the enemy with our superior weaponry and did not suffer any casualties.

The battle eventually died out towards last light and the main operation to our north had been a significant success, without any interference from the teams we engaged.

We moved on to the next operation.

That day could have gone very differently, but in retrospect I realise that the success had less to do with the decisions I took on the day, and much more to do with the years of teamwork that preceded it. At that point my team had been together for two years and I knew I could trust my junior commander's opinions, and I believe they had faith in my ability to coordinate.

Regardless of the sector, the leader's role is primarily done in advance, by building the right team, explaining the mission and ensuring that everyone has the information and resources to deliver.

The benefit of drawing the junior leaders deep into the decision-making process is that they intimately understand every aspect of the plan. They have faith in their role because they will generally have designed or, at the very least, heavily influenced it.

The final benefit is initiative, because when things go awry, as they always will in a fast-moving, complex situation, the junior commanders have enough information, context and confidence to intervene immediately and decisively.

Every crisis gets worse when people have to wait for the boss to arrive!

Adapt and Overcome

Succeeding in a complex and volatile environment means accepting change and adapting to meet it.

Invariably, this means challenging 'the way things are always done' and often leaving behind the traditions and people that are tied to that past. This is difficult enough for an individual, but it takes real courage of purpose and weight of personality to impose dramatic cultural change on an organization, especially one that is intrinsically secretive, steeped in tradition and full of combative egos.

The rise of Al Qaeda presented a new and deadly challenge for the intelligence services and Special Operations Community that had developed during the slow, secretive and highly paranoid Cold War period.

Despite the overwhelming resources at their collective disposal, the complex, over-specialized and often competitive mix of organizations did not present a single coherent response. This limitation was exacerbated by the highly agile threat that the Al Qaeda network now presented.

I arrived in Baghdad in June 2005, and joined the US-led Joint Special Operations Command (JSOC) Headquarters that was running the international battle against Al Qaeda.

I had only recently joined the Special Operations community and had very quickly become used to the highly secretive and often elitist atmosphere that pervades that world.

In stark contrast, at the centre of the most sophisticated Special Operations campaign in history, I found a culture that was inclusive, open and positively embracing.

Leaders set the culture, and Lt Gen Stanley McChrystal, a man who would later command in Afghanistan before publicly falling out with Barak Obama, commanded JSOC.

McChrystal is an excellent leader and a true visionary. Unquestionably, his Spike is willingness to challenge and impose change on convention. He had recognized early in the campaign against Al Qaeda that he needed to break down the traditional silos that naturally operate in the Special Operations and Intelligence community, and build a single integrated team.

As is often the case in the commercial sector, the constraint was not resource, but rather the lack of teamwork. First, he needed to get information flowing quickly and easily around the network he was intent on creating. The mantra became: "A network to defeat a [terrorist] network", and the following is an extract from an article he wrote not long after leaving Afghanistan:

"Ultimately, a network is defined by how well it allows its members to see, decide, and effectively act.

Although we got our message out differently than did our enemies, both organizations increasingly shared basic attributes that define an effective network.

Decisions were decentralized and cut laterally across the organization. Traditional institutional boundaries fell away and diverse cultures meshed. The network expanded to include more groups, including unconventional actors.

It valued competency above all else – including rank. It sought a clear and evolving definition of the problem and constantly self-analyzed, revisiting its structure, aims, and processes, as well as those of the enemy. Most importantly, the network continually grew the capacity to inform itself."

It is worth re-reading that excerpt from a commercial perspective. Whilst McChrystal was describing both Al Qaeda and the network he built to defeat it, he was also inadvertently describing any modern organization that is optimised to thrive in any complex environment, regardless of the sector.

Easy to see – more challenging to do, because whilst it takes a visionary to see a new way of working, it takes a radical to challenge the accepted norms and it takes a determined and inspirational leader to drive through the requisite changes.

McChrystal was all those things and he created a culture that was built on trust and mutuality – scarce commodities in the intelligence community.

Looking from the outside, I would say that one of his most powerful tactics was to create a team collective with a higher purpose.

He brought together members of the various 'Three Letter Organizations', such as the CIA, DEA, NSA etc., and made them work together in a single integrated team alongside the various military elements.

I once asked him how he had overcome the institutionalized reticence to collaborate. He told me quite simply: "You take young operators, bring them close to the battle, put them all in the same room and ensure they all understand the mission. In those conditions the team naturally gels together around the joint mission."

The team was known as the Joint Inter Agency Task Force (JIATF), and the integrated intelligence picture, which they helped frame, would form the heartbeat of the global fight against Al Qaeda.

The second strand in McChrystal's strategy was to adhere doggedly to Claustwitz's First Principle of War, 'The Selection and Maintenance of the Aim', which meant that he stayed focused on the mission and resisted any distraction.

The Special Operations team in Baghdad was richly resourced and focused entirely on defeating Al Qaeda in Iraq (AQ-I), and the wider global battle against Al Qaeda.

At the same time, the Coalition's conventional forces were engaged in a far larger battle against a wide variety of belligerents in Iraq. The situation was further confused, because many of these belligerents cooperated with Al Qaeda on a tactical level, whilst maintaining distinct strategic agendas.

On a number of occasions, conventional force commanders asked McChrystal for assistance, and for any good soldier that creates a difficult dilemma, as I know it did for him. For a good leader, the answer was more straightforward. The JSOC mission was to defeat Al Qaeda, so JSOC would offer support where we could, but it would not be distracted from the mission.

As savage battles raged across Iraq, and more young American lives were lost, I know that this position was difficult to maintain.

Leaders are paid to take tough decisions.

Politics firmly aside, it is important to understand the context that created the complex tactical situation in Iraq at that time. JSOC clearly derived its mission to defeat Al Qaeda from the 9/11 attacks, but Al Qaeda had little or no effective presence in Iraq prior to the Coalition invasion.

Saddam Hussein's Baathist party ruthlessly suppressed any Sunni Muslim militia throughout his tenure. A Pentagon report published in 2008 finally debunked speculative links which had been suggested by the Bush administration.

Following the rapid ground offensive in Iraq, the de-Baathification policy removed this internal suppression and Al Qaeda rapidly expanded, exploiting the power vacuum under the brutal leadership of Abu Musab al-Zarqawi.

He led a savagely violent campaign of attacks against coalition forces, the Iraqi government and Iraqi Shiites. His aim was to defeat coalition forces, suppress any Shiite governance and, ultimately, establish an Islamic caliphate.

Al-Zarqawi was killed the month I arrived in Baghdad, and whilst the details of that operation remain restricted, the operation was a vindication of McChrystal's vision and methods. The operation was a JSOC team effort, involving diligent intelligence, highly skilled surveillance and brave decision-making.

Such was the level of chaos and violence at that time in Baghdad, that the removal of the titular head of Al Qaeda in Iraq (AQ-I) had made no discernible difference to the tactical situation. With an average of 800 sectarian murders being committed a month, the politicians refused to admit that the country had effectively slid into civil war. The reason that AQ-I could carry on unfettered by the loss of its leaders was due to a unique leadership structure, which did not rely on central decision-making.

McChrystal's paper goes on to explain:

Al Qaeda in Iraq's (AQ-I) lieutenants did not wait for memos from their superiors, much less orders from bin Laden. Decisions were not centralized, but were made quickly and communicated laterally across the organization.

"Zarqawi's fighters were adapted to the areas they haunted, like Fallujah and Qaim in Iraq's western Anbar province, and yet through modern technology were closely linked to the rest of the province and country. Money, propaganda, and information flowed at alarming rates, allowing for powerful, nimble coordination."

Al Qaeda in Iraq had built a leadership model that was highly suited to the VUCA (volatile, uncertain, complex and ambiguous) environment, and so McChrystal countered by building a network, both within Iraq and globally, to counter this capability.

Following the death of Al-Zarqawi, the tide slowly began to turn against Al Qaeda and it became a less dominant force within Iraq under the withering attention of the JSOC team. Whilst the volatile tactical situation remained, it was no longer being orchestrated by AQ-I. So, the JSOC team kept to their 'global' mission and turned their attention to Afghanistan and the Pakistan border region.

Although McChrystal moved on, his legacy remained and, ultimately, they got their man when Bin Laden was finally hunted down in Pakistan in 2011.

From a personal perspective, I have no doubt that this ultimate success owes a great deal to the early and dedicated leadership of McChrystal.

Whilst leaders are naturally remembered for events and victories, the most decisive element of his leadership was in creating a change in culture.

In the midst of a ruthless battle and unwavering political attention, he transformed cold-war paranoia to an inclusive agile network, primed to meet the military challenges of the modern world.

FROM HUMBLE ORIGINS

Paul grew up outside Liverpool, in the north west of England, in a working class family. He was always that little bit different from the crowd and freely admits that he was difficult to control as an adolescent. He always had determination and was never afraid to follow his own path, but he needed to learn to control the frustration that life never appeared to be moving fast enough for him.

Paul saw a different future than the jobs and careers of those around him and his family, although initially he followed the advice of his teachers and built on his academic strengths to qualify as a dentist.

This gave him a respectable profession and career, but Paul was never settled, knowing that he was still searching for something different. His Spikes of courage and the ability to acquire new skills very quickly would mark him out from the pack for the rest of his career.

The call of adventure coupled with his spirit of curiosity led him to the Royal Marines recruitment centre. The Marines instantly spotted his leadership potential and gave him all the encouragement and opportunity to develop and further hone his embryonic – at that time – leadership skills. Having worked with Paul during his time with the Marines, and also having him join a very successful Marketing start-up business, of which I was the non-executive chairman, I have had the privilege of observing him from close proximity.

His ability to absorb complex information and instantly break it down into digestible smaller constituent parts was fine-tuned by his time in the militia. However, it was always there. It was his natural Spike.

His summaries were ruthlessly devoid of any 'flannel' or prose. His ability to listen to all around him with both respect and purpose, and then, having made his mind up, to 'cut directly to the chase' and still take people with him, has become a huge Spike.

Paul is a very special leader. He is prepared to make big and bold decisions having taken the time to share the situation with his colleagues, taken on board their views and can then rapidly formulate the most inclusive, yet decisive course of action.

This sounds a lot like Lt Gen Stanley McChrystal, who he described so eloquently.

Good leaders create followers – great leaders create leaders.

SPIKE SPARKS

Loyalty is everything. The best mentoring relationships are fuelled by mutual confidentiality and respect. If you are getting value from the relationship – value it. Don't take it for granted; fuel it and keep it alive.

If you've never made mistakes, you are probably not pushing hard enough.

Far too many leaders tend to like people who are just like them. Be bold enough to look for those who have Spikes different to your own – this is how high-performing teams are built.

On your way to the top, it is vital you learn to trust your intuition: as you move up, judgment becomes more essential than data.

When was the last time you made a mistake? Owned up to it and consequently enabled others to learn from it? If you are not sharing your errors, then shame on you!

ON THE SAME PAGE

"Teamwork makes the dream work, but a vision becomes a nightmare when the leader has a big dream and a bad team."
– John C. Maxwell

A common and familiar quote is, 'Fail early, and often'. Glenn Llopis explains: "Managing mistakes is much like leading change management. Everyone is in search of the clarity and understanding to minimize risk and discover the short- and long-term rewards of change.

"We focus so much time on maximizing our strengths but not enough time on understanding how and why we fail – which is equally important to success in the marketplace. Becoming the most effective leader requires us to take on the responsibility of dissecting both the why and the how of both our successes and our failures.

"Making mistakes is such an important part of the leadership journey. I am certainly not suggesting being reckless when leading – but be responsible to know why things didn't work in your favour and how you could have approached things differently. Because we live in a more short-term, rapid-paced world of work, we need to be more mindful of pacing ourselves, to take the time to self-evaluate and learn from our mistakes."[36]

Jack Welch, author of *Jack: straight from the Gut*, says that "When people make mistakes, the last thing they need is discipline. It's time for encouragement and confidence building. The job at this point is to restore self-confidence. I think 'piling on' when someone is down is one of the worst things any of us can do."

"True leadership lies in guiding others to success – in ensuring that everyone is performing at their best, doing the work they are pledged to do and doing it well." – Bill Owens

---

[36] Glenn Llopis (2015) "4 Reasons Great Leaders Admit Their Mistakes" (online) *Forbes / Leadership*. Available at: http://www.forbes.com/sites/glennllopis/2015/07/23/4-reasons-great-leaders- admit-their-mistakes/#6aaa177f7e21 [Accessed 23 Apr 2016]

CHAPTER XV

~~SHAVE STANDARDS.~~

SHOOT FOR TOTAL COMMITMENT

Despair is readily available to all of us. Hope is so much tougher to access every day – but it's so worth the effort.

What's your personal vision or mantra that keeps you full of hope and moving forward every day?

Change has a way of bringing out the best, the worst and the 'so-so' in people. The 'iffy' behavior – this 'so-so' stuff – occurs when people make a habit out of shaving standards and dropping them, in their efforts to cope.

Pressed to keep up with change – to do more with less – some people play fast and loose. They shrug off the idea of excellence in an effort to pick up a little speed.

Scrambling to cover the necessary ground, they make sacrifices in the quality of their performance. If everyone was playing to their Spikes, the collaboration and interdependency would catch this careless behaviour instantly.

The slippage begins when employees cut themselves some slack. They excuse themselves for giving less than their best and thus create a culture of mediocrity.

Considering the circumstances – the pressure, the stress, all the new demands – they rationalise that it's okay to go the quick-and-dirty route, to settle for lower commitment to their work – or to relax on issues relating to ethics and integrity.

Maybe there's even a little revenge at work here sometimes. For example, shaving standards is a way of getting even with life or the organization, when you don't like what's going on.

Shaving standards doesn't look like a major violation. But when enough people get lax in the chase to get things done, theirs and the organization's reputation get a little shabby. Customers start to drift towards the competition. Naturally, this puts you and the organization at even greater risk.

Find your Spikes. Raise your standards and pursue a culture of total commitment. Make no compromises in your personal ethics, the caliber of your output, or your overall productivity. Instead of accepting less than your best, improve on it. Reach for new and higher benchmarks. Stay on the highroad with your ethical standards.

Don't tolerate 'so-so' performance, in yourself or anybody else. Energise each other's Spikes.

Now, during the tough times, is when you really define the character of the culture; and the organization with the most leaders, capitalising on their differing Spikes, wins.

"YOU CAN PUT YOUR BOOTS IN THE OVEN, BUT THAT DON'T MAKE THEM BISCUITS."

DALLAS DJ ON COUNTRY RADIO 105.3 FM

MORE MUTUAL MENTORING

Some of our richest relationships are delivered through the strangest of circumstances, but only if we are bold enough to allow and enable them to happen.

As I sat waiting to have my haircut at Andy's barber shop in Paddington, west London, I considered that the shop had certainly seen better days. Like many black barber shops around London, they were more than just mere shops – they were a regular meeting point at the heart of the community for the local men.

This was a little different to the standard black barber shop, as the founder and owner, Andy, was a proud Greek Cypriot. He had arrived in Paddington armed only with the half crown (12.5 pence) coin that his father had given him before putting him on the plane to London from Nicosia back in 1974. He found the means to rent the shop and taught himself how to cut black hair. He soon became a popular mainstay and stalwart of the local community – everybody knew Andy.

My father had taken me to the shop many years ago. I was to find myself frequenting Andy's, after my regular local barber had suddenly been taken from us by throat cancer.

I loved the cut and thrust of the extremely quick-witted customers. Andy and his sidekick, Ron, were merciless catalysts for endless fun and satire. Andy's shop was ageless and classless and despite being a black barber, it was inclusive and friendly. Youngsters of all races would come in for the latest 'hip hop' shaved styles.

On a Saturday morning in early 2011, I overheard a conversation about a British title fight. Black barber shops are loud and vibrant centres of male camaraderie. Conversations are interrupted, arguments are the norm and you quickly decide whether to sit quietly and decently away from the fray, or become instantly embroiled.

Without any malice or forethought, I jumped into the conversation about the British title fight. Andy asked a softly spoken man with his hood over his head to repeat what he had said about the title fight. He instantly closed down and bowed his head and never spoke again. He appeared sullen and withdrawn.

How could someone with such an apparently negative disposition be fighting for the British boxing light-welterweight title? Andy gently asked the boxer again to explain to me what he did and what lay ahead. He said nothing at all.

Something just didn't add up. Andy was an excellent judge of character and he obviously and manifestly really liked and had time for this distant man.

I offered to take the barbers to see the fight and offer the boxer, Ashley, some local support. He was still clearly unimpressed and indifferent towards me. Why? Whilst there was absolutely no reason whatsoever for him to engage with me or even to be polite, still, to go out of his way to totally blank me seemed very odd behaviour.

We had great ringside seats, but I didn't enjoy seeing Ashley being hit. It was obvious that he was operating on the tightest of budgets. His corner was spartan and there was hardly any support for him in the cavernous Wembley Arena. However, it was impossible to miss the steely-eyed determination and focus which was written all over Ashley's face.

He entered the ring to a chorus of boos. It felt like the auditorium was full of the Champion's fans. The Champion had a loud and vociferous corner of the arena full of his boisterous local following. Even the neutrals were jeering our stone-faced man and cheering for Lenny Daws, the Champion.

Ashley was not in any way intimidated; he stood upright and unmoved. The more the crowd cheered Lenny, the harder Ashley fought. Before long, he had worked Lenny out and, having put him down twice in the 9th round, went on win a unanimous victory. I didn't enjoy seeing him in some of the torrid exchanges – it is a brutal sport. But I had nothing but admiration for him. He came out into the crowd amongst us wearing his prized Lonsdale belt, which is given only to British champions.

I shared and enjoyed his pride. He was transformed. Pumped up by his win, he couldn't stop talking and he was bright, positive and very engaging. I just listened and observed. This was the man the public needed to see. How could you not admire and support such a decent and hard-working individual?

His secret was out – and I was determined to let the rest of the world in on his best-kept secret. This engaging genie was never going back in the bottle.

On my next visit to the shop, Andy was delivering his usual dose of cutting sarcasm to his loyal clientele and thoroughly enjoying himself. Once the shop had emptied, he sat down and spoke privately to me about Ashley.

He said "these kids lived on a 'diet of disappointment'. Ashley especially." Andy explained how every now and again someone "turns up and offers him support and then lets him down again and disappears".

He didn't need to say anything else – I left him my business card to give to Ashley.

ASHLEY'S STORY

It's just another normal day. A Friday or Saturday, as I always try to get my hair cut for the weekend. Something about personal pride means looking good over the weekend, even though I don't go to the clubs. I'm just training, as usual.

In essence, just another day.

But I can still remember this particular day clearly, just like it was yesterday. I'm sitting on the old worn-out leather seats in my local barber shop; Andy has not refurbished the shop in years, but it's still home to me. I wouldn't have it any other way. There's better looking barber shops, but I had my very first haircut here. This is my barbershop. Andy is my barber.

I'm busy and distracted on my BlackBerry phone, messaging someone or just playing with the functions.

Andy starts talking to a man sitting opposite me. He tells the man I'm a boxer and that I'm fighting for the British title soon. The man replies, "Is he any good? Will he win?"

Andy tells him I'm training in America and that I beat Danny Garcia (who would go on to win a world title) a year ago, but was robbed. I'm sitting there, listening, but not joining into the conversation.

The man tells Andy, "Do you want to go to his title fight? I'll buy us some ringside tickets."

The last thing I would have ever thought is that this man and I would go on to build a friendship founded on trust and loyalty.

He was a successful busines man. I was a young man doing okay in my chosen profession; of course I could be doing better, but I was on my own. And in my profession, you can only do so much on your own.

So the man comes back the following week and tells Andy he's bought some ringside tickets.

I won the British title in style. Lenny Daws was dominant at that time in Britain. I was the world-travelled fighter and the world number four fighter, but I was still the underdog in Britain. I couldn't help feeling that this was disrespectful.

On February 19th 2011, I became British champion. A day I'll never forget. For years the British boxing industry had shut its doors on me. This was my opportunity to show all those promoters who had never given me a chance, that they had made a mistake.

The man who had bought ringside tickets for himself and for the guys in the barbershop had left his business card with Andy. He'd told Andy he'd like to help me.

I didn't know how he could ever help me. In my mind, I didn't need his help. I was world-ranked. I was British Champion. I was guaranteed some nice paydays in Britain now. These British fighters couldn't beat me.

But Andy, whom I've always respected, told me, "Just meet him – he's a good guy." So I eventually emailed this man called René Carayol. I had nothing to lose by meeting this man. When you're doing good, everyone wants to be part of your team. It's when you need help that there's no one around you.

I'd been on my own for years, so I'm used to relying on myself for help. But I thought, "Let me see what this man wants."

So we arranged to meet up. I met him at Andy's. I got into his nice car and he drove me to his house in Swiss Cottage.

He lived the opposite to me. A life of relative luxury. I've never known any form of luxury in my life. I was born into poverty. Being poor is normal to me. He had a nice house. I didn't know what this man did or who he was.

I was just there to listen and then go home.

René mentioned how I'd won the British title, but the media was more focused on Lenny Daws losing his title. That didn't especially bother me. The British public have, unfortunately, never shown me any love or even made me feel wanted.

René said how he believed in me and that I put in a very good performance, which should have gathered more love and certainly more acknowledgement. He went on about helping me get my name out there and building a 'brand'. I never knew what this 'brand' thing was before him. But it would be something that would stay in my mind for years to come.

This 'brand' he had in mind soon became who I really am.

René said he'd like a 'trial run'. I'd work with him to meet his tight timescale. He would arrange a photo-shoot and he said he would build me a new website. If I then wanted to part ways afterwards, then I could, with NO strings attached.

In my mind, I had nothing to lose. I would get a new website out of it and I would get to do a photo-shoot. Why not?

AGAINST ALL THE ODDS

Trust is something earned, not given, so René and I had an interesting start.

I didn't trust the man's motives. Why help me? What was he getting out of it? In my line of work, fighters are always being taken advantage of. There are former world champions, like Iran Barkley, who made millions, but ended up penniless and homeless.

So, weeks and months went by. René and I would meet up for lunch on a Saturday afternoon, after I finished my morning workout at All Stars Boxing Club. He would drive us to one of his favourite restaurants, Mediterraneo, in swanky Notting Hill.

We would talk about my week and his plans for me. Many of his plans, and his vision, I just didn't (or couldn't) believe in, but over the years the majority have actually come to fruition.

He put a new tailored suit on me; we had a fabulous photo-shoot and I, obviously, looked the part. The photographers, Amit and Naroop, clearly loved the session and we have since also become good friends, and they have worked with me on a number of assignments since.

To my surprise he had a director and cameraman also in the studio, and I soon learned that he was also an experienced BBC TV presenter. He somehow set me at ease and we had a fascinating and revealing conversation – on camera. It all seemed very easy going and he managed to encourage me to answer all his questions brutally honestly and from the heart.

As soon as we had stopped shooting, René's team who had obviously been through this process with many of his clients before, just broke out into spontaneous applause. It felt good and the positive atmosphere made it even better. This interview became the signature part of the new website that he and his team had designed and built for me.

I'm not sure what he had seen or felt but he was really energized and excited at the prospect of working with me.

He encouraged me to write a regular blog. I'm not sure how he knew that I loved writing because I had never shared that with anyone. I was soon sharing my thoughts, hopes, dreams and frustrations with my growing number of followers on Twitter and leading them to my website.

Before long, many boxing platforms started asking to publish my blogs – nearly all were in the USA; we even had a Canadian boxing site asking for my blog. Strangely, hardly any requests came from the UK!

I have to admit, the photos were fantastic. The photographers certainly knew their stuff. They had made me relax and smile. We laughed a lot and they caught the real essence of who I am. Chris, the tailor, was also a champion in his own field. He couldn't do enough for me. He was also calm and charming. He had prepared me a total collection: the suit, shirts, ties, cufflinks – he was a professional with everything at his disposal.

I looked (and felt) so different. The photos were telling their own story, but it was really my story.

René declared that we were now ready to take me "out there". He was very pleased with my early blogs, and the photo-shoot had given him the ammunition he was looking for. The video was the main bait and it was all working to plan.

René stated that we owned the copyright to all we had done and would now give it all away freely to any media companies or journalists who were interested. Photos, copy and videos – all high quality and all readily available.

BUILD IT AND THEY WILL COME

One of my early sponsors, Vitabiotics, the UK's leading nutrition business, saw this new imagery and 'brand' and asked if they could now feature me in their magazine promotions for their Wellman vitamins. The magazine adverts were everywhere: GQ, Esquire, Boxing News, Men's Fitness and many more.

Before long, the adverts were transferred to local and national billboards – I would have photos of the adverts sent to me from all over the UK. The adverts were now on the sides of trains, in underground stations and in many other places.

My new image was everywhere. Without René this wouldn't have been possible. It's funny how much you can achieve with a little bit of help and someone believing in you. I'd achieved a fair amount in boxing, reaching this point on my own. I'd been ranked world number four, become British champion, won boxing matches in five different countries, and fought some of the best fighters of my generation in boxing – all on my own.

But now, René was helping me take that next step. He wanted me to be known by normal everyday people – those that had zero interest in boxing. He insisted that I could be a strong role model for many who came from the most humble of origins and had very few positive 'local' role models.

We had discussed how we could better capitalize upon my new image and more confident appearance. He took me to see the head of 'brand' at Ted Baker, the highly successful British fashion brand at their HQ in north London.

As usual, René did all the talking. I would sometimes blush at the way he talked about me. It took me a while to eventually accept that the person he described with such pride and praise was actually really me. Ted Baker have provided me with a wide collection of their best gear and we really do 'suit' each other (if you will excuse the pun).

"The Best of British Boxing wears the Best of British Clothing."

By May 2012 I was no longer British champion. It took a very controversial decision and I had lost my title. Even the fighter who was given the benefit of this decision told me that he thought I had won the fight.

This was no longer acceptable. I had had enough of British boxing. I felt strongly that I'd been robbed and cheated by the powers that be – far too many times now. I headed back to America for a win in North Carolina.

My new promoter, Ricky Hatton, had put me on his comeback show. I warmed up all night, only to be told I wasn't fighting. I was still paid – but that was a small consolation. It was the last straw. I packed my bags and travelled to Luxembourg just after Christmas, picking up a title for my troubles.

René was at ringside on his own to watch me win.

I had some deep thinking to do about what I was going to do next. I couldn't rely on British boxing, if I did – I'd have to retire.

MY AMERICAN DREAM

It was time to think big and realise that there was no risk-free approach to which ever direction I chose.

The Money Team! Las Vegas.

Floyd Mayweather had been so nice to me the year before, when I visited Las Vegas to train and workout for two weeks – I just had to go back. That was my only option. No promoter in Europe was willing to give me a serious opportunity.

René fully agreed with me. He supported me with some resources for my training camp out in Las Vegas. I was on my own again, but somehow it felt like the right thing at the right time. Floyd clearly remembered me from the first day I returned to his gym.

I killed myself for two months in Las Vegas. I engaged in fearsome sparring daily, with the biggest names in the gym. World champions, former world champions, contenders and Olympians.

I held my own with everyone.

Word soon got back to Floyd, and he confided in me that he could help my career.

He agreed that I had been robbed against Danny Garcia, and knew that I'd been an opponent for ten years but had still racked up a respectable 33 wins and five losses.

He invited me to his fight against Robert Guerrero at the MGM Grand in Las Vegas. After the fight, he called me over and told me, in front of the media, that I was "his fighter". This was an unsolicited and nearly unbelievable compliment.

Two months later, he told me that I would be opening up his next Pay Per View telecast. I thanked him; it was a dream come true. To be signed to a legend. It was his choice (and his choice alone) to sign me.

I was also on his sparring team for his mega-fight with Saul Alvarez. The first time we sparred, I remember getting into the ring, looking across and seeing Floyd Mayweather. That was an incredible feeling: to be sharing the ring with this all-time great.

On August 1st 2013, when I was officially signed to Mayweather Promotions, I went out for a run with Floyd and thanked him for the opportunity. He told me that he believed I would be World Champion someday and that I'd beat Adrian Broner, the then-undefeated welterweight world champion. I just thanked Floyd again and kept running.

Floyd showed his belief in me by matching me against the tough and highly ranked Pablo Cesar Cano. A two-time world title challenger. The man had bricks in his hands. I went on to lose a hard-fought split decision.

Floyd could have easily dropped me after losing my first fight with him – I would have understood. But instead he said, "Don't worry Ashley. Get some wins and you'll be back."

So I did just that. I won six fights straight over the next two years, knowing and believing that my ultimate test would come. My career-defining fight. The super fight I craved. The dream fight I'd wanted as a child. I'd dreamt about fighting for a world title and now it was coming.

Thirty years after telling my Mum and Dad that I wanted to be a boxer, my ultimate test arrived.

Adrien Broner won his fourth world title and immediately called me out. It gets no bigger (or better) than that. A highly charged and lively five months of build-up followed.

Floyd even came to London and told the UK media that I would be world champion.

The build-up was everything to me. I gave my all in training camp. This is what my career had been destined for. Despite the low and lonely moments when I hadn't been able to get a fight in the UK, I'd never stopped believing. I'd known I had no future there.

I always knew I'd have to go America to achieve my goals.

Thirty minutes before my fight with Adrien, Floyd came into my dressing room. He told JP to stop filming. He sat down and spoke to me like he had never done before.

He told me that I now had "a chance to change my life, a chance to be part of boxing history. Some fighters never get this opportunity." He told me to "give everything you've got in every round. If you're not happy with what your trainer wants you to do in the ring, let him know."

He said, "This is for your parents, your Mum and Dad." The talk was hugely motivational and quite emotional for me. Floyd spoke to me for maybe 20 minutes. I listened intensely and took everything in.

I gave my all during the fight. It felt like the fight was close. He'd win some rounds then I'd come back and win some. I was outworking him, but he had the power advantage. He was explosive.

I got hit with an uppercut, I moved away to the other side of the ring. Adrien chased me and swung a left hook to my groin. I looked at the referee, Luis Pabon, and raised my hand to complain about the low blow, but, incredibly, he stopped the fight.

He would say afterwards that he thought I was quitting. Why would I quit when I'd just won the previous two rounds?

I shouted "No! No! I'm alright! I'm alright!" But he'd stopped the fight. His mistake had cost me the fight.

Floyd came up to the ring and hugged me. He said, "I'm proud of you. A few wins and you'll fight for the world title again."

Most people don't see the good that Floyd does. He has definitely helped change my life for the better.

In the following weeks, many fans would tell me they thought I was winning, the fight was a draw or I was starting to take over.

It felt close from where I stood. It was tough and grueling – we gave each other no respite whatsoever. I'm proud of myself. I wanted to give my all – to give my best – and I did. I held my own with a young legend for eight rounds.

Without René Carayol this might not have been possible. He's backed me and helped me along the way. I did the work to get onto TMT. I won the fights to get the world title shot, but René has always been there in the background. Whenever I've needed him, he's never let me down.

I'm very fortunate to have some inspirational men in my life: Isola Akay, René Carayol and Floyd Mayweather.

My experience has taught me that you have to be incredibly mentally strong to pursue your goals. People will always tell you that you 'can't do this' or you 'can't do that'. The majority of the time, you're doing far better than the people trying to put doubt in your mind are.

Stay strong. Believe in yourself and give your best.

I remember back in 2011 being interviewed by René; he asked me on camera whether I really thought I could win a world title. I was positive that I could fight for the world title but it seemed so far away then, that it was too hard to really imagine it happening.

So to eventually challenge for it, against the biggest name in the division, was one of the most significant of milestones in my life. Even if we didn't get the result we desired.

To get to that level is success and a grand achievement.

I've battled the odds all my life, coming from where I grew up in London, where broken dreams surrounded me as a kid. Low employment rates were the norm – nearly everyone I knew was on state benefits for the unemployed. High crime was all around us.

Given the context and the circumstances, I'm a success.

I intend to be even more successful after boxing. I want to contribute by managing the next generation of fighters, helping them to achieve their dreams, opening gyms around the inner city of London, touring the world speaking about my career and telling people how to fulfill their ambitions.

I want to continue to beat the odds.

You can do so much good on your own – but with a team you can do great things. My career showed me that. I did well on my own, but having René Carayol and Floyd Mayweather behind me lifted me to the highest of heights.

TRUST

The tailor I'd had for years had taken complete control of Ashley's outfit. Chris is the ultimate perfectionist and he always delivers.

As soon as Ashley put on the tailored suit, he looked the part. I stepped over and, knotted his tie carefully and properly. Something instantly changed. He was now fully present and what a presence!

All his anxiety just evaporated, and this charming, handsome and intelligent man just instantly appeared to trust me.

I went for a hard-hitting and no nonsense type interview,

but with an unwavering and friendly smile on my face. He was focused, honest, and quite remarkable. He had a story to tell and could tell it effortlessly.

His smile was a million dollars and when he spoke so sincerely about his mother, the studio instantly lit up.

My very discerning team, without thought, just broke out into sustained applause and cheering.

A star was born.

We played the video back and watched it, unedited, together. Was it just chemistry? Was it a mutual understanding and respect? I don't really know, but I do know that when it happens, you must walk towards – walk towards your complementary Spikes.

We've been together as a team ever since. The genie had escaped the bottle – forever.

Ashley was right from the start; we were opposites, but perhaps not in the way he initially thought.

Ashley has a deep resilience and determination, like no other person I've ever met. He's careful and thorough. He's not shy, but he's no extrovert. He's the most reliable and dependable friend one could ever wish for. Coupled with his intellect and charm, he has an amazing set of Spikes and we continue to bring the best out in each other.

"CHALLENGES ARE GIFTS THAT FORCE US TO SEARCH FOR A NEW CENTER OF GRAVITY. DON'T FIGHT THEM. JUST FIND A DIFFERENT WAY TO STAND."

OPRAH WINFREY

SPIKE SPARKS

Your attitude determines your altitude.

Always aim to be the best you can be. You may not achieve it all the time, but you will always feel better for having given your best.

Bring in some really 'scary' people – but ensure you support them as they are often in danger of being marginalized or ostracized.

Establish an inspiring personal dream or vision for this year, thinking as BIG as you can. Then ensure you spend a little time every day, taking just one step closer to that compelling dream; others will then start to be energized by your vision.

Why do losing football teams have so many injuries? When teams are winning, everybody wants to play – despite the niggling injuries. Winning soothes many pains and ailments. Winning is infectious, habit-forming, fun, and so much better than losing.

ON THE SAME PAGE

"Leadership is lifting a person's vision to high sights, the raising of a person's performance to a higher standard, the building of a personality beyond its normal limitations." – Peter Drucker

In an interview with Gary Insull (Champions Club Community Founder), Brian Tracy stated, "One leadership requirement is the ability to focus excellence. A commitment to excellence is one of the most powerful of all motivators. All leaders who inspire people and change organizations are enthusiastic about achieving excellence in a particular area.[37] As a leader, your job is to be excellent at what you do, to be the best in your chosen field. Have a vision of high standards in serving people. You not only exemplify excellence in your own behavior, but you also translate it to others so that they, too, become committed to your vision."

Harvard Business Review article of 2010 states that "As team members earn small wins, their confidence grows and seemingly insurmountable problems appear less daunting. Roadblocks become interesting puzzles for the team to solve."[38]

Mentors act in a way to shake up their mentees' thinking processes. Erik Thompson explains that, "They develop penetrating insights about the professional blind spots of those they want to develop, and then challenge people to face them. Along with technical and business skills, they pay attention to people skills. Whether a talented team member is hesitant or arrogant, clumsy-with-ambition or talented-but-lazy, true mentors skillfully put what they see on the table.

Great mentors 'go for it' when it comes to giving people all the insight they have in the service of professional growth. The question: Do you want to know what I think about you? is not out of bounds. Subordinates are wondering anyway, and they will make up the answers if they are not hearing them directly. True mentors are blessed with the opportunity to evaluate how various team members respond to this level of challenge. The most mature rise up to meet it; the least mature can't handle it.[39]

---

[37] Tracy, B. (2009) "As a leader, what does doing your best really mean?" (online) Taugher – Change Catalyst Consulting. Available at: http://www.taugher.com/What-Does-Doing-Your-Best-Really- Mean.htm [Accessed 22 Apr 2016]

[38] Wiseman, L. and McKeown, G. (2010) "Managing Yourself: Bringing Out the Best in Your People"(online), *Harvard Business Review*

[39] Thompson, E. (2010) "How to Be a Better Mentor" (online) *Journal of Accountancy*. Available at: http://www.journalofaccountancy.com/issues/2010/nov/20091446.html [Accessed 22 Apr 2016]

CHAPTER XVI
~~BLAME OTHERS FOR WHAT YOU DON'T LIKE.~~ TAKE RESPONSIBILITY FOR FIXING THINGS

Don't waste time and spirit on blaming others. Figure out what you can do really well to alleviate the pressure. When do you ever look for guidance and direction from those who are junior to you, or just different from you? They have Spikes too.

Today's accelerating rate of change is like a breeder reactor for problems. That's just the nature of progress. But as people watch one problem give birth to several more, they start searching for somebody to blame.

Badmouthing those in authority and the bosses becomes a favourite pastime.

Pointing fingers becomes the most popular form of exercise. The growing number of problems proves nothing, but is offered as hard evidence that the changes are wrong, or that the changes are being managed poorly. The changes are therefore not for you.

Of course, none of this has a crying chance of slowing down change, or reducing the rate of problems. All it does is create a culture of blame.

Blaming comes easy. Complaining is a cakewalk. But this culture needs encouragers instead of complainers, fixers rather than blamers. Blaming uses up a lot of energy, but doesn't provide any real relief. Rather than lightening anyone's load, it just creates additional burdens.

Often blaming is employed as a defensive tactic. Pointing your finger at another person diverts attention from yourself. Accuse someone else of taking the wrong action, and that sort of gives you grounds for expecting them to fix things you don't like.

Overall, blaming is a devious way of delegating responsibility. Rather than offer solid help to resolve problems, you put the 'monkey' on someone else's back. Start believing it's YOUR problem, but the team can help.

Identifying problems is fine. Just make sure you package top-notch solutions with your complaints. Come up with constructive ideas of your own, instead of waiting for somebody else to fix things. Own up to where you are not at your best – quickly and honestly.

Get busy doing what you can do instead of second-guessing somebody else's efforts.

'Monday morning quarterbacking' gives some people the notion that they're contributing something meaningful, but it's just a cheap, backhanded way of throwing more blame.

Spend the time identifying your own Spikes, and start to find a new path, based on the things you know you excel in, and the future will instantly start to feel better.

Simultaneously identify and inspire those whose Spikes complement your own.

There are more than enough problems to go around, so take your share of the responsibility for fixing things. Push for a culture of personal accountability and push your Spikes to the forefront of all you do – whilst recognizing those who differ and excel at what you do not.

That's Leadership.

"DON'T YOU WISH YOU WERE ME?
I KNOW I DO."

SIGN TAPED ABOVE ELEVATOR BUTTON IN OFFICE BUILDING

IT TAKES TWO

Things were going very well at Dixon's: I was being allowed more and more freedom to act and my confidence was at an all-time high. We didn't really have a day-to-day boss; Terry was engrossed in 'strategy', so we did all the work.

I loved the confidence Terry had in us, and there was absolutely no way that I would abuse that trust. In fact, it was quite the opposite. We worked forever harder. Kin and I were the only two analyst programmers on the team; he had such a marvelous work ethic and was also ultracompetitive.

Kin was from Hong Kong, and we could not have been more different. Kin was usually first in the office with his head stuck in the Financial Times. He had learned to play the stock markets and was obsessed with the movement of shares of 'Mid Cap' companies. As soon as I arrived he would hit me with all his thoughts and bets that he was thinking of placing. He was so enthusiastic that I just had to take an interest. My growing understanding of his world cemented our friendship.

He was exceedingly bright and could crash out code at top speed. He treated his work the way many would treat a crossword. It was a temporary challenge and, once solved, was forgotten about as he moved to the next challenge. He was fast and always cracked the problem at hand, but when things changed (as they always did), he could never amend his existing program but would have to start all over again.

The approach that I had been so painstakingly taught by Geoff was paying off yet again. Geoff had called it 'functional decomposition', or 'tree structure' – the branches could be changed quickly and effectively without ever having to change the 'trunk'. It was elegant and reusable because of its modular design. Kin dismissed it as "over-engineering". We would argue and laugh about our differing approaches.

One day, Kin was in early again and couldn't wait for me to arrive. He just couldn't contain himself. He had won big with his latest gamble on stock picking. He had won enough to buy himself a really smart, bright red Alfa Romeo sports hatchback car. Sharp, high performance sporty hatchbacks were all the rage back then, and he was hugely proud.

The following day we went for a spin at lunchtime. What a car! I found myself being as pleased and proud as Kin was. He was really surprised that I was proud and not envious. He was hoping that I would be massively jealous. Again, we laughed and our bond became even closer.

Our workload started to increase, and there were so many changes to the requirements that Kin was falling behind, as he had to rewrite his programs nearly every couple of days.

It wasn't long afterwards that I could hear myself repeating Geoff's words of wisdom and patient approach. I shared with Kin how to design his programs using a method similar to the one I had learned from the master coder.

It was somehow strange for me to become Kin's coach and mentor, but I had learned from the best and we now became a truly formidable team. We sliced through any and all changes at great pace and competed fiercely, whilst never letting our rivalry damage our friendship.

We hardly ever saw Terry, but we rarely let him down. A year flew by. I loved coming into work, our camaraderie blossomed, and then, surprisingly, I was promoted. This hurt Kin badly. I felt for him and we both fought together to have him promoted as well.

On a bitterly cold winter day, Kin insisted that we went out for dinner that evening. He of course would be driving us in his swish Alfa Romeo. Kin was not one for bothering to wash or clean the car. The appalling winter weather had rusted his prized sports hatchback, and as we approached it, he confessed that the two doors had become so corroded with rust that they could no longer be opened. We both climbed in via the hatchback rear door. It really did look like we were breaking into the car.

We clambered out on all fours when we reached his favourite Chinese restaurant and fell out on the snow-covered road.

As we ate and our conversation moved to work, he confessed that he would be leaving to go back to Hong Kong with his girlfriend. I was devastated.

He said that they had decided to get married back in Hong Kong, from where they both originated.

Deep down, we both knew that he couldn't work in the environment any more, as no one would tell him what he had to do to be promoted. He was just constantly told all the things he was not that good at. He had been given a 12-month Personal Development Plan that was fixated on his 'Areas for Improvement'. He wanted a plan for promotion. Why could no one see his towering, problem-solving strengths?

The following day I went to see Terry. He was a kind and calm man, but obsessed with what could go wrong. He just couldn't understand why I was so keen for Kin to be promoted too.

Eventually, I found myself with our HR officer. At least Terry indulged me by listening to my case for Kin. But, as far as the company was concerned, Kin's Spikes of hard work, commitment, loyalty, plus his ability to crack any and all problems at pace, stood for nothing at all compared to his perceived 'weaknesses'.

When Kin left, I knew my time was also coming to a close. I had lost my partner with complementary Spikes, and our once-brilliant environment had lost its sparkle.

By now, I was an avid reader of the Computer press. They were flooded with appointments pages. Every company appeared to be recruiting for their young IT departments. Marks and Spencer (M&S) were on a massive recruitment drive and they were offering mouth-watering packages. I had never noticed their ads before. How could I have missed them? Well, easily in fact, as I had been far too busy enjoying working at Dixons.

My brother in law, Owen, had a really good friend who I knew worked at M&S. The next time Owen came over to the

pushed themselves even further than the previous year, which had been an outstanding one.

At that moment, he noticed me standing by the stage and asked me what I was doing in the conference room. I don't think, at this point in my career I had ever seen a Board Director, and certainly had never spoken to one, so in a choking voice I muttered, "Just ensuring everything is okay."

Joe said with a mischievous smile: "I thought that was my job", and everybody laughed. It broke the ice and the collective anxiety, but at my cost. Seeing that I was clearly embarrassed, feeling small and looking out of place, he asked me what my name was. I just managed to mumble my reply: "René."

He asked me to come and join him at the front on the stage. He announced that, "René will be performing the review with me." For a moment, I could neither breathe nor move.

I had barely sat down and already he was asking me in front of everyone to state my job title and where I worked.

He then asked me what I thought of the range. Not seasoned enough to understand the politics of the situation, I took the question at face value and answered, "Not bad at all, but I have to say that I thought it was much better before they made the final changes before you arrived."

I had been there earlier when lots of the really creative displays were removed on the sharp instruction of a late arriving senior manager. I sensed that those who had spent the night carefully putting these garments up with such care and attention to detail were crushed by this rather sweeping diktat.

With very little understanding of the bigger picture or the politically correct approach, I responded to Joe's gentle probing and told him everything 'unvarnished' in front of the Lingerie department's finest!

Despite my gauche style and language, it was an unbelievable moment. This was a huge learning point for me: when things are going well, it should never just be about the task at hand; it is vital to always spare a thought for the feelings of others. This was a lesson that was about to be brought alive for me by a true master operator.

Joe went on to provide individual feedback regarding almost all of the garments. He commented on the quality of the fabric, colours, pricing, volume and who the manufacturer was. He consistently used the most positive and encouraging language, but after a while even I could work out that he wasn't pleased with what he saw.

He was saying things like, "I can see what you are trying to achieve, but can you think about it again please?" or "I really like the fabric, but I'm not so sure about that particular shade," and "I completely understand why you are being this ambitious on these garments, but maybe you've pushed it that little bit too far."

This went on for nearly three hours.

He was jovial, well-mannered and good-humoured, but in the end he totally decimated the range. Crucially, he did this without ruining morale or making any individual feel as though they had wasted their time and efforts. It was a master class of how to deliver tough feedback without ruining the feelings of those who had worked so hard, but had got it wrong.

At the end he stood up, with me by his side, and gave a beautiful summary that motivated everyone to try that little bit harder and said he would be back in three weeks for another review. He delivered this so authentically and sincerely that the chastised audience were encouraged to look forward and become excited about having to do it all over again. Now, this was inspirational leadership.

This was the first time in my career I had actually been in the presence of a great leader.

It was a master class of sensitive and positive communication, underpinned by a strong emotional connection, which was conveyed through Joe's incredible humility. He made it so easy for someone in my position, as a relatively new and junior manager, to bridge the gap with him, a fully-fledged board director of the UK's most admired company. I so wanted to be able to do that. Who doesn't want to be liked and admired?

As we walked out of the conference room, an opportunity not to be missed presented itself to me; on impulse, I asked Joe if he would be my mentor. Was it courage that gripped me? Was it a special insight? Who knows? As far as I was concerned, it was the effect his behaviour had on me. It just instantly reflected what I inherently believed was the right way to get things done.

The feeling inside of me could not be denied, and I just had to act or I would regret it forever. I might not have this golden opportunity again and I certainly could not live with that.

Joe was not sure what was involved in being a 'mentor'. I myself had only found out a few weeks before from reading an article in *The Economist*.

I quickly responded with a short analogy, comparing our situations to that of the young King Arthur and Merlin. He smiled out loud, and we agreed that I would meet him in his office for a chicken salad lunch the following week; he committed to sparing me one hour.

Before turning away down the corridor, he shared how this would work: I had to book the meetings in advance with his PA, Sue, set the agenda, and everything we discussed would be totally confidential.

The onus and accountability would clearly reside with me. He had already started: he had given me trust and ownership. What an opportunity!

I strode away, feeling six inches taller. After turning the corner, I sprinted back to my office. I instantly dived across the desk and grabbed the telephone. I dialled Sue's number and a warm and friendly voice listened to my breathless delivery. Sue responded, "Is that René?" How had she known? She replied, "Joe called and mentioned that you might call me immediately."

Come the following Thursday, I sat in Joe's secretary's office a full 30 minutes prior to our appointment. Sue knew that I was both nervous and excited at the same time. She shared with me that Joe was the best boss she had ever had, and that he was as much looking forward to our lunch as I was. Her Spikes were clear for me to see and benefit from.

After a short while, she invited me into Joe's office; there was a small table laid out tidily for lunch for two, with two chicken salads carefully prepared and wrapped in cling film. Joe came over from behind his desk and invited me to join him at the table and he instantly proceeded to give me a damn good listening to.

He picked over his salad, saying little, but coaxing everything out of me. It was amazing how much I blurted out and in no sort of order. I tried to remain methodical and structured in my delivery, but he was skilled at getting me to switch subjects, to go ever deeper, and the honesty just sailed out in return.

In no time at all, I was realising the power of really listening. Joe not only heard everything I said, but he played it back in a language I could only dream of using. After about 40 minutes, he had stopped eating and after encouraging me to eat, it was his turn to speak. I just listened to every word and every pause, and digested absolutely everything. He knew so much; he'd achieved so much and, most of all, he appeared to completely understand and empathize with my career dilemmas and concerns. Time seemed to just evaporate when I was in his company.

I wanted to be like Joe. His candour was delivered with total sensitivity but, vitally, he never avoided honest feedback. Unbelievable brilliance – this was it.

When I left his office, I was now a full 12 inches taller.

I went back to my office and wrote everything down. This was easy, as he had made it such an unforgettable experience.

We were to meet for a further two years, every month on a Thursday, in his office with me setting the agenda and him providing the wisdom and the chicken salad. A monthly master class that always made me feel 'hungry for more'.

Amazingly, I was promoted three times during my time there, and I just know it was because Joe had enabled me to understand how to better 'navigate' the complex business that was M&S. But even more than that, I'd had the benefit of close proximity to a fabulous role model, with no feeling of training or studying whatsoever.

Very powerful indeed. I never missed a moment of his advice, let alone missed a mentoring meeting.

At what would be our last lunch, Joe shared that he could no longer mentor me. I was devastated – what had I done wrong? He never gave me a reason, but said it would all make sense shortly.

A month or so later it was announced that I would be moving from IT to Menswear as a merchandiser. This was a dream come true for me. Most of the board directors at M&S were merchandisers by training. I just knew, having been carefully coached by Joe, that without the experience and wisdom that commercial acumen brings, at M&S I couldn't get to the top.

Joe had moved from Ladies' Lingerie to lead Menswear. I would effectively now be working in his new area. Unfortunately, even I could work out that it was a potential conflict of interest, as I effectively now reported to him. It was a fantastic opportunity to be working in Menswear, but in retrospect, for me it was less about working in Menswear and more about having Joe as a leader.

I was initially placed in Men's Leisurewear. Ray was the Senior Selector in Men's Leisurewear, and he had been the creative inspiration in its meteoric rise in both performance and importance. Seeing him in action only increased my admiration for him. He had all the energy and passion necessary to back himself to the hilt with his bold choices and visionary zeal.

It goes without saying that I learned so much from Ray. He had an amazing gift to spot creative talent and then provide the necessary 'air cover' to enable them to grow.

We are still best friends to this day.

LEAVING IS NEVER EASY

Joe had also, unwittingly, prepared me very well for my move out of M&S and into the world of Pepsi and then on to the board of IPC Magazines – I was seriously better equipped. He had given me the confidence and tools to try my hand at leadership, but inadvertently, after 10 good years, he had also inspired in me the impatience to want far more influence.

Despite my strong desire to move on, I just could not initiate leaving an organization that had done so much for me. Eventually the phone rang and the offer was irresistible. I moved on.

After leaving M&S, I immersed myself in my new challenges; I had not spoken to or heard from Joe for a good number of years and Marks and Spencer were now underperforming and beginning to drift quite badly. Whilst going through the business press early one morning, the banner headlines were all about the travails of the UK's favourite retailer.

How could it all have gone so wrong? There was nothing more hurtful than reading about the place where I'd 'cut my teeth' in business and seeing it struggling so hopelessly. It was impossible to stop reading and despairing over M&S, in a very personal way. The whole experience was ugly and brutally public.

As I read the hard-hitting, relentless criticisms of M&S and opinions on why it was failing, I saw Joe's name mentioned and it was not good news. He was now back, looking after Ladies' Lingerie, and their performance had been dire for some time. Speculation was mounting in the press that he would (and should) be voted off the board at the coming Annual General Meeting (AGM).

It hurt. I could barely continue reading, I instinctively grabbed the phone, called Marks and Spencer and got through to Sue (who was still Joe's secretary) and asked if I could possibly have a mentoring session with Joe next Thursday in his office.

We both laughed. She said warmly: "He would love that, René." She even remembered the chicken salad.

Walking back into the M&S HQ, Michael House, was a galling experience, having been away just over five years and seeing and feeling that absolutely nothing had changed. The place looked the same and smelled the same; the only real change was a palpable lack of urgency.

I was shown in through some uninviting turnstiles, which employees never experienced – this was for visitors. I had my bag searched in a brusque and officious manner, and the stern-looking security guards pointed me at a rather long queue in front of three receptionists, who hardly seemed human, with their eyes focused on their PC screens and their headphones on.

After a silent and unfriendly 15-minute wait I was eventually brought up in front of one of the receptionists. This was my second visit in two weeks as Joe had had to cancel our initial appointment after I'd arrived: he was called away at very short notice. That never used to happen before.

The blank and unfriendly receptionist shrieked out, "NAME?" just as she had done the week before.

This was not the warm, friendly business I had left five years before. Having given her my name, she then barked: "CONTACT NUMBER?" Feeling a little threatened, I blurted out my mobile phone number. There was a long unfriendly pause and she looked up at me, and informed me, "You haven't returned your security pass from your previous visit last week." She then proceeded to glare at me and then barked again. "Do you have it with you?" Feeling extremely chastised,

I responded "No" in a soft and friendly voice. To my horror, she then demanded, "You will have to pay £10 or you will not be allowed to enter the building."

In that single exchange, it became very clear to me that this once proud and first class organization had changed for the worse.

M&S had always prided itself on its paternal and family approach to its people and suppliers, but it had become harsh and unfeeling. 'Process' had become more important than people.

I was incensed and angry and just about to leave the building when an old colleague of mine from Menswear shouted out my name from the staircase. He came swiftly over and we shook hands and chatted. When I explained how outraged I was at being charged to come in, he told me not to worry and that he would sort this out. With an air of indifference, he asked the receptionist to place the £10 charge on his cost centre! Not quite the response I was expecting or hoping for.

This learning was to become part of my future test of corporate culture. Before accepting any new assignment, I now try and spend 30 minutes alone in the reception of the business. This short time reveals so much about the prevailing corporate culture. What would an outsider think of your business if they had to spend 30 minutes in your reception?

I now trudged in, like everyone else, in a forlorn and listless manner, before sitting in the grey and uninviting supplier waiting room. Junior members of staff from various buying departments were coming in and out, picking up suppliers and escorting them to their buying departments in the brusquest and most charmless of manners. This was not the business I had joined, or indeed left, not too many years ago.

Joe's secretary came in. She looked so much older and all her energy and charm had disappeared. We walked silently up to Joe's office. No eye contact, no small talk; in fact nothing whatsoever.

Even the chicken salad didn't look as fresh. It didn't matter – I could hardly taste it. There were more pressing thoughts on my mind.

Joe appeared to have shrunk. The smooth operator of old was long gone: now he was shy, introspective and a little nervous.

Something strange happened during our meeting. Whilst it was brilliant to see him again, Joe looked so much smaller and the spark had all but gone. Something was wrong. It was only after about 40 minutes or so that I realized what it was – he was doing all the talking and I was doing all the listening.

It was obvious that he was no longer enjoying the role he had and it was time for him to leave.

When our hour was up, I gave him a huge hug (this was not M&S behaviour), not really knowing what else to say. He left me with the words that, "Marks and Spencer has always looked after my career and I've never bothered about applying for any external positions since joining; the company has always looked after me – and will continue to do so." As I left the building, I knew the company had changed and that it was time for Joe to also leave… and soon.

The trouble was, he just didn't know how to: the company had not given him permission. He had 'outsourced' the whole of his career to M&S and had no idea how to get his hands back on the steering wheel of his professional life.

On arriving home, it was really clear to me that I must help Joe, but how could I? He was my hero and my mentor.

When I got to my office the following day, it dawned on me that I had some experience and exposure that Joe didn't. This was very hard for me to believe – he knew everything, didn't he?

I needed to help save him from his current predicament, the way that he had helped me. I had the experience of taking my career into my own hands and wrestling it back from Marks and Spencer. I now knew how to resign and I'd done it twice since having Joe as a brilliant mentor.

This was something I needed to share with Joe and coach him through it, before it was too late. Mentee or mentor? It didn't matter: this was about friendship and trust.

Very carefully I spoke to Sue and invited Joe to have lunch with me at the offices of IPC Magazines at King's Reach Tower on the South Bank of the River Thames.

When Joe arrived, it was obvious that my world was alien to the only world he knew so well. This was a far more glamorous industry, with loads of attitude. We were Europe's largest consumer magazine business. We published a hundred magazines ranging from *Marie Clare* to *Loaded* to *Country Life* to *NME*.

We also had a hundred different, vibrant sub-cultures, from the fashionistas who worked on Marie Claire to the introverted train spotters of Railway Magazine, or to the men behaving very badly on Loaded. This was a very different place to the lone monolith culture of M&S.

Joe met me up on the 29th floor where we had one of London's finest entertainment suites, with glorious views across London from the all-glass walls. Our meal was skillfully prepared at our private table. The team looking after us knew me very well and afforded us the space and privacy to talk quietly and peacefully.

Joe and I had a very difficult lunch, where I carefully advised him it was time to leave and assisted him in composing his letter of resignation. This was not easy for either of us. It hurt to listen and it hurt even more to say, but we owed honesty to each other. We shared each other's pain whilst trusting each other's empathy and candour.

The toughest love.

Two weeks later, Joe had gone from Marks and Spencer and I sadly haven't heard from him since, but I will never forget him.

THE WORLD HAS CHANGED

Why haven't I made contact with Joe? How have I let this happen? I'm not sure I can answer this, but I do know that when he left me at IPC Magazines, we were both embarrassed but fortified.

Sometimes it might be best just to leave things unsaid. When he walked away that day, we both had tears in our eyes. Here was a man that had taught me virtually everything I knew in the business world up to that point.

Now I found myself suggesting to him what he might do, and that can be a very tough pill to swallow. He has left an indelible and positive mark on my life.

Sometimes you can feel the 'end' of any relationship – you just know that the time has come to let go. In Joe's case, I wanted to keep in contact just to let him know how I was doing, and how important he was to me.

I know he just knows. And that's the legacy that does remain: not a resignation letter, but a pathway to a better place.

Late in 2015, there was another announcement on the Today Programme on BBC Radio regarding a still beleaguered M&S, who had a new Chief Executive. I held my breath, hoping for the best. His name is Steve Rowe – the son of Joe, my fabulous mentor.

SPIKE SPARKS

It is up to you to identify your Spikes and enable them; only then you will begin having your desired impact on the world.

You have to believe in yourself before others can start believing in you.

Be sure to surround yourself with high-quality individuals, whether they be colleagues or friends.

We mentor best by passing on not just our knowledge but also our care.

The best leaders spend more time listening than they do talking. Listen effectively and deeply – all the time.

ON THE SAME PAGE

"A good leader takes a little more than his share of the blame, a little less than his share of the credit." – Arnold H. Glasow

"Meaning is not something you stumble across, like the answer to a riddle or the prize in a treasure hunt. Meaning is something you build into your life. You build it out of your own past, out of your affections and loyalties, out of the experience of humankind as it is passed on to you, out of your own talent and understanding, out of the things you believe in, out of the things and people you love, out of the values for which you are willing to sacrifice something. The ingredients are there. You are the only one who can put them together into that unique pattern that will be your life. Let it be a life that has dignity and meaning for you. If it does, then the particular balance of success or failure is of less account."[40]

"People spend too much time finding other people to blame, too much energy finding excuses for not being what they are capable of being, and not enough energy putting themselves on the line, growing out of the past, and getting on with their lives." – J. Michael Straczynski

Robbie Bach, former Microsoft President and Chief Xbox Officer explains, "Great leaders utilize their strengths to great effect, but they also understand areas where they need help from others. The real magic as a leader is understanding how to shape strategy and operational plans by integrating ideas from others and empowering them to bring those concepts to life."[41]

Based on a groundbreaking 1985 study, Michael Scheier states, "We know why optimists do better than pessimists. The answer lies in the differences between the coping strategies they use. Optimists are not simply being Pollyannas; they're problem solvers who try to improve the situation . . . Pessimists, on the other hand, tend to deny, avoid, and distort the problems they confront, and dwell on their negative feelings. It's easy to see now why pessimists don't do so well compared to optimists."[42]

---

[40] Gardner, J. (1994) "The Road to Self-Renewal." *Stanford Alumni Magazine*

[41] Bach, R. (2015) "Xbox Revisited: A Game Plan for Corporate and Civic Renewal." Dallas, *Texas: Brown Books Publishing Group*

[42] Scheier, M. and Carver, C. (1985) "Optimism, Coping, and Health: Assessment and Implications of Generalized Outcome Expectancies." *Health Psychology*, Vol 4(3), 219-247

PART FIVE

THE STORY OF THE STORIES

CHAPTER XVII
~~ACT LIKE AN ADULT.~~
ACT LIKE A CHILD

When was the last time you asked an under 25 for guidance and direction? Talked to a newly graduated student about how they use technology to help them with deadlines? Maybe listened to a teenager on how to get the best from your smartphone? Or even asked a child how to use a tablet? Eight-year-olds have little fear of the 'new', as they have no memory of having done things differently before.

In our technology-driven world young people usually have a more intuitive understanding of what we may fear.

Kids have a reputation for handling change a lot better than adults do. Children enjoy it and take it in their stride. It's in their nature to flex, to adapt. They readily bend, while grown-ups get set in their ways. Instead of resenting the difficulties of change the way older people do, kids just treat problems like another plaything.

Adults also become mired in routine and habit, but children won't settle for the boredom of 'sameness'. Kids insist on variety. Change is what keeps them from getting sleepy. They crave surprises and seek novel experiences. They love to learn. Youngsters are explorers at heart and they're open to the unexpected. As a result, their life is a constant stream of 'breakthroughs'.

We need to approach the 'new' in the same way we did when we were just a few years old: with curiosity, rather than with worry. We should be willing to fumble our way along in the process of figuring out what works best; quick to abandon any behaviour in favour of more efficient new-found solutions. We need to be relentless in our determination to learn and consumed with our search for mastery, for continuous improvement, intent on finding a better way every day.

Adults try to cope with the challenge of change by 'using their heads', trusting in logic and drawing on experience. But as kids we followed our hearts as much as our heads. We trusted our creative instincts, our intuition, because our logical thinking skills had not yet developed. And since we had not been around long enough to learn much from the past, we did not become trapped by old solutions. We did not get hung up on tradition.

Language can play a significant role in stimulating both learning and curiosity. And the learning of new words – not by their strict definition, but also their sometimes colloquial meaning, can help shape a whole new and vibrant understanding. We need to employ this creative approach to all areas of learning: expanding and being flexible with ideas, in the same way that children are flexible with language.

As kids we did not dread the future, even though it was unpredictable, challenging and full of problems for which we were unprepared. We had fun with change. And we learned more – and faster – than we ever have as adults.

We need to act like children again – to create a culture that knows how to learn and can give the organization the keys to the kingdom.

Being 'young at heart' can be a strong and necessary Spike for those involved in continuous change or transformation. Be more accepting that even languages can evolve by accepting new words, new meanings and new ideas, and not staying trapped or shackled by the purity of old 'texts' and definitions.

"WHY DON'T PEOPLE GET BRAVER AS THEY GET OLDER?"

ASHLEIGH BRILLIANT, AUTHOR

UNIQUE, SPECIAL AND DIFFERENT
BACK IN THE DAY – CIRCA 1500 IN MEDIEVAL ENGLAND

*Urine was once used to tan animal skins, so families used to all pee in the pot. And once it was full, it was taken and sold to the tannery. If you had to do this to survive, you were '**piss poor**'.*

*But there were some who were even poorer, who could not even afford to buy a pot. They consequently "**didn't have a pot to piss in**", and were the lowest of the low.*

*The not-so-frequent ritual of having a bath consisted of a tub filled with hot water. The man of the house always went in first, having the privilege of the nice clean water. He was followed by all the sons and the other men, then the women and finally the children, and last of all, the babies. By then the water was so dirty and murky you could actually lose someone in it. Hence the saying "**Don't throw the baby out with the bath water**".*

*Most houses had thatched roofs – thick straw piled high, with no firm platform of wood underneath. It was the only place for animals to keep warm. So, all the cats, mice and bugs lived in the roof. When it rained, it became slippery and sometimes the animals would slip and fall off the roof. Hence the saying "**it's raining cats and dogs**". There was nothing to stop them falling into the house.*

*The floor was dirt. Only the wealthy had something other than dirt. Hence the saying "**dirt poor**".*

*On rare occasions people could obtain pork, which made them feel quite special. When visitors came over, they would hang up their bacon to show off. It was a sign of wealth that a man could "**bring home the bacon**". They would cut a little off to share with guests and all would sit around to "**chew the fat**".*

*When there was enough to bake or buy bread, it was divided according to status. Workers got the burnt bottom of the loaf, the family got the middle, and guests got the top or "**upper crust**".*

Lead cups were used to drink ale or whisky. When the lead

became mixed with the alcohol, the combination would sometimes knock the drinkers out for a couple of days. Someone walking along the road would come across a prone lifeless body, mistake them for dead and prepare them for burial. They were laid out on the kitchen table for a couple of days and the family would gather around and eat and drink and wait and see if they would wake up. Hence the custom ***"holding a wake"****.*

As the villages and towns started running out of places to bury people, they would dig up coffins, then take the bones to a bone-house, and re-use the grave. When reopening these coffins, one out of 25 would have scratch marks on the inside, and they realised that they had been burying people alive. So, they would tie a string on the wrist of the corpse; the string would hang out of the coffin and be tied to a bell. Someone would then have to sit out in the graveyard all night ***('the graveyard shift')*** *to listen for the bell. This someone could be* ***'saved by the bell'*** *or could be considered a* ***"dead ringer"****.*

IN THE DAYS OF SPIKE ETYMOLOGY

Understanding the origins of the words and phrases we use today can be both fun and instructive. The words we use throughout *Spike* may mean slightly different things to different people, and that is precisely what is intended.

Some of the Spikes that are experienced throughout the book are provided with a flavour of how the use of the word, which has been adapted through the lens of our Strengths-based Revolution.

Audacity – Having the ability to challenge received wisdom that would lead to a negative outcome and replace it with the audacity to dream about positive outcomes only. Paul's story is built around the audacity of his belief in his team's capability.

Collaboration – Nothing is best done alone anymore. The more complementary Spikes we find to surround ourselves with, the easier and more enriching our lives become. Collaboration is the new leadership, as is clearly shown in Paul's story.

Compassion – There was a time, not so long ago, when talking about 'love' and 'compassion' was not deemed appropriate for our places of work. Today, it is everyone's dream to do a job that they truly love. Geraldine's story shows how much she was in love with all she did, and everyone she touched felt her authentic compassion.

Creativity – When you are brave enough to dare to think about doing things differently from the way they've always been done, you are on to something. If you're prepared to move from thoughts to action, you are already very special indeed. Camila's story demonstrated her constant brave attitude towards finding a different route, where possible.

Diversity – The best teams are always diverse, thriving on an array of different Spikes. This arrangement of complementary Spikes by design makes the whole team so much greater and stronger than just a random grouping of individual capabilities. Camila's story brings this diversity alive.

Drive – When surrounded by those who have Spikes that are complementary to yours, all concerned will feel compelled and propelled to move towards the same goal. This creates that extra drive for everyone involved. It is the power of consistently exposing and capitalizing upon your Spikes. René's mum's story inadvertently helped spark his endless drive.

Empathy – Sharing as much as we can helps us, and also those we share with; nothing is more powerful than understanding the feelings of others and sharing our feelings. This empathy is vital when building trust. Ashley's story had empathy underpinning his change of heart.

Energy – Every team looks for the energizers: those who give off and share their positive energy. Long gone are the times when energy was all about exercising on your own and driving towards your isolated, individual goals. We now share each-other's energy and can achieve so much more together because we do. Having a peer or partner who complements your Spikes can drive the other's energy levels: Kin's story perfectly models this outcome.

EQ – Emotional Quotient – As our life networks bring us into many different and sometimes new worlds, the need for better empathy and self-awareness makes demands of our EQ much more than our IQ. Camila's story shared her most amazing deft touch with all who entered Kids Company but perhaps her self-awareness was swamped by her all-consuming mission and purpose.

Failure – As we see throughout the book, the only mistake is the one you don't learn from. Failure can be a great teacher, as long as you and those around you view it as such. To never have made a mistake is to never have really tried; without embracing risk nothing much is ever achieved. Ashley and Shalimar took every disappointment as great learning in their stories.

Humility – Despite having achieved so much and having served so many and delivered so much, some retain the most compelling of traits: humility. Being humble ranks extremely highly with those you come into contact with for the very first time. Ashley's story is one built on humility and pride.

Imagination – Safety used to be about doing the same things over and over, but increasingly, today it is essential to think the unthinkable and have the conviction to share these different and new thoughts with those around you. Joe's story shows just how hard it is to escape the pull of the past.

Ingenuity – Everyone has the capacity to see the world a little differently, but some environments can crush any desire to challenge the status quo. Having complementary Spikes around, which feel free to challenge and support different thinking and creative approaches, can liberate ingenuity. Paul's story was about learning from those who were chosen because they were different.

Insight – Not so long ago, the 'data' provided us with all the insight we needed. Now, as the pace of change has multiplied, the data is now struggling to keep up. We have to find understanding and clarity from our experience, our people and our customers. The data-gathering techniques applied in Paul's story bring alive this new approach to acquiring much needed insights.

Inspiration – Having someone to believe in or something special to belong to can raise not just our horizons, but also our performance. Mandela's stories epitomise how the infectious hopes and dreams of one can infuse so many around them.

Integrity – The new complexities of networks and relationships have made strong demands on the trust and values of all those who are both engaged and engaging with each other. Integrity has become a key requirement for team membership. Joe's story highlighted a sustained friendship, built on integrity.

Leadership – This is the art of accomplishing more than the science of management says is possible. At the heart of true leadership are the qualities of Vision, People, Teams and Culture. Geraldine's story displays how a New Age leader behaves.

Management – Management is still imperative for running all teams and organizations, but its focus is on controlling people and their activities. Management requires the balancing force of even more leadership, in order to successfully deal with today's far greater levels of uncertainty. Ernest's story shares his insights on trying to break free from a world where he only ever experienced strong and controlling management.

Optimism – This is no longer an empty gesture or hollow words, but is an essential oxygen and fuel for all we attempt to do, as exemplified in Shalimar's story.

Originality – As society moves from demanding conformance to beyond tolerating difference and is now increasingly requiring originality, it becomes more positively inclusive. Keith's story is underpinned by a desire for inclusion that fosters an environment that encourages originality.

Passion – An act of passion has often been used to explain sometimes outrageous or damaging behaviour. Passion, when positively induced, can completely transform the most mundane of atmospheres and assist in creating positive environments for others to feed off. Ken's story at Cardinal Hinsley School was all about his contagious and intoxicating passion.

Recognition – Recognition was always constrained by the feeling that 'we have seen it all before'. Today, recognition is about always feeling excited and proud when seeing the right behaviours and values – no matter how many times you've seen them before – and openly acknowledging them. Matt Barrett's story showed how he had made the art of recognition one of the cornerstones of his leadership style.

Spike – We all have our limitations, but they should no longer define us, or our horizons. We all also have huge standout strengths: not things we are just good at but things we are great at. Once we have discovered what our Spikes are and we are prepared to work on honing and fine-tuning them, they can soon become defining superpowers. Every chapter and every story identifies Spikes and will enable and assist you to start to identify your Spikes.

Talent – Everybody has talent and it's always been different for all of us, because we are all Unique, Special and Different. The new goal for all of us is to develop our talents into our Spikes. Every story in *Spike* is a story of talents becoming Spikes.

Trust – Historically, trust has always been hard-earned and it took time to prove one's reliability. In the new world, trust is now given. This extended trust lubricates relationships and enables richer outcomes, but it involves an element of clear risk. There are always more gains than losses but it requires adjustment. Ashley's story saw him change his approach to trust, and it paid off.

Understanding – The ability to understand has become far more than simple intellectual comprehension: it is as much an empathetic 'feeling' for the situation or person. Donald's story demonstrated how his understanding and care for someone from such a different background and environment could be so transformational.

Values – Businesses have always focused on creating value, and this is still true and necessary today. Smart businesses and progressive leaders now know that they also need to create values that will drive the pursuit of value. Values provide the beliefs that positively support us in the tough times and jet-propel us in the good times. When there was not so much around to feel great about, Shalimar's story enshrined the power of values.

Vision – There was a time when vision was constrained by only what you could see with your eyes. Today, vision is much better defined by what you can imagine without your eyes. René's parents had the vision of going to a place they had never seen, with a life-changing purpose.

Every chapter has a story for you. Each chapter has heroes or heroines. The language is that of Spike and the Strengths-Based Revolution.

Whilst there are many winners on the pages of Spike, there are no losers. With Spike, there never need be losers anymore.

Everybody wants to be good at something: we all deserve that and are all capable of it.

"PREDICTING THE FUTURE IS EASY. IT'S TRYING TO FIGURE OUT WHAT'S GOING ON NOW THAT'S HARD."

FRITZ R.S. DRESSLER, PRESIDENT, FRS DRESSLER ASSOCIATES

ABOUT THE AUTHOR

RENÉ CARAYOL'S FOCUS IS ON INSPIRATIONAL LEADERSHIP AND HIGH-PERFORMING CULTURES, BOUND TOGETHER THROUGH HIS COMPELLING 'SPIKE' PHILOSOPHY, WHICH IS FOUNDED ON HIS EXTENSIVE BOARD-LEVEL EXPERIENCE.

Extraordinary times demand extraordinary leadership and make no mistake about it: we currently find ourselves in unchartered and turbulent waters.

If there was ever a time when we needed leaders with the speed, agility and the ability to 'think the unthinkable', it is now. Digital and mobile networks are ubiquitous and have dramatically disrupted how the world and businesses operate at all levels.

Much of René's success in creating a lasting impression has come from his ability to tell stories, narrated in his inimitable and powerful style and raising the spirits of his audience. He inspires his readers and listeners to win, and not just the next battle: he motivates them to transform their teams and businesses.

René Carayol is a hard man to classify.

Business icon or TV personality? Mentor or radio voice? Broadsheet journalist or leadership expert? Guru or inspired leader? Devoted father or best-selling author?

He's all of these. And more.

In short, he is a business guru who is able to adapt and evolve his concepts alongside the rapidly changing marketplace, offering unique solutions in a world full of increasing problems.

Many organizations can appear to be afraid and distrustful of their people, and inadvertently constrain them with far too many rules and processes. To achieve seemingly impossible results, organizations have to learn how to release their people from the shackles of hierarchy and control, thereby enabling them to find and exercise their personal Spikes.

This may involve tolerating weaknesses in individuals, but will also lead to capitalising upon their Spikes within teams, thus creating a new definition of leadership and a new route to success.

René inspires organizations to embrace their Spikes and the Spikes of their people: he motivates businesses to change the game, achieve breakthroughs, and generate the restless energy that comes from releasing their people to focus on their Spikes. By allowing their people free rein, businesses learn to practise a less controlling culture, which ensures that the energy and Spikes in their people become liberated and unleashed.

Small steps can have huge and positive consequences.

René asks awkward and uncomfortable questions. How do you change the old-fashioned, risk-averse processes that are ill-suited to emerging global markets? How do you secure and nurture the talents of a new generation of leaders? How do you overcome cynicism and complacency, and replace them with resolve?

René tailors every keynote to fit the actual challenges or opportunities faced by his clients – embracing regional differences and cultural nuances learned from his years of experience working across the globe.

His style has always been not to simply talk to people, but to make his audience feel that he is confiding only in them. This inimitable style helps René to deliver an honest and heartfelt message for change.

René's ideas are based on practical, real-life experiences, presented with electrifying effect. He both shakes up and inspires his audiences, showing them not only what lies within their grasp, but also that vital strategy for any successful individual or business: how to keep one step ahead of the chasing pack.

He presents a formula for change and success, which capitalizes on the skills of the individual and galvanizes the entire team. The result is a winning and unique approach, which brings out the Spikes in everyone he encounters.